I0762568

CONTENTS

7 **The Animal Side of Life**
Thomas Meaney

17 **Good Medicine**
Sheila Heti

72 **Steal, Erik**
Natalie Shapero

75 **Transference in the Afternoon**
Jesse Barron

103 **Whatever Creek Meadows**
Benjamin Kunkel

123 **Every Dark Corner**
Deborah Levy

128 **Therapy Rooms**
Nigel Shafran

139 **The Orange Ship**
Christopher Bollas, in conversation with Granta

157 **Mother**
Elfriede Jelinek, tr. Gitta Honegger

160 **I missed, Poem Interrupted by Mary Ruefle**
Olive Franklin

164 **Plant Teachers**
Musuk Nolte, with an introduction by Guadalupe Nettel, tr. Rosalind Harvey

187 **Mozart Balls**
Camilla Grudova

199 **Dropped from the Sky**
Juliet Mitchell, in conversation with Granta

209 **Psychoanalytic Writings**
Louise Bourgeois

216 **Inhabiting Light**
Rinko Kawauchi, with an introduction by Granta

GRANTA

12 Addison Avenue, London W11 4QR | email: editorial@granta.com
To subscribe visit subscribe.granta.com, or call +44 (0)1371 851873

ISSUE 174: WINTER 2026

p.128–136 'Therapy Rooms' by Nigel Shafran thanks Khiron Clinics, Marco Cortez, Marina Lorenzato, Agnes Otzelberger, Colbun Psychology, Harvest Therapy and City Road Therapy for locations. Thanks also to Rhiannon Bowden for production; p.157–159 'Mother' by Elfriede Jelinek is excerpted from *Winterreise*, her response to Franz Schubert's song cycle; p.209–214 Courtesy of The Easton Foundation, New York. All work pictured by Louise Bourgeois and displayed in the following order: c. 1986 (LB-0506); 1986 (*I Feel Threatened*); 1 March 1986 (LB-0427); c. 1990 (LB-0009); c. 1958 (LB-0127); c. 1961 (LB-0019). © The Easton Foundation / DACS, UK; p.234–247 © 2024 by Estate of Victor Heringer; p.263–266 'Madame Gandi' from *Au coeur d'un été tout en or* © Mercure de France, 2020.

Granta (ISSN 173231 USPS 508) is published four times a year by Granta Trust, 12 Addison Avenue, London, W11 4QR, UK.

Airfreight and mailing in the USA by agent named World Container Inc., 150–15, 183rd Street, Jamaica, NY 11413, USA.

Periodicals postage paid at Brooklyn, NY 11256.

Postmaster: Send address changes to *Granta*, ESco, Trinity House, Sculpins Lane, Wethersfield, Braintree, CM7 4AY, UK.

Subscription records are maintained at *Granta*, c/o ESco Business Services Ltd, Wethersfield, Essex, CM7 4AY, UK.

Air Business Ltd is acting as our mailing agent.

The manufacturer's authorised representative in the EU for product safety is Authorised Rep Compliance Ltd, 71 Lower Baggot Street, Dublin D02 P593, Ireland (arccompliance.com)

Granta is printed and bound in Italy by Legoprint. This magazine is printed on paper that fulfils the criteria for 'Paper for permanent document' according to ISO 9706 and the American Library Standard ANSI/NIZO Z39.48-1992 and has been certified by the Forest Stewardship Council® (FSC®). *Granta* is indexed in the American Humanities Index.

ISBN 978-1-909-889-78-1

234 **The Love of Singular Men, News for Nira, My Grandfather Is the Future, The First Gulf War, I Am Not a Poet**
Victor Heringer, tr. James Young and Justin Greene

249 **Secondhand Smoke**
Dushko Petrovich Córdova

263 **Madame Gandi**
Anne Serre, tr. Mark Hutchinson

269 **The Perec Case**
Paul Keegan

281 **Her Enemy's Phrase**
Missouri Williams

287 **We Are Creatures Who Mourn**
Jonathan Lear, in conversation with Benjamin Y. Fong

300 **To Adam Zagajewski, Thinking of Adam, Politics**
Robert Hass

307 **Notes on contributors**

The moment you ask about the meaning and value of life, you are sick, because neither of those things objectively exist; you have only admitted that you have stored up too much unsatisfied libido, and something has happened to it, a kind of fermentation process that leads to grief and depression. My explanations might not be the best. Perhaps because I am too pessimistic. An advertisement is running through my head, which would make for a bold and successful American jingle: 'Why live, if you can be buried for ten dollars?'

Sigmund Freud to Marie Bonaparte, 13 August 1937

The Animal Side of Life

'There has been nothing like this since the spread of the potato and of maize,' Ernest Gellner wrote of psychoanalysis, 'and this diffusion was even faster and may have deeper implications.' The worldwide dissemination of forms of therapy, many with their origins in Freud's consulting room in fin-de-siècle Vienna, was the great underdog intellectual development of the last century. Within the space of three decades, the theories of a miniscule scientific sect overturned the mores of the middle classes. The result was a new climate of self-scrutiny, and a novel ritual of confession. The way individuals thought about their passions, deceptions, selves, and the trivia of their lives changed in ways that would have baffled previous generations. Ordinary people began to speak of their libidos, their egos, and their unconscious. Not long after Freud's death, the US military was training psychotherapists at an industrial scale and offering free sessions to soldiers. Psychotherapy has saturated online China, where smartphone apps and chatbots answer the overwhelming demand for mental health professionals. In 2017, Pope Francis reported he had undergone weekly psychoanalysis in his forties. It is hard to imagine a better scalp for the therapeutic.

Freud correctly identified his leading enemy as America – 'Dollarland' – where psychotherapy has been turned into a business; banalized, and medicalized beyond recognition. The rise of pharmaceuticals – anti-depressants, mood stabilizers, anxiolytics – may in theory be complementary to psychotherapy, but in practice they take the lead. In the realm of psychoanalysis itself, Freudianism was long ago eclipsed. The most prevalent form of the 'talking cure' today is cognitive behavioral therapy, which is explicitly premised on treating symptoms as efficiently as possible, and avoids probing the depths of trauma or unconscious conflicts. Therapy as a concept has now been extended to cover counseling of almost any kind, from coaching to interacting with animals to psychedelic experiences, craniosacral massages and desensitization to trauma by mimicking the rapid eye movements experienced during sleep (EMDR). When one considers the amount of time and money and the delicacy of the social arrangements required, it seems likely that more rigorous forms of psychotherapy – not to mention psychoanalysis itself – are poised to become a rarified pursuit, even if some of the old Freudian vocabulary remains unmovable.

It did not take long for critics, such as the Soviet V.N. Voloshinov, to expose the limits of Freudianism as a way of understanding the world. Freud, Voloshinov argued, had developed a picture of individual psychology that sealed it off from the ideologies, social relations, and language in which it swam. The result was an overly individualistic picture of human life that put the onus on biological, mostly sexual, drives. This turn inward was itself a symptom of eras in which a ruling class in decline preferred to remain insensible to larger material forces. 'It is almost as if people of such periods desire to leave the atmosphere of history, which has become too cold and comfortless, and take refuge in the organic warmth of the animal side of life,' Voloshinov wrote.

Freud himself was interested in intellectual revolutions but not politics. 'Patients are a rabble,' he joked to Sándor Ferenczi, but they were the only rabble who concerned him. The mission of psychoanalysis was to reconcile patients with the world as it was: capitalist, imperial, inevitably disappointing. Grievances could be addressed by more therapists and more therapy, but certainly not revolution. 'The standard-issue psychoanalytic understanding of politics is that we carry over the inarticulate needs of childhood into the tumult of society,' writes the therapist and scholar Ben Parker.

'Politics, as a way of relating to others, is a garbled translation of the solipsism, envy, sullen exclusions, and arbitrary permissions of an unconscious past.' Mass movements were, almost by definition, pathological.

In the cheapest psychoanalytical political commentary, historical forces were reduced to internal psychological malfunctions: the iniquities of American politics are blamed on the narcissism of a single man, and Brexit, as Parker writes, becomes 'an aversion to emotional dependence, as if a commitment to free trade and open markets was a milestone of personal maturity'. In the richer psychoanalytic contributions to politics, work by Adorno and Fanon shows how economic arrangements alone are insufficient to explain how inferiority is internalized, classes are naturalized, desires are manufactured, and neuroses nurtured.

Freud's ideas were rickety in places, and his intellectual insecurity could be overwhelming – he dismissed even legitimate challenges to his thinking as 'resistance'. But he was a charismatic writer, who, even when he was mistaken, could imbue the minutiae of everyday life with the interpretive richness only found in novels. It would be churlish to deny that some of the most perceptive modern literary critics have come equipped with profound psychoanalytical sensitivity. Nor would it be a stretch to view each of the three psychoanalysts interviewed in this issue of *Granta* – Jonathan Lear, Juliet Mitchell, Christopher Bollas – as literary critics. Their texts range from *Gilgamesh* to Platonic dialogues to the English novel to modern American poetry. Nevertheless, there is a faultline between viewing human subjectivity from a literary perspective and from a psychoanalytic one. The faultline comes into view in the exchange Lear has with Benjamin Y. Fong:

> FONG: There is a common idea about therapy that it is not necessarily about coming to the truth, but about giving patients a story about themselves, a story with which they can more contentedly live their lives. What do you make of that conception?

LEAR: […] I think it's pretty importantly wrong. Stories are nice . . . but they can have a very defensive use. The construction of a story, however nuanced or sensitive or insightful, can be used as a defense to cover over real problems that are getting ignored precisely by the narrative. I think that's bad.

Lear makes a plea for classical psychoanalysis: if therapy does not attempt to get to the bottom of things, then it is not doing its work. But what if we constantly trade in updated fictions of ourselves? What if the self is mostly made up of the stories we tell and the stories other people tell us about us? 'Most people reveal more truths about themselves through fictive representations than they do by stating the solemn and verifiable truths of their lives,' Christopher Bollas, the British Object Relation School's grandest inheritor, told *Granta*. 'No analyst I know in the United Kingdom would maintain that he or she was trying to get to the "truth" beyond self-fictionalization. That is because to create fiction is to unconsciously tell the truth.' The irony is that just as psychotherapy more fully adopts this literary way of seeing, the profession faces its severest threats since the Nazi menace. Lear worries about the drugs that suppress feeling; Mitchell laments a crisis in confidentiality and the effects of social media, which allow therapy to spread but thins the experience; Bollas speaks plainly of the 'death wish' of psychoanalysis, as it restricts credentialization and undergoes hyper-factionalization.

The subject of therapy in this issue is approached with our house prejudice: that of literature. Literature has finer antennae than its peers in the social sciences, which often admit this by pillaging novels and poetry for examples of what they are trying to explain, without approaching the same density of insight. We set out to avoid the jargon and in-speak of contemporary therapeutic writing, whether in its technical vocabulary or in its pop variants. In the 1950s, Bruno Bettelheim complained that many of Freud's finest terms – *Seele* ('Soul'), *Ich* ('I'), *Fehlleistung* ('faulty achievement') – had been needlessly translated into highfalutin Greek: psyche, ego, parapraxis. The German was meant to bring the concepts closer to people; the Greek made them feel more distanced. From the perspective of a literary magazine, the protocols of psychotherapy still appear to be jealously guarded by those who insist that we learn their language and pledge fidelity to their master thinkers.

In this issue, on behalf of *Granta* and with the encouragement of her boyfriend, the novelist Sheila Heti risked her mind, which is a terrible thing to lose. In 'Good Medicine,' she tours the underworld of drug therapies in Western Canada, and undergoes ketamine, DMT, and LSD/MDMA treatments. Heti restricts herself to relaying and trusting the images and impressions that came to her, which, last summer, culminated in a resplendent vision of God. In the course of her treatments, a delicate rebalancing of her life and memories transpires, as she learns to experience in a new way the love around her. 'Perhaps I had never before been open enough to feel it,' she writes, 'how fragile a person was in loving you, and the terrible responsibility that came with it.'

In 2025, the Los Angeles journalist Jesse Barron received a phone call from Michael Pollack, a one-time Wall Street hedge fund manager, who was suing his former therapist for malpractice. The two had been in a sexual relationship for a decade. When it ended, Pollack claimed that he was the victim of 'erotic transference'. In Barron's noirish narrative, both sides have a case to make, and both try on each other's idioms: Pollack argues in the language of therapy, the therapist in the language of romantic love. That a doctor cannot fall in love with a patient is an assumed view of the therapeutically minded, but this kind of relationship – between professors and students, between executives and assistants – happens regardless. Prohibition only invites transgression. Who has the moral upper hand: the therapist or the banker?

Paul Keegan, author of a marvelous introduction to Freud's *The Psychopathology of Everyday Life*, returns to the psychoanalytic fray – this time, to Paris in the 1960s, when Georges Perec first stepped into the consulting room of Jean-Bertrand Pontalis. Keegan recreates a dream-like pas de deux in which both men tried to enlist the therapy sessions into the service of their own art, all while deflecting the effects that each had on the other.

Another word for case history is memoir. In 'Secondhand Smoke', the Chicago painter Dushko Petrovich Córdova confesses to having neglected his sense of smell, and finds an extreme remedy in perfume. The pursuit leads him to manic corners of the internet and back to the Quito of his childhood. In 'Every Dark Corner', the novelist Deborah Levy analyzes the language and theater of the consultation room: how it's arranged, decorated, and entered. In her novel, *The Piano Teacher*, Elfriede Jelinek depicted the intensity, aggression and co-dependency that can develop between mother and daughter. In 'Mother', a tumbling account of the search for intimacy and recognition in the internet age, the author returns to the perverse threads that bind parent and child.

The fiction in this issue does not indulge the received ideas of therapy, but approaches analysis in its own language. Newly-engaged and hoping to share their happiness, the couple in Benjamin Kunkel's 'Whatever Creek Meadows' hike into the Colorado mountains with their close friend, but the trip does not go as planned. Accusations flash, neuroses are fueled, and in comically controlled prose, Kunkel sets in motion the triangulated desire among his characters. Anne Serre's light, teasing story, 'Madame Gandi', relays an older man's reaction when he finds that his therapy session is to be conducted by his cousin. In 'Her Enemy's Phrase', a story of a conversation between two writers, one aspiring, the other established, Missouri Williams deconstructs an artist's obsessive impulse – how a desire to strike on the *mot juste* can take over a life. In Camilla Grudova's 'Mozart Balls', an eccentric psychoanalyst offers an encyclopedic tour of his consultation room, detailing the many objects that have earned him his reputation as a hoarder. Characteristically revolting and maximalist, Grudova's arresting tale of incest and obsessive compulsion delivers a send-up of Freud's most famous themes.

Like psychoanalysis, the central preoccupations of poetry are love and death. Robert Hass, one of the great elegists of our time, remembers his friend, the Polish poet Adam Zagajewski. Natalie Shapero's wry, associative verses express her muted disbelief at death's constant presence in American life. Olive Franklin writes love poetry that is clipped, comic, and full of strange joy. The issue features five poems by the Brazilian writer Victor Heringer (1988-2018), whose incandescent story, 'Lígia', *Granta* published in 2024. His subject is the past, present, and future of Rio de Janeiro, a city where dandies and drug lords mingle with the poets who immortalize them: 'I write sambas for the tango and tangos for men / in good health. They don't need them, since they die / at any bend in the hour hand, in the stupidest ways, / senhora.'

Musuk Nolte's photographs draw on his familiarity with the ayahuasca traditions of the Asháninka, Shawi and Shipibo-Konibo peoples in the Peruvian Amazon. The Mexican writer Guadalupe Nettel introduces them with an account of her own encounter with *la medicina* in the Tepozteco Valley. The photographer Nigel Shafran, known for his relentless commitment to the details of everyday life, meticulously inspects therapy rooms in London. He limited himself to fifty minutes – the length of a session – in each room. In 'Inhabiting Light', Rinko Kawauchi, another photographer of the quotidian, strips down the visual field more radically than in her past work. Here, she makes the elemental qualities of light appear: an acrylic prism rearranges the rays of the sun, a glowing mist is turned opaque and solid, as if it is barricading a dark path. We include as well six images of Louise Bourgeois's psychoanalytic writings. Bourgeois began analysis in 1951, soon after her father died. In the first eleven years, she produced very little art but wrote prodigiously, recording her dreams and process notes on loose sheets of paper. Across almost a thousand pages, she moves between past and present, French and English:

> The analysis is a jip is a trap is a job is a privilege is a luxury is a duty is a duty towards myself my husband. my parents my children my is a shame is a farce is a love affair is a rendez-vous is a cat + mouse game is a boat to drive is an internment is a joke makes me powerless makes me into a cop is a bad dream is my interest is my field of study – is more than I can manage makes me furious is a bore is a nuisance is a pain in the neck –

This issue of *Granta* was a more involved undertaking than we expected. At least one editor went into therapy with at least one contributor. If this kind of thing continues, we may no longer have a magazine. ■

TM

JULIAN STANCZAK
Inward - Yellow Filtration, 1981
Courtesy of the Stanczak Foundation

GOOD MEDICINE

Sheila Heti

Sometime during my forty-eighth year, I began to overhear myself saying, in conversation, 'I don't really need to live much longer,' or, 'If I died tomorrow, that would be fine.' I felt uneasy, surprised and disturbed every time this came out of my mouth. One friend said, 'That's very wise, very enlightened of you,' and I suppose it could have been. But in my case, it didn't feel like wisdom. I felt like I knew who I was, and what my life was, and looking to the future, I saw only repetition. My work, my friendships, my relationship with my boyfriend were all good. I just didn't see the value in decades more of living.

That spring, I had posted to Reddit for the first time, a question I titled, 'What happened to you after fifty that was new?' The post included the sentence, 'I wonder if this age represents a natural downturn in a person's life, where things sort of plateau, and all you were working toward reveals itself, and then you have it: a life . . . I know age forty-nine is statistically the hardest time for people. Thanks!'

I was told to try lifting weights, asked if it might be perimenopause; someone said her life had improved when she had bought a house. I felt grateful for their answers, but they didn't touch the central point: I was simply tired of being me.

★

It was early June. I was standing in a lush garden of old, amazing, twisting trees, on a volcanic island in the Azores, in the middle of the Atlantic Ocean, feeling happy and relieved at having just officiated the marriage of my lovely, bright young sister-in-law and the devoted man who was now her husband. I had never wanted to marry anyone before, but they were family, and their relationship a beautiful one. She had said, 'Make up a new ceremony. I trust you. You just do whatever you want.' Wanting to do the best possible job, I naturally worried I'd make a mess of it.

Now I stood there with the sun in my eyes, the final month and a half of summer stretching out before me, uneventful and stress-free. Checking my phone, I noticed a message from the editor of this magazine, asking if I would write something for their 'Therapy' issue. I mentioned this to my boyfriend of fifteen years, a criminal defense lawyer, who requested, for this article, that I call him Handsome Jack. What could I write about? I asked him. After thinking about it for a moment, he said, 'You're so interesting when you write about your own mind. Why don't you try a bunch of psychedelic therapies and report on what they feel like?' Beyond him, in the distance, the bride and groom were laughing and hugging their guests.

It was an interesting idea, but it scared me: although I'd smoked pot daily in my late teens, living in Montreal and attending theater school, after a few years marijuana began making me paranoid, and I had to stop, and since then, I have rarely touched it. And while Jack and I sometimes take mushrooms, whenever he proposes it, my stomach starts to ache and I feel like I don't want to. I remember the day after I took ecstasy in my early twenties as the most suicidally dark day of my life. And I have a lifelong fear of LSD: I had awful nightmares as a child, for years on end, and I have always worried acid would be like one of those bad dreams. The one time I tried cocaine, I had the awful feeling that I was being an asshole to all my friends. I guess I like being sober: that hard-won, delicate feeling of equilibrium. (Although I don't know if I can call it sobriety, exactly: I've been on a low dose of Prozac these past nine years.)

As for therapy, I have done many different kinds, after, for years, resisting the idea as creativity-killing and self-indulgent: I've tried regular talk therapy, CBT for anxiety, Jungian therapy for growing up, and twice-a-week visits to a Freudian psychiatrist to talk about my dad. Sometimes it seemed helpful, sometimes it felt like a waste of time. Mostly it felt like a near-invisible remedy, like taking vitamins; you mostly had to believe, *Yes, I do feel better when I'm taking vitamin D.*

Over the next few days, I tried, with difficulty, to come up with other ideas for this article – and was close to saying no. Writing articles always takes up so much time, and gives me the bad feeling of being in school, of being tested. But I needed the money and liked the people at the magazine.

And yet it wasn't just that. The imp of provocation had come into my life, and my reluctance to take on Jack's suggestion began to feel like cowardice, like turning my back on a fear I didn't want to name. And so, instead of naming it, I replied to the editor and proposed this piece.

*

Back at home, after the wedding, I started Googling 'psychedelic therapies in Toronto'. Nothing came up. Increasingly panicky over the next several days, I began casting my mind across everyone I knew, finally calling the sister of a guy Jack was friendly with, who offered 'psychedelic integration' as part of her therapy practice. She and I talked for half an hour, and I asked her if this was going to be impossible. She said that ketamine was legal in Canada, and there were clinics where you *could* try it, and that psychedelics were being used in clinical trials, and that psilocybin was available for end-of-life care, and to first responders suffering with PTSD. 'But beyond that,' she said, 'you're in the underground world.'

So I began looking into ketamine clinics. I would find my way to the underground later, to take the illegal drugs they offered there.

All I really knew about ketamine was that friends of mine in New York took it sometimes, then went out dancing all night, and that its original use was to tranquilize horses. How it could lead one species to fall asleep and the other to dance was not really clear to me, and I had no idea what effect it might have on the mind of a person who was sitting in a chair, in a clinic, talking.

'Have you ever had a traumatic brain injury?' a nurse asked me over Zoom, during one of the clinic's many intake sessions. I had already filled out so many forms. 'No,' I said.

'Do you ever use support aids, such as a walker or a cane?'

'Nope.'

'How's your sleep?'

'Fine.'

'Do you or have you ever considered yourself a risk to others?'

I really had to think about this one. 'No.'

There would be three intake sessions in total, and three integration sessions after the ketamine treatment ('integration' is what the psychedelic-therapy world calls 'making sense of what happened to you while you were on the drugs'). I signed up to do one lower-dose treatment, during which I'd talk with a therapist, and one higher-dose treatment, which would be silent; together this would cost $1,500 CAD.

★

The morning of the talk-therapy treatment, I carefully chose nice underwear in case I died on the drug, then took an Uber forty-five minutes north to a newish industrial park somewhat outside the city. The complex held a strange assortment of businesses: a tailor shop called Lady Needle, a karate studio, a novelty fun palace called Batl: The Home of Throwing, two dental offices, an art supply store, something called Touch of Modern, and something else called Futurity Gate. I went into the bland, four-story office building and exited onto a floor where I passed two chartered accountants before finding the clinic.

Inside, there was no one waiting. A giant photograph of a wheat field was framed above a basic couch. The only thing that distinguished the office from a dental clinic were two, foot-high mushroom statues placed in front of the reception desk, and, stenciled onto the wall, a symbol suggesting a woman meditating inside a flower, with the words 'Atma Cena: Psychedelic Therapy'.

The nurse, an older woman, came and led me into a room, where Richard Utama, the therapist I'd chosen from the website, was waiting, sitting on the floor, cross-legged and smiling. He was slender and fit and seemed slightly older than me; a relaxing presence, yet animated. We had spoken twice already, most recently for an hour-long 'intention-setting' session. He was wearing a friendship bracelet with his name on it that a co-worker got for him at a Taylor Swift concert. ('I prefer Kylie,' he said.) As we made small talk, the nurse took my blood pressure and measured my oxygen levels with a little finger clamp.

Then they explained what would happen: I would take two 125 mg pills of ketamine, let them dissolve in my mouth, then swish them around as the nurse read a meditation. Resting in the La-Z-Boy, I pressed the buttons that controlled the chair, and pushed off my shoes and pulled the weighted blanket over me, lowering the eye shades and leaning back.

NURSE

Now, as you settle in, take a moment to become aware of your body. Slowly begin to feel it soften, letting go of any tension in your head, shoulders or arms. Feel the weight of your body begin to sink into the surface beneath you, giving yourself permission to unwind.

SHEILA

I can swallow this, right?

NURSE

No. Did you swallow it?

SHEILA

Yeah.

NURSE

Okay. It's okay.

SHEILA

Wait – I didn't understand. I feel like I've been swishing it for a long time. You're supposed to swish it for the full fifteen minutes? Oh my God.

NURSE

It's a small enough dose, my dear. We'll just kind of like – okay, you might be here a little longer.

SHEILA

I thought I wasn't supposed to swallow the *pill*! I didn't realize I wasn't supposed to swallow the *liquid*.

NURSE

No – that's why I said to expel the saliva at the end.

SHEILA

I'm sorry.

NURSE

It's okay. Like I said, nerves and anxiety sometimes come along with it. Trust me, it happens to . . . a few people.

She then returned to the meditation, and I began to feel dreamy, the way one gets when falling asleep, although I also felt weirdly lucid.

NURSE

(*reading*) With each breath give yourself permission to be vulnerable, to let go of any expectations. Your only task today is to exist in peace and curiosity. There is no need to impress anyone. No need to be anything other than exactly who you –

SHEILA

(*suddenly*) Can I interrupt for one second?

NURSE

Of course.

SHEILA

Richard, I just had a thought that I'd like to come back to, if we can at some point. Just – I've always had, like, a negative feeling about relationships in general. So I'd like to come back to that.

RICHARD

Yep.

SHEILA

Sorry for interrupting.

NURSE

It's your journey, my dear, whatever you need.

SHEILA

You said to be your authentic self, so I was like, okay, I can interrupt. I normally like to be polite and not interrupt.

NURSE

No, no. Thank you. See, the next line is 'There's no need to impress . . .'

SHEILA

Yes, you said that. So I thought, 'Here's my chance.'

Already I was starting to act a bit strangely. Normally, I would never have interrupted the nurse, feeling obliged to honor the work she was doing to get me into a meditative state. But it was like some learned politeness was being pulled back, and instead I was being led by this surging urgency.

Fifteen minutes later, Richard finished reading *his* meditation, during which time I'd swished the second set of pills, and beckoned for a Kleenex because it felt as though the solution of ketamine and saliva was overrunning my lips and spilling out of my mouth, which had gone numb. And I felt an emotionally volatile, bluntly honest version of me was pressing itself to the surface.

After I spat, I felt myself speaking incredibly rapidly, in a strangely high voice. (Listening back to the transcript, this was not true.) But it felt like there was no distance between thinking and speaking. The part of me that was speaking seemed to be drawing itself forth from a shut-away corner of me that I had never before visited.

SHEILA

Wow, ketamine's really weird! Wooh! I feel really high! (*laughs*) One, why do they tranquilize horses? Like, why do horses need to be tranquilized? Second, I want to say that I'm very happy to be doing this with you, Richard. I think you're really cool (*laughing hysterically*) and so funny! I don't even understand why I'm here today! It's so strange!

RICHARD

You're sounding really good! (*laughter*) You're super-upbeat, Sheila!

SHEILA

Oh my God, this is so strange to do therapy while high! This is, like, the craziest thing a person could ever choose to do! (*laughter*) This is so weird. Oh my God, why did I decide to do this?

RICHARD

How are you feeling right now in your body?

SHEILA

(*suddenly aware of the sadness*) Like, there's some real sadness behind all this laughter, but they're basically balanced. (*stretching out a leg from under the blanket*) Whatever I do with my body is okay, right?

RICHARD

That's fine, yeah.

SHEILA

I feel like I want more drugs. (*laughs*) Is that wrong?

RICHARD

(*laughs*) No, it's not wrong. Because you love this feeling of balance, equilibrium, right? You understand that these two ideals could coexist. All these different emotions.

SHEILA

Sadness, happiness. They're so close to each other! And this is where, when I was saying about relationships earlier – like, I love my boyfriend so much (*suddenly crying*), like I couldn't love anybody more in the whole entire world, but (*sounding so sad*) my parents didn't have a good relationship, and my little brother – really, he was the only person I had. I just loved him so much! He was like, my best friend and (*crying more*) my favorite person in the whole world, and I just wanted to make the world so nice for him and, like (*sobbing*) I just didn't want my parents to be *his* parents. And so I wanted to be his – is it okay if I just talk and talk?

RICHARD

Yeah! This is how it is. Talk, talk.

SHEILA

Oh! Please don't say anything, because I'm too responsive to people! I just need to speak!

RICHARD

Yeah, I'm here.

SHEILA

So my brother –

RICHARD

Mm-hmm.

SHEILA

(*desperate*) Oh, please don't even say *hmm*, because everything I hear from you, I just feel like I have to react to it, because I have to react to everything around me (*sobbing*) and it's so hard, because I really want to respond to everyone, but it's almost impossible (*crying harder*) and that's why it's so hard to be in a relationship. Because here's this one person who has all these needs, and you want to, like, give them everything . . .

In two decades of therapy, I had only cried a few times. And apart from after the deaths of my father and my last dog, Feldman, I never, in real life, sobbed. But these thoughts were all new to me. I remembered that I'd felt like I was my brother's true parent, but I had imagined myself as an overconfident little girl, playing real-life dolls. But it was because *I didn't want my brother to have the same parents I had*? I had never known that! I had to make sure to tell him. It suddenly felt *so important* to think perfectly clearly, and I became super-sensitive to anything that might get in the way and distort my mental progress. In sober life, I almost took pride in not asking for what I needed; that I could adapt to other people was my strength. When, during the intake, a nurse had asked me whether I wanted a room with windows or not, and what scent I might want burning, I had been so irritated, even insulted: I wasn't so delicate! Do it whichever way – I'd live!

The conversation went on, through how when my parents were upset, they often reacted with the silent treatment, and I realized that I *always still* interpret someone's silence (even a late email from an editor, say) as that person punishing me, which also explained why I was forever scanning myself for the last thing I might have done wrong. There were moments of push-back (so unlike me!) and nonsense, like when I objected to Richard referring to my 'inner child'.

SHEILA

Oh, please don't say 'inner child'. I really don't like clichés! I'm a writer! I just . . . I *really* think things should have their own words. Every word needs its own word!

And I kept talking about my problems in relationships.

SHEILA

But that's where I – there's always a part of me holding myself a bit aloof, that thinks I should break away.

RICHARD

What is that thing? Can you name it?

SHEILA

I'm just thinking, just let me think . . .

Normally, saying 'let me think' always led to me thinking of everything *except* the thing I was trying to think about, but somehow, on this drug, I was able to think deeply and directly in whatever direction I turned my mind.

SHEILA

Fear of being tainted or diminished or trapped or consumed, or not the full expression of myself. I assume when I was a child and my dad and I were alone together, he seemed full of joy. And then my parents, when I would see them together, he would seem diminished. (*reasoning this out logically for the first time in my life*) Yes, that's probably what it was! And then when I was alone with my mother, I'm sure she would have been . . . brighter. And then when she was with my father, she would have been dimmer. (*very emotional*) So a relationship dims you. I think that's my fear.

RICHARD

And that's what you still carry today in this relationship. That's the story that you're still carrying.

SHEILA

What's the story?

RICHARD

That being together is not good for each other, dimming each other's light.

Richard then asked me if there was evidence for this in my relationship, but all I could see were the ways Jack had made me a brighter, healthier person. But if my unconscious belief was that a relationship dimmed you, was I unconsciously doing things to dim *him*? I knew right away that the answer was yes. And into my mind came one of his biggest disappointments ('the one thing I would change about you', he once told me), which was that I didn't like music, an art form he loved. Before we lived together, he would listen to music all the time. But I preferred silence, so we lived in a mostly unmusical home.

Ten minutes later, we were still on the difficult subject of love.

SHEILA

Often in a relationship, I feel that I want to leave. I think because I want to leave the darkness. But I'm mature enough to know that there's always going to be darkness with *anybody*. It's just – a different darkness. It looks different, it feels different, but there's still darkness. I want to be with Jack for the rest of my life, (*really emotional*) I really want to be with Jack! But he has a lot of pain and suffering that he feels came about because of me. And I have a lot of pain and suffering that came about because of him.

RICHARD

Yeah. Sharing those pains, sharing the burden. That's part of love.

SHEILA

But you create – but you are a burden to each other, *also*. You don't only *share* your burdens. You *are* each other's burden. Like you give – you *cause* pain to the other.

RICHARD

But also each other's happiness.

SHEILA

(*very simply*) Yes.

We both laughed. I felt some new lightness and relief at the simplicity of this equation. 'Darkness and lightness,' Richard said. Then, a little bit later, I brought up another difficult thing about relationships: how when other people talked about theirs, or when I saw them depicted in the media or in films or books, it didn't seem like what we had, and that often made me feel insecure, like there was something wrong with the way that we were doing it, or like there was something wrong with me.

RICHARD

And what's wrong with not relating to those people?

SHEILA

Because I feel like that's the way it's supposed to be.

RICHARD

The way it's supposed to be is programming. How about . . . 'the way it's supposed to be *for you in this relationship with Jack*'. Right? Not those other people's 'supposed to be'.

SHEILA

Right. Yeah. Maybe it feels kind of scary to – to have no model. To just say 'this is for *me*'. Why does it feel sort of scary and threatening and uneasy to go out on a limb, to feel like our relationship doesn't have a model? That it's just ours?

RICHARD

How about if we scrap those models and build a model, your own model?

SHEILA

(*little laugh*) It's nice.

RICHARD

Scrap those programs, scrap those operating systems, create your own OS. Yeah, we can work to build your own moral compass and discard those models. Patterns as well. Yeah. This is amazing! There are always patterns. From a mathematician's point of view, life is mathematics, patterns, shapes . . .

SHEILA

Right.

RICHARD

A commitment to look into those patterns. They used to serve us, typically when we're younger, because we're more, for lack of a better word, dumb. (*laughs*) And then those patterns no longer serve us as we grow, mature.

I then talked about how I often felt cowardly, being in a relationship – even in a friendship: that I had a picture of a person alone in the world, discovering the world in a completely alone sort of way. My fear was that this was the only way to write great books, to get at the Truth, and to arrive at the truest understanding of Life.

RICHARD

Oh, my God, that's huge! (*big laugh*) That's a huge responsibility, to understand the Truth of Life! How about if we scale it down . . . the truth of *your* life?

SHEILA

(*long pause, sweet, relaxed feeling emerging*) Yeah, and this is the truth of my life, that I have Jack, yeah. (*relieved*) Why do you think I abstract things so much, generalize?

RICHARD

But that's also a question for you to ask.

SHEILA

What's the question?

RICHARD

You just asked the question.

SHEILA

Why am I always abstracting things?

RICHARD

For yourself to answer that, too.

SHEILA

Yeah. (*thinks*) Because I feel like I'm not enough.

Almost an hour and a half had passed since the drug had taken effect, and I understood we were coming to the end now.

SHEILA

My God, that was so incredible. Should I take the eye shades off? Are we at the end?

RICHARD

(*laughter*) Yeah. Water?

SHEILA

(*big sigh of relief*) Yeah, water, sure. Oh my God, that was nuts. I want to do that again!

★

Calling the taxi, I had a sense of bewilderment and disorientation. And I felt a touch embarrassed, saying goodbye to Richard, at having behaved with so little regard to how I was 'supposed' to be in the presence of another person. But once I was downstairs, standing outside the building, in the hot sun, waiting for my ride, I detected inside me some clarity and peace.

In the back seat of the car, it suddenly seemed obvious why one might need to tranquilize a horse: like maybe the horse broke his leg. But as the drug was coming on, the idea of a horse tranquilizer had only filled me with terror: did they use it to kill horses, or did they . . . cut off their hooves? For *glue*?

The next few days I felt very physically tired – perhaps because I had swallowed the drug. But in little ways, which are always big ways, I felt myself acting and thinking differently. For one thing, silence from other people didn't seem like punishment. Unreturned emails felt like nothing. And I really paid attention to brightening, not dimming, Jack. *Maybe I could wash his car?* I thought, imagining other ways I might help him, for he was always, in practical ways, helping me. And so I did wash his car, and it was even fun. And he seemed happier, too.

I also felt less tentative in the physical world, which had always felt like it didn't belong to me. When I washed the dishes, or his car, or looped the garden hose to put it away, I didn't feel like the dishes or the hose or the car were going to crumble beneath my hands, as I hadn't even realized it had always seemed. The world began to feel more real, like matter, not wisps from a dream. Had a multitude of denials of reality – so many of which I'd uncovered in the session – made my entire waking life feel like a dream?

I began telling people, 'I'm never again doing therapy without ketamine. What would be the point?' I saw how in normal talk therapy, you remain your usual defensive self, making up stories with your defended mind, pretty much treading water, performing for the therapist, despite your best wishes not to.

In the ten days that followed, before my next appointment, I found it fun, in small and daily ways, to press myself, testingly, against the world, and to feel it, gently, pressing back.

★

Six days later, it was time for me to do the higher 'psychedelic' dose. But I didn't want to. My fear of doing drugs had returned. I slept poorly the night before, out of anxiety, continually resetting my alarm clock, knowing I needed to be at the clinic by 9 a.m. If I could have canceled without financial penalty, I would have.

As I dressed, I thought back to something Richard had said when I'd discussed my reluctance to do drugs; how I always took it to mean *I really shouldn't.*

RICHARD

> In the body, there's always a sense of resistance. Resistance to the unknown. It operates to protect us. It's pretty much in all of us. It's in our genetic makeup. But soon we can think, 'Okay, this is resistance. I understand the resistance, and I'm also open-minded about trying different things.' Sometimes we need to go against our intuition, our instincts, right?

As the taxi driver drove us north through the city, I watched through the side window as the numbers of the houses on Dufferin Street passed: 1977, 1983, 1987, 1995. I felt like I was passing through all the years of my life. And now we were driving into the future: 2027, 2061, 2095, 2145, 2304. Then the car turned east onto Eglinton, and suddenly we were plunged into the past, back before any of the living had been born: 1807, 1801, 1745, 1685, 1592. I felt dizzy, bewildered, and in awe of time. I was making myself high.

★

I sat in the darkened room with a new nurse. It wasn't the same room as before, and I wished that Richard was there, too. But this was supposed to be a different experience: a higher-dose treatment, where you were meant to 'go inward', while the nurse sat quietly as a 'compassionate witness'. This nurse was short, like me, and she had an apologetic way about her. I swished the ketamine, as before, and perhaps it was that I was tired, but the feeling was different, less intense.

The nurse was sitting on a chair in front of me, looking into her laptop, as I closed my eyes and pulled down the eye shade. The lightly psychedelic music coming through the headphones began to scare me, so I asked her if we could change it. She did, but I didn't like the new song. Finally I asked her for the iPad, scrolling through the playlist myself, but every song I tried was too dreamily spiritual. Missing how the meditation sounded when Richard read it, I reached for my own earpods and tried to listen to the audiobook of *The Courage to Be Disliked*, which Richard had recommended, and which I had been finding illuminating. Very quickly, I knew it wasn't right. I tried silence for a while, but was distracted by the sound of the building's air conditioning. I imagined returning home and saying to Jack, 'It was a disappointment.' Thinking of Jack reminded me of a frustration he'd had when, early in our relationship, we got the strange idea to take dancing lessons. 'You're terrible at being led,' he'd said, in our first session. I thought to myself, 'Stop fussing; let yourself be led,' and so I put on the clinic's headphones once more, and let their ketamine playlist play, and closed my eyes and began to settle.

Very soon I felt I was deep inside myself. Perhaps the music had a heartbeat to it, because I began to think of how my father had apparently played records for me when I was in my mother's womb. And then I saw myself being, or perhaps felt myself to be, inside her body, listening to the music, which now sounded both echoing and far away, as if separated by a barrier of human flesh. Then I really understood that I had once been a fetus, and that I had really been born, and had lain in my parents' bed, between them, when they were still young, and full of love for me and each other, and feeling a new excitement about life.

And then my awareness moved forward in time, and I was in my childhood bedroom, and I was able to move through our house, into my brother's bedroom, as it had been back then, seeing details I had long forgotten about.

And then it just continued: I was on the bus I had taken to grade school; then I saw the photographs in my high school locker; then I was in New York, one summer in my late twenties – a thick and slow panning across my whole life, until I was nearly thirty. I understood that this had been 'my childhood'. And the atmosphere of my past had a gentle warmth, and I felt the real affection and love I had been given as a small child, which was something I had come to forget.

Then I felt myself wondering, 'What *is* that song?' It was a tinkly, instrumental version of 'Dancing on My Own'. And I realized, 'Oh, I'm no longer high.'

The whole trip had lasted an hour.

★

The taxi dropped me off in the little town of Georgina, about an hour north of the ketamine clinic, where I was meeting Jack. I went into a café on the modest high street; a new restaurant had just opened, and I was amazed to see that along the walls were glass-fronted display shelves of memorabilia that I recognized so well from the 1970s and 1980s, when I had been a child. Behind the counter was the owner, who had also been a kid back then, and he and I started talking. All this stuff was from his mother's basement; he'd kept his ALF doll, and his yellow Sony Sports Walkman, and all his VHS tapes – the covers were burned into my brain from hours spent wandering the video store with my brother and dad. *Amadeus*. *E.T.* *Weekend at Bernie's*. It was a physical embodiment of what my trip had shown me: the past was *a real place*. I had really lived in it. There was concrete evidence.

I went outside, and Jack pulled up in the car. I got in and nuzzled our dog, Fritzi, who was leaning forward happily from the back seat. Jack looked at me briefly but carefully, and said, his voice containing both wryness and relief, 'You still look like the same Sheila.'

★

The following week, I visited my mother. We sat in her kitchen, as usual, in the house in which my brother and I had grown up; my father had moved out when they'd divorced, after twenty years of marriage.

SHEILA

Did I tell you about the article I'm doing? Psychedelic drugs with therapy? So ketamine, DMT, MDMA, LSD, but in conjunction with therapy. So they talk to you while you're on these drugs.

MOM

Oh, you're getting the therapy while you're high? How did you apply for it? How did they pick you?

SHEILA

How did they pick me? I'm writing an article about it. And with the second session – I kind of felt like I wanted to remember my childhood, and I felt like I was able to sensually feel being a baby in your womb, being born, and then the early days, when you and Dad were still happy. And I pictured the three of us in your bed, and you two being really happy and in love, and you two having this baby you loved. And it was such a nice feeling – just the warmth and the intimacy of that. But . . . do you think it's true?

MOM

(*thinks*) Possibly. Yeah, I mean, why not, sure. I mean, we were still in love, and we were very happy about the new baby. So it's very possible.

SHEILA

Can you imagine lying in the bed and having the baby between you?

MOM

I can imagine.

Then I read her some of what I'd transcribed from the session with Richard.

SHEILA

(*reading*) 'So it's like . . . my brother was *my* child. But that's a crazy thing to say, because I was *five and a half* when he was born! And my niece, she's seven. That's a *child*! She's not . . . but she *is* at the age where she could be a mother, because she knows what's right and what's wrong. She knows what's what. Like, she actually has a full brain already. And even two years ago, she had a completely full brain. Your brain actually is there at five. Like, I guess . . . I guess you're working with your five-year-old brain forever.'

MOM

Weird, really weird.

SHEILA

It's crazy that I thought that Evie was old enough to be a mother!

MOM

I mean, you were on drugs, come on, what do you expect? It's a good thing you knew that your name was Sheila.

★

In the weeks that followed, the actual sensation of being myself slightly shifted: I felt more dimensional, having experienced my past in such an embodied way. I wasn't just a racing mind in the present. I carried around an entire life. And memories, long ago forgotten, started coming back to me at the slightest touch – while watching movies, or talking to friends.

It was about three years into taking the Prozac – I had started it during an especially difficult patch – that I first began to wonder if I could function without it. And in the four years since then, I'd continued to wonder: it doesn't feel great to be dependent on a drug, and I'd always remained slightly concerned about whether there was an important part of myself that I was being cut off from, which might be harming my writing – though when I first began taking the drug, I was actually able to *start* writing again. I had tried quitting a couple of times since year three, but each attempt had failed: I'd become angry, teary, despairing; I almost ruined a friendship. I took these episodes as 'how I am without Prozac', rather than as symptoms of withdrawal. Each time, I had given up and gone back on.

In the wake of the first ketamine sessions, I developed a theory: because over the course of the next six weeks, I would be flooding my mind with all these new chemicals, could I successfully titrate off the Prozac at the same time? (I was taking the lowest dose, 10 mg a day.) Would my brain, distracted and confused by all these new inputs, barely even register the absence of the SSRI? Plus, SSRIs were known to dampen the effects of hallucinogenic drugs. I wanted the full effects, which also made it seem like a good time to quit.

After talking about it with my doctor (although I didn't mention the psychedelic project), I lowered my dose to every other day.

Then I called my mother and apologized to her for some of the things I had told her about my ketamine trip; I didn't want her to feel bad about how she had mothered me. We'd been through all of that, pretty thoroughly, ten years earlier. I started crying as I was apologizing and she said hurriedly, 'It's okay, thank you, I'm not upset. Just please . . . please stop crying.'

★

The underground world, I came to learn, was actually quite far away, on the west coast of British Columbia, a five-hour flight from Toronto. There, through connections of connections, I managed to find a man, Bruce, a former minister turned psychotherapist, who would dose me with either mushrooms or LSD, and would sit with me for four hours until a friend took over. I would also meet a woman who I'm here calling Ellis, who would arrange for me to try DMT (dimethyltryptamine). She asked that I download Signal (the encrypted messaging app) to communicate with her.

As I bought myself a plane ticket, I explained all this to Jack.

He said, 'So you're going to Vancouver to do drugs with criminals.'

I hesitated. 'Yes.'

★

I was staying with family friends in Vancouver – the man, Janos, had been a close friend of my father's from childhood, he had worked with Greenpeace since the 1980s. When I explained the reason I was in Vancouver, he and his wife, Noni, seemed completely unsurprised. The city had been a hippie Mecca, not unlike San Francisco, a straight shot, fifteen-hour drive, down Highway I-5. Sitting in their living room shortly after I arrived, I listened as Noni recalled the first time they had done acid, in the 1960s, with two friends who were a couple. The woman had gotten high, but the man – the only one of them who had tried LSD – remained sober.

Noni said, 'We laughed and giggled for four hours until finally he said, "Okay, enough giggling. Time to get serious. Listen to this." And he put on an album that had just come out: it was the first time any of us heard "Here Comes the Sun". We said, *Whooooooaaawww!!* It was a completely new sound for the Beatles.'

At the wedding in the Azores, Jack had become friendly with a man who ran breathwork seminars and who worked with psychedelics in Vancouver. He had passed around a glass of liquid MDMA after the wedding, when everyone was dancing. (Jack and I had declined.) When I was unsure of how to find DMT, Jack suggested I get in touch with him. He was lovely and helpful and put me in touch with Ellis.

Ellis seemed somewhat younger than me; we had spoken a few times over Zoom. She seemed warm and efficient, wore her dirty-blonde hair long, and dressed in tank tops and sweatshirts in a way that suggested the sort of woman who was always running off to the next emergency. She had been working as a senior therapist in a psychiatric hospital, a 'secure facility', for the past twenty-five years. 'It's for those who are found by our court system not criminally responsible due to mental illness.'

She explained how they used cognitive behavioral therapy with patients who were suffering from psychosis. 'Like, if they're hearing a happy, benevolent voice that's not causing them any harm, we say, "So be it, have the voice, because some are actually saying really nice things." But if they're having voices that cause distress, we work with them on tolerance. We give them exercises to be like, "How believable is this? Like, are you *actually* God? Or is there another possibility?" It's interesting. It's its own nuanced, little version of CBT.'

What was important to recognize about her psychedelic work, and the work of others like her, was that it was not just about the medicines they offered, but 'your alliance with the people holding space for you – the container. The ethos of "big pharma" is, "I'll just take this pill". But it's more than that, it's all of it.' She said if she didn't feel a connection with the person who was coming to her, or if *they* didn't feel a connection, she wouldn't proceed with the dosing.

She emphasized the importance, on the day of the ceremony, of letting your body do whatever it wanted. Once, after doing DMT, she had been 'shaking for an hour'. This seemed awful – I didn't want to shake! She said, 'Most people are worried about doing something embarrassing at some point,' but that she had seen everything. She reassured me, 'I've worked with some of the most psychotic people in Canada.'

★

After three preparatory therapy sessions, each one lasting an hour, I felt I knew what to expect: DMT was an immediate and fast-acting drug ('Medicine,' she reminded me. 'We don't say drug.') that affects the mind almost instantaneously. It is naturally produced in humans in trace amounts, and in certain plants and animals – most famously, the Sonoran Desert toad. The reason I wanted to try DMT was not only because the high lasts just fifteen minutes, but because she said I might meet creatures.

Ellis suggested we do N, N-DMT, not 5-MeO-DMT, because N, N was less likely to be dampened by an SSRI. Also, she was concerned that with 5-MeO, part of me would be trying to keep one toe in reality; that even unconsciously I would be wanting to take notes for the article, and fighting it, and this could result in a difficult trip. With N, N there wasn't that risk of 'gripping': it just 'blasted you off into the stratosphere'.

She also shared with me an incredible N, N experience she'd had, in which she was 'up somewhere very high' and these 'little gray, translucent beings with red glowing lights in them' hurried up to her and were like 'we only have ten minutes, we're going to get all the trauma out of you'. They meant the trauma she'd absorbed from her patients. And they started pulling it out of her as fast as they could. She told me, 'That night my Apple Watch logged the best sleep of my life. I got an AWARD.'

Ellis didn't love that I was doing all these therapies over the course of a month. There'd be too much to unpack, and it would be exhausting for my body. 'But I have this deadline,' I explained. I had given myself until the end of the summer to do the drugs, at which point I'd be leaving town for a month; I'd have the first two weeks of September to write the article. 'Yeah. If you didn't have a deadline, I'd say do them over six months.' She reassured me, however, that I wasn't going to die, and that 'the experience unfolds over a lifetime, really'. We would have three integration sessions in the month and a half following the DMT ceremony. 'So it's not like you just came and did some drugs and had a fun time,' she said. 'If someone's not offering integration, you're going to be getting a medicine ceremony, but it's not therapy.'

The evening before I flew out to Vancouver, we talked and she prepared me for an hour, then we finished with this exchange:

ELLIS

One last thing I wanted to ask: when you're feeling stressed or overwhelmed, what do you have that would anchor you into a happy moment, that would immediately bring a smile to your face?

SHEILA

(*thinks*) I guess my dog?

ELLIS

Yeah, I just wanted to check in on that. People always pick their dogs.

★

Janos drove me to my DMT experience, which was to be held at 10 a.m. in a refashioned garage – the headquarters of Lucinor. Ellis would meet me there. She had suggested we do the medicine with the Lucinor people, because they had a good space, and were experienced at offering DMT.

Lucinor was run by David Chin and his partner, who I'm calling

'Kay'. (Her day job as a therapist made her nervous about being identified in this article, same as Ellis.) David toured the world talking about DMT, and he and Kay hosted 'covenant ceremonies' and 'communication ceremonies' in their space, and Lucinor sent microdose supplements of DMT and mushrooms all across the country.

David was warm and authoritative and handsome (his acting website notes that 'there's a psychological intensity and a physical presence within David that makes him a convincing criminal, corrupt cop or broken soldier', which seemed true). He was wearing flip-flops, long shorts, and a kimono over a *Back to the Future* T-shirt that read 'Where we're going, we don't need roads.' Kay was petite and elegantly tattooed, her black hair dyed purple at the ends. I had met her (David had just poked his head in) several weeks earlier in an online session with Ellis, and Kay was, in person, sweet and unhurried, with a clear and patient way of explaining everything.

The medicine space was in their garage, in an alley out behind their house. Inside, a cream-colored, painted wood ceiling rose up from the walls to a peak in the center. There was dim lighting, and a round rug with a mandala pattern on it, and in the center stood six thick candles, around which the four of us sat, and the garage smelled of incense and oils, and there were so many pillows, and something like a futon cushion lay flush on the tatami mat–covered floor, and it was a restful and good place to be.

It was an hour and a half before I took the medicine. Together we chose the music. Kay lit incense and put some DMT on the 'altar'. She thanked the land. We went over to the low bed, and did a practice run of David holding the bubbler, and me inhaling (though I didn't yet inhale) then lying down; the pillow was carefully placed so it would be right beneath my head when I lay back. I went to the washroom and found that I had suddenly gotten my period – two weeks early! When I returned and told them this, feeling a bit shocked, they all nodded as if it was just one of those things that happened around DMT. David explained that the medicine – a yellow crystal powder; he showed it to me – had been extracted by one of his best friends from the bark of a *Mimosa hostilis* tree in Mexico. And Ellis reminded me that I was welcome to take the medicine a second time if I wanted; only half an hour of rest would be needed between the journeys because DMT leaves the system so rapidly.

I pulled two cards from a divination deck and Kay read them, and I reflected on how the card Let It Go made me think about our last dog, Feldman, a Rottweiler, who had died a year ago at the age of ten, and here I started to talk about how much I missed him, and how he was 'such a good dog and just my best friend and protector', and how I had a feeling that I was betraying Feldman by loving our new young Rottie, Fritzi, which was making it hard for me to really love her.

Then I was told to speak my intentions with the DMT out loud, since, as David said, 'this medicine is particularly sensitive to intentions'. The prospect of doing so made me feel really shy, but I did the best I could, thinking on the spot.

SHEILA

Um . . . my intention for this ceremony is to access deeper clarity about the relationship between the spirit world and the material world, and the purpose of . . . our relationships with each other, and how I can access more . . . giving love and receiving love. But, yeah, I'm just interested in that word. Clarity. And that feeling.

Then we went over to the low bed, and I sat up in it, preparing for when I'd have to suddenly lie down. Kay was by my feet, Ellis was on my left side, and David was on my right, holding in his hand the large bubbler, into which he'd packed a high dose of 30 mg of DMT. He would push the button, and it would melt, and then I was to inhale for ten seconds, filling up my lungs with the smoke until I reached 70 or 80 percent of my lung capacity – then I was to take one last sip of air, hold it in for ten seconds, then exhale. He would again bring the bubbler to my lips, I would do it again, and then I would do it a third time. They had frequently made the point that many people felt unable to inhale a third time, feeling too high already; but the risk of this was ending up in the 'waiting room' and not getting all the way to the other side. This sounded very bad to me. Yet if I couldn't inhale a third time, not to worry. 'There's no rush to enlightenment,' David said.

Finally he said that if the experience was too intense, 'there's a very simple solution, which is just to open your eyes. And the experience that you're feeling of being elsewhere, or being with entities, or what have you, will generally dissipate. It's sort of like pulling your parachute'.

Kay made the lights go pink, and put on the music we had chosen, of a woman with a celestial voice singing slowly and reverently. I inhaled from the bubbler, and the smoke tasted like nothing I had ever tasted – perhaps a bit like if you smoked one of those dense, hard, red-white-and-blue rubber balls from childhood. Yet the smoke also tasted oddly familiar, an uncanniness I didn't like at all.

In the seconds between the second and the third inhale, sounds and colors became severely distorted, everything was larger or smaller than normal, and David's hand in front of my face with the bubbler was the largest hand I had ever seen. Then I lay down and pulled on the eye shades and felt plunged into the darkest darkness, and I was traveling up into the stratosphere, leaving my life and myself behind: I did not know what city I was in, what room, I saw a flash of myself drinking coffee that morning, way down below on Earth, where I had gone for coffee that morning, and this seemed to me the sweetest and very best thing in life, and I did not want to be where I was now, so far away from everything familiar, why had I done this when life was so good and now it was so hopelessly far away, and then this was gone too, and I had the sensation of repeating lines and angles, a totally nauseating, strict geometry that allowed for no accidents, like at the base of everything was just math, and I didn't want to be there, wherever I was, or seeing this, and I had lost all sense of my body, or how long had it been since I'd taken my last breath.

And how were you supposed to breathe? In and . . . *out*? I couldn't remember. I guessed that a whole minute had passed since my last breath inward or outward. And then I laboriously tried one way, and I felt the terrible difficulty of breathing, and knew if I didn't figure this out, I was going to die. I tried telling myself, *This is a drug, you have chosen to take it, nothing is wrong*, but my body didn't believe me. And I said, sort of raspily, 'I'm forgetting how to breathe or something.' Most frightening of all, there was even a disconnect from the idea that the responsibility for breathing had to do with 'me'. Then suddenly a sweet smell came over me – Kay wafted some oils beneath my nose, I later learned – and smelling this very quickly soothed me; I understood that if I was smelling, I probably *was* breathing. And she leaned over me and said, 'In through your nose . . . and out through your mouth . . .' and I just did it in time with her speaking. And I felt safe and cared for.

At some point, I was back.

'How long has it been since I smoked that?'

'Ten minutes,' someone said.

Nobody could have convinced me that this was therapeutic, or anything but maybe the stupidest drug in existence. I lay there still feeling the terror of not knowing how to breathe, and then I thought about my dog, Feldman, and I realized that that was probably how frightened *he* had felt when he was dying – exactly that bewildered and scared – and I felt so sad and heartbroken for him, and I started crying, and I felt such sadness for my lost Feldman, and I kept on weeping with longing and grief. I knew they were sitting there, watching me, but I let myself cry and feel all the sorrow, and I made little animal sounds of grieving that normally I wouldn't ever have made. After about two minutes, I stopped, and I felt in the stillness inside me the presence of Fritzi, our new dog; for the first time I could see her clearly; how she was such a bright spirit, and so stimulated by the world, eagerly taking everything in, and I was seeing her not in comparison to Feldman. And I had such a desire to be there at home with her, and to connect with her.

Then I heard David whispering, 'This is Dimitri. It's a . . . journey buddy.' He was crouched beside me with a stuffed doll – a worm about a foot in length and made of patchwork fabric, wearing a felt hat and smiling, and in that moment, nothing in the world could have comforted me more, and I felt the tenderest gratitude toward David and the doll. 'Dimitri?' I asked.

'It's the street name for DMT.'

Then I asked if it had looked like I couldn't breathe, and Ellis said she always watched people's chests and stomachs ('that's one of the cues I look for') but apart from breathing up in my chest, I seemed fine; the breathing in the chest 'was nothing concerning'. I could hardly believe it. I explained that I thought I was going to die. David said it was 'incredibly normal', and that 'the difference between poison and medicine is dosage, and you just introduced *a lot* of a molecule that your body *does* recognize, but in the quantity that it generally reserves for birth and death. It is believed that DMT is released at birth and death, in large quantities, in the human body, and that's what near-death experiences are. They're DMT experiences'.

Twenty minutes later, after having fully come down from the drug, I was feeling more settled. The thought of now getting up and leaving the garage and saying goodbye felt wrong. I hadn't flown all the way to Vancouver to forget how to breathe.

'I think I'm going to want to do that again,' I said.

★

After all the women left the garage to use the washroom in the house, we gathered again and picked a new, more playfully upbeat song, and everyone settled themselves, and then I was back on the mattress, and there was David's hand with the bubbler.

Sometime later . . .

DAVID

Welcome back.

SHEILA

How long was I gone for?

ELLIS

Twenty minutes.

SHEILA

I wasn't scared that time.

DAVID

You're a natural!

SHEILA

(*laughs, delighted*) Really?

KAY

Yeah! You're really good at this! By the time you got it – after the first time – then it was like, your body knows. I could tell with the way you were inhaling.

SHEILA

It felt like an almost infinite . . . like a honeycomb, kind of . . .

KAY

Oh, you went there.

SHEILA

With little things dancing in unison . . . in every honeycomb?

KAY

Yeah, I'd say don't try to figure it out today.

★

It was now two in the afternoon. David went into the kitchen to start cooking, and I sat in the dining room with Kay and Ellis. Kay offered that I could stay for lunch, but I felt the need to just walk and walk.

I *did* want to figure it out today. The visuals in the second trip had been astonishing. The music was really different: moody, looping, electronic rhythms. As the medicine was rapidly coming on, I reminded myself that I *could* breathe, and I did, with some effort – deeply and deliberately – and then I was traveling infinitely far from my body, and then again I was in that world that was uncomfortably geometric, devoid of any curves. The reality I found myself in was an infinite and interlocking pattern of honeycomb shapes, unfolding in all directions, and across *all* the dimensions – not just space and time, but dimensions I was intuiting for the first time. And as complex and recursive as these honeycombs were, my vision was so sharp that I could see, even into the ones at an infinite distance, their most intricate details, like that inside each hexagram was a little creature dancing, doing a regular, sort of regimented dance, like in the Bangles' 'Walk Like an Egyptian' video, and the music I was hearing was a deeply essential part of their world, and there was a perfect equivalence between what I was seeing and what I was hearing, or like seeing and hearing were really the same sense, and the bodies of these creatures were sort of flipping right and left, each in sync with the others, but in perfect time to the music, and all perfect copies of each other, not completely unlike the Grateful Dead bears, but angular, and all wearing the same mischievous, suggestive, ironic, almost winking smile, looking at me, but their bodies also looking, and widening their eyes, as if to say, '*Hey SHEILA . . . but have you ever heard . . . MUSIC?*'

Then, after what felt like one or two minutes, I found myself back in the garage, and I must have coughed or cleared my throat in a normal way, for David very gently said, 'As the effect of the medicine begins to diminish, you may want to remove the eye shades and take a look around. You'll have some of the DMT world still left. And things can look a little different.' Removing the eye shades, the light in the room seemed soft and rosy, and looking around at each of their smiling faces, I thought I saw in the corner of each of their right eyes a cartoonishly large and glistening tear, each in the shape of a perfect teardrop.

★

Walking toward the ocean – in the direction Kay had pointed me (although I never did reach the ocean) – passing slowly through their placid West Vancouver neighborhood, the sun out and the sky clear, I began writing notes into my phone, pausing every half-block to jot down something new.

> Feeling a slight disappointment
>
> That apartment building looks like the DMT trip: those windows in a structure
>
> My vision of that morning's coffee: is the DMT talking about how deep repetition is in a human life? Is that the very thing we'll miss most when we die?
>
> Is there something playful about logic? About order and structure? About repetition? Is repetition funny? Is it funny to have a schedule? To do the same thing every day?

How much activity breathing is! Really it's this very laborious activity that's keeping you alive

Gripped David's hand the third time when he was holding out the bubbler. 'I got you,' he said

Felt more like a 'drug' than any drug I've ever done

Pride at being told that I'm good at smoking DMT. Like being told you're good at blow jobs. Kind of a sordid thing to be good at. Doesn't really make a difference in the world. Not something you can go around bragging about

The DMT experience is like a dream; how it rapidly disappears and withdraws from you

Visuals a bit like those screensavers from the early 2000s, those colored lines moving through the darkness, or those star-bits of light racing toward you

Or like when you're a kid and you press down on your eyelids to make shapes and colors come

Still can't believe I looked completely normal from the outside

Feel unable to interpret what happened in the language of 'meaning'

How could that come from the bark of a tree?

Then I was on a main street, unsure if I was hungry. I went into a bakery and was overpowered by the smell of DMT. Disgusted, I went next door, into the deli, and again the air smelled pungently of DMT. What was happening? The exhaust of a passing car smelled like DMT. I passed a pharmacy called Boomer Drugs. I sat at a bus stop and took more notes.

> Am not looking forward to doing acid. Will be glad when this is all done with. If someone foretold that I'd never do drugs the rest of my life, I'd feel relieved
>
> Doesn't matter that I can't quite remember what I saw in the DMT world, because even if I did, I wouldn't be able to describe it anyway
>
> Feeling very positive toward every human I encounter
>
> How can you describe an altered state of consciousness when you can't even describe the resting state?
>
> Crows and dogs everywhere

★

When I returned to the house where I was staying, my hosts were lying on separate couches, reading their books. Noni looked up at me and said, 'How was the DMT? Did it feel like a profound drug?'

I hesitated. 'Not for me.'

'Did you get any insights into yourself?' Janos asked. I don't know what my face did then, but he said, 'I guess you realized you don't really like drugs.'

★

I had made the decision, before I even left for Vancouver, to buy a DMT pen from Kay and David – a 'low-relational dose', which meant that, smoking it, you would only get a tenth as high as I'd gotten in their garage. It had cost me two hundred dollars, which now seemed like such a waste. Why didn't I wait until I'd seen whether I even *liked* DMT?

I went to sleep that night, and the next day, I spent a nice afternoon with a few friends at the beach. That evening, I got into bed, thinking I wanted to listen to the song Kay had played during the second DMT trip, in case it would bring back some of the visuals, the memory of which was already fading. In the darkness, I put on my earpods and, after taking a drag from the vape pen – essentially a microdose – I turned on the music.

With the very first notes, I experienced a ticklish feeling inside my brain, around the edges and at numerous points in the interior – I had never before felt my brain as being composed of different physical regions. Then a deep shiver went all the way down through my body. As far back as I could remember, music had a distant, two-dimensional quality, like words on a page. But as the song continued, it was like I was hearing it in a different place: not flatly in my ears, but in this resonant amphitheater that was as dark and vast as outer space and as small as my skull, as if the dark, infinitude of outer space lived behind my eyes, in my skull there. I could, for the first time, distinctly pick out every instrument, and I felt music's depth and mystery and the miracle of it, and its complex and beautiful strangeness, and I started to laugh in disbelief: it was as if I'd been given a new brain, and a new perceptiveness with it, and there was the music, pinging around in my brain, as if the notes were pinballs lighting up bumpers in the galaxy.

After laughing at this wonderful gift, I began crying. Tears were running down my cheeks from joy. And for the next four hours, until three in the morning, I continued to lie there, playing songs, those I knew, but also songs I'd never heard. And part of my excitement was about telling Jack – who had recently set up the speakers so carefully – that I finally *got it,* this art form he'd despaired of me ever enjoying, this passion he felt I would never share. And each individual song changed the atmosphere of my interior world completely, flooding me, and it was the most wonderful feeling in the whole world.

Before I went to sleep, I wrote these notes:

> I think that DMT trip was the greatest thing to ever happen to me
>
> I don't understand how it did what it did
>
> Whole mind an amphitheater now

And one little note about my dad:

> My dad wanted me to stay with him in his narrow little world. To be confined within his own consciousness somehow. To live in there forever with him

★

I didn't mention the music thing to Jack until I had been home from Vancouver for two weeks, in case it turned out to have just been one night of magic. But by the time I told him, it was obvious that I'd been altered: whereas before I preferred silence, now I couldn't stop listening to music.

★

In the weeks after leaving Vancouver, I began to wonder why I had flattened 'therapeutic' into meaning being able to tell stories about myself and my childhood. What could be more therapeutic than the gift of sensitivity in one of our primary senses, and sensitivity to the art that touched it? Since my early twenties, music had often made me uncomfortable. *Why do I want these sad feelings? Why do I want these nostalgic feelings?* But those feelings were suddenly exciting and no longer threatening.

Back in Toronto, I was having an online integration session with Ellis and Kay, five weeks after taking DMT in the Lucinor garage, trying to talk through my thoughts around music. 'If your brain can't hear music, what else is your brain not able to access? Like, which emotions? What else are you not perceiving in the world? And what aren't you perceiving about your own body?'

Kay agreed and explained how she understood it: 'Over time, as we age, we start shutting down certain functions, or they start disconnecting because they haven't been used, or we've learned to distance ourselves from them because they overwhelm, or for protection mechanism purposes. And when we do that over time, we just forget how to use them.'

I wanted to know how the DMT changed all this.

KAY

What psychedelics do is, they allow you to fire all those parts of your brain, to reactivate it and make it more malleable. It's almost like a clean slate, and you're like, 'Oh, this is what it's like to experience something fully connected.' The whole brain is lighting up. Psychedelics are such a beautiful medicine. It depends on how the container is created, but it can almost allow your brain to completely shut down and reboot, because it's such a fast experience, and it's so short. But just because the experience is short, it doesn't mean it's any less profound.

SHEILA

You know, after the DMT, I just thought, 'Oh my God, I really love gin and tonics.' Like, that's the best drug humans have developed. That's the thought I had all day! Like, I'm never doing DMT again. And then the music thing happened! And then a few days passed, and I just became so curious about that world that I entered, even though it was scary. I was like, What *was* that bizarre place? I felt like I wanted to go there again. And then, returning to Toronto, I just felt so much love for Fritzi – like there was this new, open channel of love for Fritzi!

ELLIS

Maybe because you got the grief out of the way, or because of having expressed it. There are some unexplained things that happen in the body that are hard to make sense of with the DMTs. Like with blockages. Some people talk about it as a wringing out of the nervous system, almost like a reset or a clearing. It's really cool that you're able to feel that with Fritzi.

SHEILA

Yes. My heart feels sort of clean and clear, and I don't feel guilty about loving Fritzi.

Then Ellis reminded me of something I'd said at our first integration session. 'You were like, "I'm not sure what the therapeutic part is."'

'Yeah,' I said. 'I was like, "How is this therapeutic – to see a bunch of honeycombs?"'

★

Back in August, it was the morning after my DMT-inspired night of music, and I was traveling from Vancouver to Bowen Island, a twenty-minute ferry ride. The next day, I would be meeting Bruce Sanguin, a man who appeared to be in his late sixties, with long hair and glasses, who had been a minister in the United Church of Canada for twenty-eight years, before leaving to work as a therapist. I had been given his name by Jack's stepmother, a therapist who had taken an online course with him on how to do psychedelic therapy with patients; a version of a course he also taught to psychiatrists and doctors.

The first time we had spoken, back in July, I had told him I thought I wanted to do mushrooms together, since I was comfortable with mushrooms. But when I asked him what drug he preferred to work with, he said LSD. When I asked why, he said, 'I feel like it's *clean*. They call it "light medicine", so there's a lot of clarity, and a lot of intuitive knowing sort of comes online. I tend to get big ideas that are connected to reality, but nevertheless they become . . . orienting principles for my life. I find mushrooms are a little more earthy, embodied. I think because of the mycelial network thing, you tend to want to sort of get down and roll in the earth. They take you into your body – and there's obviously deep wisdom there as well. It's just a different direction. Acid is more airy, up into the light.'

I'd never heard acid described in this way. When I thought about it, mushrooms were for me almost *too* bodily: I'd be taking off my clothes, then putting them on again, then getting in the bath, then needing to be outside, then needing to be inside again, always too aware of what was physically comfortable and what was not. It sounded like on LSD you floated above all that.

'I think I'd like to try LSD,' I said.

'And we'd do it with MDMA,' he said, 'because it puts you in a good space, and in that good space, you're able to surrender. That's the key: just being able to relax.'

When I asked him what he brought to the experience, he said he didn't impose 'any sort of protocols', and that 'people tend to find a rhythm of going inward, and then coming out and connecting. And the medicines – they're not putting anything into your mind. They're *showing you* your mind. R.D. Laing said we're "psychophobic" – we're afraid of what's in our mind. So sometimes it's a matter of reminding the person, "It's okay, you're not being invaded by some alien species. This is a paranoid part of your mind." I can provide a corrective perspective fairly quickly, but I try to stay out of the role of therapist, and just be Bruce, and connect with you.'

His only concern was about how long an LSD trip lasted – at least eight hours – which would be difficult for him as he had a small child at home, 'and I don't feel comfortable leaving a person at the four-hour mark, when they're, like, tripping balls, you know?' He said if I could find someone to sit with me for the tapering period, I should come to Bowen and rent a place for a couple of nights. I said I was sure I could find somebody and agreed to bring his fee in cash (his usual rate as a therapist – $200 per hour, multiplied by five hours – plus about $20 for the medicine).

I texted a writer who I had been friends with for twenty-five years to see if he could do it – he lived on an island near Bowen – and he said, yes, sure, it would be fun! I suggested he bring his girlfriend along and stay for both nights, make it a bit of a vacation, and I rented for us a modern, minimalist, light-filled Airbnb, with soft white couches and raw oak ceilings, and a master suite for the two of them.

★

Bowen Island (population: 4,256) was warm and sparkling when I arrived: a sweet, tidy seaport with some charming, modest cafes and restaurants running along the shoreline. There was a gravel path a short distance from where the ferries docked, leading to acres of natural forest, and another path, past a dusty trail over which I dragged my luggage, leading to a residential neighborhood. I crossed a pebbly beach, and a bench on a lookout. Kids splashed among sea birds and there were a few small boats anchored a way off from the shore, and the scent of pine and flowers, and an unusual feeling of peace and quiet.

I let myself into the Airbnb. I still felt tired from taking DMT in the garage two days before. I considered whether I could delay the journey, but even if Bruce *was* free another time, it would be impossible for me. Today was Sunday, the next day I was supposed to see Bruce, I had reserved Tuesday to recover, and my flight home was on Wednesday afternoon.

As the sky darkened with evening, I texted my friend to make sure he would be there at 5 p.m. the next day, when Bruce would have to go. My friend had mentioned, a few days earlier, that his girlfriend was no longer coming. Now he texted that he *only just checked* how long it would take him to travel from his island to Bowen: much longer than he'd guessed. He also now had an important meeting. 'I could get there by seven or eight,' he texted. 'Or at the very latest, nine.'

Angry, I spent the next few hours scrambling through all of my Vancouver contacts, and with some relief imagined telling Bruce it was off – that we would only do MDMA. A reprieve from the gods? But early the next morning I woke to a text from someone I'd contacted in Vancouver (a woman I'd met at the wedding) saying that 'Ana' (also from the wedding) could come. Ana *lived on* Bowen! Although we had barely interacted at the wedding, I remembered her: she was blonde and serene and beautiful, and had a husband and a small child. It felt awkward to imagine being high on acid for hours in front of this total stranger. Was this a favor I could even *accept*? But Jack said I should accept it. I had flown across the country, after all. When would a chance like this come again?

★

Before sunup that morning, Bruce had deposited an MDMA capsule into a teapot that I'd placed outside, on the front porch. Then I did as I was told: swallowing the pill at 12.30 p.m., half an hour before he was set to arrive. Trembling with nervousness, I cut up the vegetables and strawberries I had bought that morning to feed him and Ana, certain I was about to cut myself. Then Bruce arrived. We sat on opposite couches, and I began to record our conversation, talking about my impulse, ever since childhood, to be pleasing and performing, and how sometimes this even ruined writing for me – my greatest pleasure! – and how I had started wondering if, in part, I chose to write the sort of books I thought my father (now seven years dead) would approve of. Could this desire, this allegiance to his taste, be preventing me from discovering a deeper or more thorough way of writing?

After about eight minutes, I decided to turn the tape recorder off. I could feel myself performing for the tape – and this was a part of myself I was trying to overcome! I was worried slightly about forgetting the trip, and so not being able to write the article, but Bruce said he thought it would be fine. 'The important things, you'll remember.' And it was true: while the DMT experience receded so quickly, my day on LSD would remain completely vivid in my mind for months and months.

After another ten or fifteen minutes of talking, Bruce stood up and came over to me and said, 'Can I see your pupils?' Satisfied, he handed me the tab of acid. I hadn't imagined it would be so tiny – hardly bigger than a lentil! I had always imagined acid to be the size of a Chiclet. I let it sit under my tongue, that little, blank piece of paper, and when I wanted to, I bit it and swallowed it. It was much easier than doing ketamine, and much easier than doing DMT.

Some time later, when we were talking in the backyard, I had the feeling that I was not quite high enough – I felt my mind was going in neurotic circles – and right then, Bruce said, 'You're tolerating this quite well. Do you want a second one?' I said yes, and he went back inside and brought out another tab, and I ate it, totaling 130 mg of MDMA in my body, and 240 micrograms of LSD.

★

How to express what happened over the next twelve hours? Lying in the brighter and bigger of the two bedrooms, the bare wood ceiling with its knots looked like little faces blowing love. And in the folds of the curtains were even more benevolent faces. It was in that brighter, bigger bedroom that a vision of God appeared in the rafters.

Then I was outside, sitting on the sofa on the shaded deck, and the trees and foliage were gently geometric, glistening and twisting. The whole world had become softly fractal and shifting, saturated with a sweet light, and I felt extremely calm, floating and happy; blissed-out by the day.

As the day progressed, difficult feelings about my father came up inside me, and I remember lying in bed, asking Bruce all sorts of questions about parents and children. Then I was alone again – for I had asked to be alone.

And then later Bruce came into the airier bedroom, where I was again lying in bed, and he said, 'It's eight minutes to five,' and I felt startled and disappointed. I had forgotten there was *even such a thing* as time.

Then Ana arrived, and they stood there talking in the front vestibule. As she was setting down her bag, and he was putting on his shoes to go, I felt myself hovering, so I made myself wander away, telling myself, 'Let the adults figure it out.' I really felt like a parent was handing me off to a babysitter for the night.

A few days later, Ana explained that Bruce more or less told her what to expect, and advised her, 'Just be yourself. But don't ask any pointed questions.' Once she returned home at the end of the night, she explained to her husband, 'I just mirrored her. If she was in the kitchen, pacing, I stood in the kitchen and moved about, too. If she was lounging on the couch outside, I lay there lounging, also.' Her husband said, 'I would never have thought of doing that.'

Ana came into the kitchen, and I thanked her for being there – on such short notice, and given that she had a small child, and as she had just returned home from a trip of her own – and I began offering her snacks, feeling so grateful and sheepish over this great gift she was giving me, until finally she said, 'This is *not* what today is about. You do not have to host me.'

Every hour – at six, and seven, and eight o'clock – I kept checking in. 'Are you sure you don't want to go home yet?' Sometimes we'd be talking and laughing, sometimes I'd be lying in bed alone, and sometimes I'd be at the computer, writing.

And what a pleasure it was to write on LSD! The white page of the screen had texture and depth to it, like it was made of rough stone. And how the letters danced! – growing slightly bigger, and slightly smaller, bigger and smaller, as the lines and curves of the letters undulated like grass in the breeze. And I just kept pressing new letters into the stone of the page, then they would be off wiggling.

Finally at nine, it really seemed safe for Ana to leave. I still felt high, and the darkest part of the trip was yet to come, but a more sober, sensible part of my mind had started to return to me. So Ana called her husband and he drove to the house and came to the door with their child, who stood there giddily in his pajamas, wearing a tiger mask. When we opened the door, the boy yelled, 'Rawr!' Then, a moment later, under his breath, he admitted, 'I'm not really a tiger.'

★

How many things in life can be called therapeutic?

Could it be called therapeutic to have argued with the spirit of my father – never once having done this, not once having articulated my most serious objections? I hadn't even known the anger I was carrying, not once in my whole life. Could it be called therapeutic to have seen a vision of God and known, *Oh, this is MY god. My god is not that other god – and it's not my father!* Could it be called therapeutic to have felt a shame so deep, for hours and hours; a shame unlike any I'd felt before – over ways I had been with Jack, at times so selfish and unseeing, so absorbed in myself that I couldn't see him, and so I had been more my own partner really than his. For, after expelling all my anger at my father, I realized that one wasn't only *hurt* in this life, but was also responsible for hurting others. So after writing about my father, I wrote a letter to Jack, kneeling on the floor, my computer on the bed, my arms stretched out on the keys, my head on my arm, completely depleted and drenched in tears.

And many more things were thought and done, to be told to only a few friends and Jack. And some things I didn't tell anyone.

Then at around one o'clock in the morning, after twelve thick hours, I went to lie down in the bed of the smaller room and tried to instruct myself, *Rest, you've done it – it's over. There's no more thinking still to do. Go to sleep!* And I was reminded of that thing they say in yoga: that the hardest pose is the one where you must lie still and rest on your mat at the end. *So it was true! The body doesn't want to rest!* I'd never believed it.

The next day I was sunk in an inner grayness, still completely emptied out, almost too tired to walk even the three blocks to the forest, where I stood about for ten minutes, before returning home.

★

That afternoon, I received a message from Noni in Vancouver, the woman who, the first time she took acid, had listened to the just-released *Abbey Road*.

'So? Did you see God?' Noni texted.

It was such a funny text, and it seemed even funnier to answer, 'Yes, thank you for asking!' So I texted that back. And I discovered that something in me wanted to explain what I'd seen, and so I did.

God – (my god? a god?) – was this huge, corpulent woman in the sky with lots of flowing, lemon-glazed hair, and her hair spread wide out in every direction, it was curly and wavy, like the clouds and the sea, and at other moments she looked like a 1940s pinup star; and she was gathering into herself all the pleasures of the earth, which she absorbed into herself, in order to also feel it, whenever we experienced pleasure, even just the sun on your face, and she could never be satiated, or too filled up with pleasures. I saw her floating above me, and all these éclairs and lollipops and sweets were hovering in the air around her, and her legs were outstretched, or she had no legs, and her arms were like a pendulum almost, alternately swinging out and gathering in, just scooping and gathering up all the world's pleasures and pushing them inside her vagina. And she did this calmly, methodically, and she never stopped gathering; in went the desserts, and she was coolly insatiable. And as I watched her, I noticed she didn't gather in pleasures that – in their pursuit – had hurt other people. So hurting other people in pursuit of your own pleasure was a sin. And anything that spoiled your own pleasure, like for instance guilt that helped no one when you were trying on clothes, or impatience to be done watching a movie when you had work to get back to – the potential pleasure of those experiences never reached her, and so could be considered neighbors of sin. All this corrected something I'd believed: that pleasure was self-indulgent. Now I realized no, it was holy. That 'pleasure is prayer'. And when I started coming down from the drugs several hours later, I realized that 'uncovering the truth' was also a kind of pleasure, one that could feed this god . . .

'Wonderful wonderful!' Noni wrote back. 'A truly insightful trip. So glad you had the experience and the self-knowledge that comes through LSD.'

Later that day, I remembered how I'd called Bruce into the sunlit room, where I'd been lying in bed, my eyes wide open, watching the god hovering in the wooden slats above me, and I described it to him so as not to forget it: the perpetual motion of her arms, the éclairs and the goodies, and I remembered saying, in a state of giddiness, 'Even the biggest cock in the world can't satisfy her desire for more and more pleasure! Some guy thinks he's got a cock big enough to satisfy *her*?!'

And I saw that it was she who had given me the special pleasure of writing, which, when it was going well, and not spoiled by some gratuitous complex, could beam right up into her. And other people had been given other gifts, like the pleasure of cooking, or running, or math, or pretty much everything.

★

Some of my notes, which I couldn't bring myself to look at until many weeks later, included the following:

> That's why I write. Because it's a pleasure TO ME and everyone else can fuck off
>
> Because my father was proud of me, *I* should be proud of me?
>
> No one would be proud of themselves for who I was
>
> What am I proud of in myself? My love for the world
>
> My father wanted me to love the world – but only the parts that he loved. And he wanted me to love only the parts of myself that he loved. And to abandon the parts of me that didn't serve him
>
> You can do whatever you want
>
> For the first time in your life
>
> *Do you feel that?*

And thousands of words more.

★

In my final session with Ellis and Kay, I explained that I seemed to have come off the Prozac fairly successfully (I'd been discussing my progress throughout our sessions); the only side effect was a dizziness that would come and go. Perhaps it was stopping the anti-depressant, or perhaps it was the ketamine, the DMT, the MDMA and the LSD, or perhaps it was everything all together. But life was feeling more detailed and new. And I said that I was experiencing more feelings – pleasant ones, and not.

Kay said, 'I tell people when they come in to work with me that these therapies are not about making you feel good all the time. *Feeling* is like looking at the whole rainbow, and you can't pick and choose which colors you see. But the beautiful thing is, as you learn to feel more, you learn how to ground yourself, and expand the spectrum, and you get to see more colors – all the different subtleties and shades you never noticed before. And even though it sounds scary, it's not, because you learn to navigate through all these feelings and emotions, and *they don't stay*. And what a beautiful gift to give yourself, isn't it?'

It was. Though of course this feeling of newness couldn't last forever. Ellis had said, in our first session, something that still haunted me, that as transformative as these medicines could be, 'The human sort of goes back to sleep. That's just part of being in the human body.'

★

About a week after returning home from Vancouver, Jack and I were having dinner with his mother and two of her friends – a lawyer and a girls' school principal – and I was telling them about the August I'd had, and the lawyer turned to Jack and said, 'Weren't you scared of her doing this? What if she changed, or decided to completely change her life; to run off and leave you?'

'If that's what she wants, better we find out sooner than later,' he joked.

As we were driving home, I brought up the exchange, and Jack said that other people, in the past month, had asked him the same thing. I'd also wondered if he wasn't concerned – although the idea had been his in the first place. He looked over at me, puzzled. 'You're a human being,' he said. 'You're an artist. You're *supposed* to change.'

★

A few nights later, I had a dream that I was visiting a squalid institution in which a group of unfortunate orphaned children were living. I was there as a reporter to learn their stories and tell them to the world in an article. At one point, I was standing by a bunk bed, and on the top bunk was a dirty, wayward, rascally boy, who was cynical about the idea that my article would help *him*. How would it get him and the others – who were so sorry and unloved and so fucked up – *out of there*? How would it convince others that they were in a terrible place and get them adopted? I thought about it for a moment, then admitted that I couldn't promise that the article would change anything for them, in terms of a new home. I said, revising my plans for the article as I spoke, *I just want to try to get down the truth of your situation.* The boy considered this, and it slightly pleased him, and he began to tell me the honest truth about his feelings and his life.

Suddenly waking up in the middle of the night, I realized that the orphan was the supposedly 'bad' feelings inside me; the ones that felt transgressive to have, that I had learned at an early age not to have, like lostness, or anger at my father, and so many more.

But it saddened me that even after everything I had been through with these medicines in the past month, these 'bad' feeling parts still wished for someone to 'adopt' them – for child welfare services to come and take them away from me, the mistress of their unloving home, and spirit them to some other place, far from my mind and my self and my brain.

I was about to get up and write down the dream, when Jack woke up, and said in a slightly confused voice, 'Sheila, I just had a dream that Bette Midler said that if a woman didn't like her body and ate pork, she would get fat, but if she loved her body and ate pork, all the fat would go to her breasts.'

'Really weird,' I said.

Then we fell back asleep.

★

It took me a few days to work out the logic of Jack's dream: if you do a transgressive thing, but you love yourself, you will be rewarded. But if you do that same transgressive thing, but you do not love yourself, you will be punished. I saw how this connected with the orphan boy in my own dream: he (my bad or unacceptable feelings), was a transgressive thing I did not love. Perhaps my disinterest in the future, which I had been blaming on midlife, had been my 'punishment'. I saw how I was only just beginning to give these taboo, orphaned feelings any kind of attention, let alone love them.

While at first the memory of the god I had seen during my LSD trip reminded me to find the pleasure of life, however small, in every moment, as the weeks progressed, feeding pleasurable moments to the lollipop-and-éclair god had gradually become a burden. I'd started to find myself being false – *pretending* I was feeling pleasure (as if God couldn't tell!) which was a recapitulation of my central problem since childhood, feeling compelled to perform for my parents that I was always happy, that I loved them without complaint and also loved everything. I could never say I was bored, or get in a fight with my brother, or express any anxiety. I'd had to *be* a lollipop, *be* an éclair for them. And now I was doing the same thing for that god.

Ellis had seemed a bit skeptical when I told her about my god; she said that many people thought the mission of life was to be happy, but for her it was 'to feel *human*, which means to feel all of the emotions, even the tricky ones'. I was understanding it better now. It seemed the two dreams were telling me that it was a mistake to wish that the orphans would be delivered to some better home, away from my mind. My god wasn't asking me abolish them; to be happy all the time. I remembered the coda that had come to me as my vision was ending: that the search for truth and the acceptance of truth was *also* a high pleasure; one that could be fed to this god.

★

I had to take another trip, and was waiting at Pearson Airport in Toronto. It was early evening, the 1st of September, and I was standing in line at the security check. I had been texting with Jack, and my mother, and my brother, who had just sent me the song 'Daniel' by Elton John. I was listening to it when suddenly I became hot, flushed all over, with the understanding that these people loved me. Perhaps I had never before been open enough to feel it, but in that moment I did: how fragile a person was in loving you, and the terrible responsibility that came with it. Maybe I hadn't ever wanted to feel it, but now every cell in me knew it for the truth: that they were real, and so was I, and so was the love that ran between us.

The line progressed, and I progressed with it, pulling my luggage a few steps forward. It is okay to cry in an airport, I told myself. People on journeys have reasons for crying. ■

Natalie Shapero

Steal

Why are you making me watch a film that is neither
set nor shot in California. Why are you having me walk
into what is so obviously a trap. Why did you
get me this job at a college when you know there's a risk
with college that the college will one day become
the most expensive school in the nation, and then
there will have to be meetings on how to make it
just a little bit cheaper. The stairwell is lined
with mental-health-themed signage. The bathroom
is plastered with what to do in the event
of an active shooter. Few parents wish for their children

to matriculate at the costliest school, but many
view the second or third on the list as equally
esteemed and therefore a steal. We just have to make
small cuts here and there: the wattage
in the weight room, pasta instead of crab
for accreditors' visits. The stairwell tells me stay
alive. The bathroom says feign being dead. Which is it.

Erik

My dad is a professional instructor of karate. Did you know that
and also who cares. When I was a kid he got socked
in the stomach during a showcase. Because of what I'd learned
about Houdini dying from a stomach punch,
I felt afraid, but then it turned out that Houdini had actually died
from appendicitis; the punch was incidental. The thing
I've always wondered about Houdini is whether he felt somehow
desensitized to death when it actually hit him,
having carried out so many actions that brought him
so close. It's certainly a stressor for me, what with my own
abiding proximity and some might say
full parallelism to what it is to be dead. Am I all alone

in this, or is it me and Houdini: fated to experience anticlimax
at what ought to be instead a space for unfettered
human awe? I really want to see the light. I don't want
to find out, when the time comes, that I don't
get the light because you only can see that one once and I've already
used it. Less of a concern for me is my whole life
flashing before my eyes – that one tbh could take or leave –

US News Metro Long Island Politics World N

METRO EXCLUSIVE

NYC hedge funder says shrink 'seduced' him into office sex sessions — and charged $250K in 'mistress money'

By Kathianne Boniello

Published March 4, 2023
Updated March 4, 2023, 1:25 p.m. ET

409

Courtesy of *New York Post*

TRANSFERENCE IN THE AFTERNOON

Jesse Barron

1

A friend sent me the newspaper story. NYC HEDGE FUNDER SAYS SHRINK 'SEDUCED' HIM INTO OFFICE SEX SESSIONS – AND CHARGED $250K IN 'MISTRESS MONEY'. The hedge funder, Michael Pollack, was suing his former therapist, Heidi Kling, for having sex with him nearly every week for ten years, all while accepting regular payments in cash.

Pollack did not claim that Kling had physically forced him to have sex. He had been an active participant in the sexual relationship for a decade. Only later, after they had stopped their meetings, did he come to view the experience as non-consensual, the destructive result of a force he called 'erotic transference'. The lawsuit, filed in February 2023, claimed Kling's actions left Pollack with severe emotional distress and panic attacks; landed a 'debilitating' blow to his self-confidence; and permanently damaged his relationship with his wife and sons.

Kling claimed that Pollack's story was all wrong. She did not dispute the existence of a sexual relationship, but said she had terminated Pollack's therapy before it began. In other words, even if she continued to meet Pollack in her office, what followed was not medical malpractice but an extramarital affair. Kling's argument raised questions about Pollack's motivations: if he had wished to break off the relationship without shouldering the blame, wouldn't being a victim of mismanaged transference be the perfect alibi?

After reading the case documents, I called Pollack's lawyer, Audrey Bedolis, and asked her to put me in touch with Pollack – who said flatly that he was not open to doing a story. I went on to other projects, but the lawsuit stayed with me. If I had some dead time in my office, I would find myself navigating the public records portal of the New York State courts, to see whether any documents had appeared in *Pollack v. Kling*. Over the next two years, as the case inched along, I sometimes called Bedolis to remind her I was interested.

Then, in March 2025, Pollack called. He said he might be open to a story after all, an article that would expose Kling's alleged malfeasance and highlight the systemic issue of sexual boundary violations on patients. Though he would not give a long interview on record, for fear of jeopardizing his case, he would be willing to provide a copy of the emails he and Kling had exchanged over their thirteen-year involvement, which he had taken from his personal computer and which he planned to submit as evidence in the case. 'So that you can see I'm not lying,' he said.

A couple of weeks later, I received a link from a third-party evidence-management company. I logged in, and a 1.67 gigabyte, 6,333 page PDF began to download. The emails were not the objective truth – the full story of what happened in the consulting room will only ever be known by Kling and Pollack themselves. But when I read the emails alongside the hundreds of pages of court filings, I felt I was looking at something remarkable: a real-time record of the encounter between a patient and a therapist. It was an encounter that started off well before veering profoundly off course.

2

Michael Pollack is a trim man in his late forties with puppyish eyes. He grew up in San Carlos, California, the son of a teacher and a social worker. In late 2007, he was working as a Wall Street trader with a specialty in short selling – making bets against companies that he thought were over-valued. A hedge fund he joined in his twenties became a success, growing from $50 million to $2.5 billion in eight years. He had by then accrued a net worth of around $30 million. He and his wife Anjali, an interior designer, had a toddler, and were expecting their second child. But the market turmoil that culminated in the financial crisis was riling him. He was having trouble sleeping and focusing, and he wanted treatment for anxiety and depression.

A friend of his wife's recommended a therapist named Heidi Kling. In her pictures, she seemed the image of an affable, non-judgmental listener, and she had experience treating 'highly productive' patients. She was a little more than a decade older than Pollack, forty-three, though this still qualified as young in a profession where many people kept working into their eighties. She studied English literature at SUNY Binghamton and public health at Yale, before getting a PhD from the Derner Institute of Advanced Psychological Studies – one of the better-known training centers in New York. She lived in the Prospect Heights neighborhood of Brooklyn, and, like Pollack, she had a young family – twins.

Pollack met Kling for the first time in January 2008, at her office in Union Square. The room was clean and modern, with a simple, monochrome couch and chair, inoffensive art, the requisite framed degree on the wall. The court filings give a sense of Kling's impression of Pollack: at first he seemed as flat and neutral as the decor. He spoke about the same topics the typical patient usually speaks about, his marriage and his parents. He was mostly concerned with the performance of his fund, and frequently brought this up. He could not understand why despite his material success, he still felt a sense of internal pressure and discomfort.

As he aired these everyday complaints, Pollack began to feel a charge. He found Kling's attention to be concentrated and direct. Full of empathy. *God, she really gets me*, he remembers thinking. The atmosphere was very different from what he was used to with Anjali. Their time together was overrun with domestic concerns, their needs as a couple being secondary to the needs of their children. When Pollack looked into Kling's eyes, he read complete acceptance.

Kling, for her part, felt frustrated with how little progress he was making. The armor of Pollack's identity as a captain of Wall Street seemed impermeable. This is a common problem in therapy. Most patients enter the consulting room like an actor walking on stage, ready with a script. The therapist tries to help the patient out of this static position, so they can develop a new awareness of themselves. There are many methods for guiding the patient toward this state. One is to interrupt the patient's flow by taking notice of what's going on, right now, in the consulting room: *I notice you're late with your payment*; *I notice you're looking at the clock*; *I wonder what this reminds you of?* The kind of interruptions that can turn a performance into an encounter.

Kling learned, over the course of six months, that no matter what she tried she could not seem to bring real emotion out of Pollack. He recited his script; she listened to him reciting it. But there was something in his eyes. When she tracked his eyes during their sessions, she noticed him taking in her body. This focus might be the way to reach him. The way to interrupt his flow.

One day, she told Pollack that she noticed he was 'fixated' on her legs.

It was June 2008 – the middle of summer, and the temperatures had climbed to the high eighties. Kling was wearing a knee-length skirt. On her left leg, she wore an ankle bracelet.

Pollack said he was looking at her legs because he found her attractive. The remark hung in the air. Then their session carried on as before.

3

In November 2008 – about four months later – Michael and Anjali flew to Mumbai, where he had a series of business meetings. They stayed with Anjali's parents. On the night of 26 November they decided to go for dinner at the Taj, where they had been married. They would have dinner at the hotel's Chinese restaurant, the Golden Dragon. When they arrived, they found their table wasn't ready, and went next door to wait at the Harbor Bar.

A sudden crash echoed through the hallway, followed by a cascade of others. Gunfire. The hostess, who could see out into the corridor, said something about a dead body. The Pollacks rushed up a stairwell with another couple and a hotel employee, and into an office. They barricaded the door with a heavy wooden table and turned off the lights. They could hear the impact of rifle butts against the door.

Peering through the keyhole, they saw one of the hotel chefs talking to someone with a semiautomatic rifle. 'Who's inside?' the gunman asked. 'Nobody,' the chef said. The gunman ran off. A sense of panic was spreading.

They left the office and went to the Chambers, a member's club inside the hotel. Someone said the terrorists were targeting white people. Pollack told Anjali to let him die, so that the kids would have at least one parent. The staff turned out the lights. Anjali went to hide in the ballroom, Pollack went to hide in a bathroom stall. He heard single shots as the terrorists conducted executions. Then grenades, and the *pop pop pop* of automatic weapons as Indian commandos, who had finally arrived, engaged the attackers. The Pollacks stayed in their hiding places until daybreak, when soldiers evacuated them.

That day, militants from Lashkar-e-Taiba moved through several high-profile locations in Mumbai with a deliberate and punishing clarity. By nightfall more than 170 people were dead, including six Americans. Their goal was territorial: to annex Kashmir into Pakistan, reversing the partition of 1947.

In the aftermath, Pollack suffered PTSD. He felt comatose, but could not sleep. The gunshots still jangled his nerves. He also felt guilty: Indian employees of an international hotel chain had died in order to protect their wealthy Western guests. Back in New York, the Pollacks' experience was covered in the media. A widely circulated photograph shows Pollack in a white shirt, crouched with other hostages behind a white fence as gunfire rains down, looking as if he expects to die. He and Anjali were invited to discuss their experience on *Charlie Rose*.

Michael wears a shirt with white and purple stripes, open at the collar, Anjali a white blouse with a gold medallion necklace. 'Why am I here and not so many other people, who made the same decisions as me?' she asks Rose. Pollack steers the conversation toward the hotel staff who saved their lives. They 'epitomize the best of humanity', he says.

Pressed by Rose on how he feels, Pollack admits to shame for thinking only of how he and his wife might survive while others acted selflessly.

'But you don't feel guilty about that, do you?'

'A little bit.'

'Do you?'

'Yes.'

What he didn't say – on air or to Anjali – was that a different kind of unease had taken hold of him that week, one harder to place within the language of trauma or PTSD. Three days before the attack on the Taj, he had confessed to a friend (as the lawsuit put it) that he had 'developed an infatuation and erotic interest in Dr Kling'.

4

In the months after the attack Pollack stepped back from the hedge fund world. Its rhythms no longer made sense to him. Money was no longer an end in itself – he had enough already that it would never be an issue again. He found himself overtaken by a broad disorientation, a crisis for which he had no language. In an interview, he chastised himself for having focused narrowly on 'wealth accumulation'. He wanted to focus now on charity work (girls' education in India), and on searching for a greater sense of meaning.

Back in Kling's office, Pollack confided that he felt 'extreme guilt' for discussing his desire for her just before he and Anjali were almost killed. Kling was reassuring. These feelings were a normal part of psychotherapy, she told him, and had nothing to do with his love for his wife. For Pollack, though, the sessions had become the place where he could acknowledge the internal forces which he felt were threatening to annihilate him – the trauma of the attack, the pressure to be a good husband and father.

At Kling's suggestion, they increased their sessions to twice a week.

Pollack began to bombard his therapist with lengthy emails. He told Kling about his dreams, his fantasies. She recommended a book: Viktor Frankl's *Man's Search for Meaning*. Suddenly he was ravenous to read. He tore through Frankl, then moved on to Irvin D. Yalom's *Staring at the Sun* and the works of Nietzsche. He was reading as much as twelve hours a day.

Pollack wrote to Kling with his thoughts on all these books, on literature, philosophy, psychoanalysis and current events. Kling wrote back, usually in a mirroring fashion. 'That we converged in this way, both in time and through the brilliance, poignancy, and compassion of Chekhov, makes it feel that much more powerful,' she told him. Pollack could be needy, insistent. He told Kling that he wished she could 'take away my suffering'. Soon he began to share everything. He forwarded letters he had written to his sons, emails from his father, drafts of messages to colleagues. Without fail, Kling replied with encouraging notes.

5

A therapeutic practice requires a rigid frame: a consistent setting, a predetermined appointment time, a regular duration (usually forty-five or fifty minutes) and an exchange of money. The relationship is expected to exist only within that frame – no socializing, no favors, no contact outside of sessions.

Because that frame is so central to the work, therapists guard it carefully. The caution with which therapists approach boundaries can verge on paranoia. There are potential violations everywhere: looking a patient up on Google; giving away a free session; communicating after hours when it's not an emergency; giving a hug; sharing personal details; asking for help. One therapist I spoke to, who attended the same training institute as Kling, told me she had declined a former patient's invitation to have a cup of coffee one afternoon after the treatment was over. 'What if she wants to restart treatment later on?' the therapist asked. 'I would have made it impossible.'

Most therapists would hesitate to correspond with a patient for anything beyond a scheduling change, out of fear of violating boundaries. Kling had begun to bend these conventions. She was writing to Pollack regularly – responding to his emails professionally, but still responding. The picture of the correspondence that emerges is of a man increasingly dependent on Kling's validation and attention. Most therapists would also hesitate to break the forty-five-minute time limit. Kling relaxed here as well: 'We can meet for longer,' she writes at one point, 'if you come at ten o'clock.'

The attraction between them, only glancingly acknowledged at first, had begun to rise to the surface. Some of their emails are mundane, but in others Kling begins to seem almost flirtatious. 'Does the dream/wish for the un-acquired object, ("perfectly preserved in the realm of fantasy") lead to madness?' she wrote at one point. In discussing the boundary, she seemed to open up the possibility of breaching it.

There are many reasons why these therapeutic boundaries are thought to matter. The most important is the phenomenon of transference – the powerful emotional current that can flow between patient and therapist. The concept, which underpins much of modern psychotherapy, goes back to Freud, who observed as early as the 1890s that a young woman seeking analysis from an older male doctor would often develop a romantic obsession. Freud's weaker disciples took this passion as evidence of their own sexual magnetism and reciprocated, having sex with – and at times even falling in love with – the vulnerable women in their care.

The intense feelings that a patient develops toward a therapist, Freud realized, can arise even when the therapist does not actively arouse them. Transference had nothing to do with the analyst's desirability: an old, shriveled man with a long gray beard could become, in the consulting room, an object of ardent longing. What explained this, Freud thought, was the patient's interior life, which projected like a magic lantern onto the blank screen of the doctor, revealing the hidden patterns – the psychic blueprint – that governed the patient's relationships with others, and was being repeated in the analytic encounter. By tracing the transference back to its source, usually in childhood, the analyst could surface the patient's unconscious motivations and, in doing so, free him from the chains of compulsive repetition.

6

In February 2011, Pollack turned up to his session to announce he was thinking of stopping therapy. The longing and intensity had become almost frightening. He wasn't sure whether to keep going or get out. Kling, who had developed strong feelings for Pollack herself, went and sat on the couch next to him. In the moment that followed, they kissed. There is disagreement about who kissed whom; Pollack says Kling, Kling says Pollack. But there is no disagreement about the kiss. Pollack came back for the next session. This time the physical contact escalated beyond kissing. In the court documents, Kling defends her actions by returning to this moment: she states that the therapy terminated when the physical relationship began – the treatment concluded with the kiss, and then their meetings morphed into a consensual affair. (In a standard treatment, termination usually unfolds over several sessions.)

They followed a few simple rules. They would conceal the relationship from their spouses, colleagues and children. Early on, when the wait between sessions was too agonizing, they met in hotels, but by the tenth or eleventh month they were meeting almost exclusively in Kling's consulting room, during the day, for an hour or ninety minutes. The perfect cover. No one arouses suspicion by walking into their therapist's office.

According to the documents, they began the meetings by talking and concluded by having sex. For the previous three years, Kling had been charging Pollack $250 per forty-five-minute session, standard for a licensed psychotherapist in a large American city. Until he and Kling first kissed, Pollack had paid his fees by cash or check. From February 2011 to 2021 – the span of their sexual relationship – Pollack began making payments to Kling in cash, usually about $1,000 per month, sometimes a little more, withdrawing the money from an ATM near her office, from an account he knew his wife never looked at.

How did Pollack make sense of the cash he handed to Kling so regularly – as gifts, or as payment for something more transactional? Was *that*, in fact, what this was – not therapy, not an affair, but sex work? The comparison between the two professions is often made. Both involve the exchange of money for things in short supply: sex and attention. Both require intimacy that starts and stops at a predetermined time. But if a man of Pollack's means wanted to spend money to buy sex in New York, he could have done so in simpler ways. Whatever the money was about, it wasn't about sex. Kling, for her part, would describe the cash payments as supportive offerings from a generous lover. The money was especially welcome during a period when her husband, an architect, was under financial strain.

7

From one angle, Pollack, the successful hedge fund manager, had a social and economic power which Kling lacked. From another angle, it was Kling who held the power, with her professional and clinical expertise. Energy that might otherwise have flowed from Pollack toward his family and business interests was now flowing instead into that simple, clean office in Union Square. In the emails, Pollack talks about his fantasy for a 'smoking woman', which a Freudian might interpret as an example of the death drive. Did Pollack represent a similar, self-destructive object to Kling?

Their dynamic is complicated by the precise nature of the risks they were taking. Both were endangering their marriages. But Kling's professional exposure was more serious. If Pollack were ever to change his view of their relationship – recasting it from love to exploitation – the resulting lawsuit could destroy her career. From the moment she began sleeping with him, Kling placed her future in his hands.

The law made that danger explicit. In New York State, sex between a patient and a mental health provider during the course of treatment is classified as statutory rape, carrying a maximum sentence of seven years in prison. In practice, prosecutors rarely pursue such cases unless the patients are underage – they are too difficult to prove. But the statute's existence hung over the relationship.

Professional regulators also take a hard line. Since the 1970s, the American Psychological Association's code of ethics has prohibited sex between a therapist and patient. In the 1990s, the prohibition was extended to include former patients: practitioners must wait two years before beginning a sexual relationship – and even then, the APA warns, may only proceed 'in the most unusual circumstances'. Psychoanalysts – those who see patients multiple times a week, often with the patient lying down – are stricter still. Most believe that sex with a former patient is never acceptable, no matter how much time has passed. The rationale for these prohibitions comes out of psychoanalytic theory.

Because patients often transfer onto the analyst the feelings they have toward their parents, acting on that transference is seen to break, symbolically, the incest taboo. Every analyst knows the refrain that goes, 'Once a parent, always a parent; once a patient, always a patient.' Pollack himself painted his mother as withholding and difficult – the theory of transference would say this withholding mother was now, in some sense, Kling. To act on such a transference, to commit a boundary violation, is to repeat an unconscious and damaging pattern, on the part of both patient and therapist. It is the ultimate, the inviolable, perhaps the *only* real rule. As Lacan wrote in his *Écrits*, 'I am talking to you. I am not fucking you.'

In 2011, Pollack asked Kling to refer him to another therapist, as what was happening between them was 'no longer therapy'. But when Kling thought of who to refer him to, her options were limited. The moment Pollack walked into a new clinician's office and began to describe what was unfolding between him and Heidi Kling – no matter how passionately he insisted it was an affair rather than an ethical breach – the new therapist was bound to receive the news with alarm.

8

Kling had already confided in someone: her supervisor, Joseph Newirth. Most therapists have a supervisor. Typically the arrangement involves a senior analyst meeting either weekly or fortnightly with a colleague to offer advice, and to provide a space for them to talk through their cases, in particular those that are proving complex. In his late sixties, Newirth was a well-known analyst and teacher, the author of several books and peer-reviewed articles, part of the inner circle of New York analysts, even if occasionally he did take provocative stances in his writing, especially when it came to the handling of transference and countertransference.

Kling first met Newirth in the mid-1990s, when he was a professor at the Derner Institute in New York and she was a candidate-in-training. The admissions process at Derner gave a taste of the institute's philosophy: a group of applicants sat on chairs in front of a faculty member. The faculty member said, 'Please get to know each other,' and then remained silent for an hour. The lesson was clear: what matters in this work is the capacity to spark a real exchange in the consulting room.

Within the faculty at Derner there were two camps. One focused on 'applied psychology', training students to use therapeutic tools for social work; the other was more interested in the psychoanalytic theory. Newirth was the king of the theoretical camp. Warm and charismatic, he attracted a circle of students who adored him, among them Heidi Kling. After she graduated, they kept in touch, and at the time she was treating Pollack, Kling was in a reading group that Newirth led.

In this tiny, esoteric world, Newirth was known for his experimental side and his unorthodox thoughts on pleasure. In his book *From Sign to Symbol*, Newirth describes the consulting room as a 'transitional space' where both patient and therapist could experience 'pleasurable, joyful, or ecstatic experiences'. He wasn't talking about sexual ecstasy, but something broader. He sometimes tried to unblock a stalled treatment, he wrote, by bursting into songs from popular operas – *Porgy and Bess*, *The Threepenny Opera*.

But that was not the only way he challenged convention. Newirth also staked out a view on how the analyst could make use of their feelings toward the patient – the countertransference – in the service of the cure. The goal, he wrote, was to transform the patient's 'repetitive, externalized experiences' into 'internal, symbolic, symmetrical experiences'. That 'symmetrical' was a bit naughty. In classic theory, the relationship is always asymmetrical: the therapist holds the frame, the patient speaks from within it. Newirth argued for a more open, playful relationship, one where a therapist could sometimes bend the rules to forge an authentic connection. None of this, however, encouraged the violation of sexual boundaries.

It was Newirth who would have taught Kling about transference and countertransference. The reading list can easily be imagined. A former Derner candidate who trained in the 1990s recalls reading Jody Davies's paper 'Love in the Afternoon', a classic account of a female analyst who becomes aware of her own erotic feelings for a male patient as he begins to idealize her. The tension simmers without either of them acknowledging it. One day, Davies gives voice to the taboo feelings; the patient flies off the handle, calling her a pervert and threatening to report her to the licensing board. Only after a long arc of treatment does he come to realize that his rage is not directed at Davies at all, but at his mother.

Former students of Newirth described him to me in varying tones. Some spoke of him with admiration and awe, and called him a master clinician. Others said he'd developed a reputation for getting a little *too* 'symmetrical', especially with female candidates. At the end of every school year, Derner students staged skits lampooning their teachers. In 1996–7, according to two former candidates, the skit about Newirth was an extended riff on his loose boundaries. A female student played Newirth, flirting with other students as they came in. At one point, a candidate sat on his lap.

9

In the summer of 2011, Kling referred Pollack to Newirth. By sending her lover, who was also her current or former patient, to her colleague, who was also her supervisor, Kling created a triangle. Now that Kling had involved Newirth directly, he would have to choose between them. He could chastise his supervisee for her boundary violation, report her, and blow up her career. Or he could go along with it, and watch as the sexual relationship progressed – something both Kling and Pollack, at the time, said they ardently wanted. According to Pollack, Newirth condoned the relationship because he believed that beforehand his patient had been a vacant Wall Street 'robot' who couldn't access his feelings – a man whose inner life was as algorithmic as the numbers on a stock ticker.

The sheer quantity of emails between Pollack and Kling – thousands – lends credibility to Newirth seeing the situation as an experience of genuine connection. But what kind of connection? On first reading, the emails sounded very warm – if more tender than hotly erotic. But on reflection I saw their neutrality could be read multiple ways: neutral because they were exchanges between a patient and a therapist (which supports Pollack's case), or neutral because they were written by lovers who worried their spouses might someday read them (supporting Kling's).

They ask after each other's children, trade links to news stories. Pollack shares quotidian dramas from his professional life – a rival achieving success; a subordinate who may have slighted him. Kling describes tensions in her marriage, the stresses of parenting, the ups and downs of her practice. She thanks Pollack for helping her draft a professional email.

Some of these exchanges are quietly moving in their everyday normalcy, in the way any long intimacy between adults – especially in midlife – can be quietly moving. 'Rough day,' she wrote him at one point. 'Thank you very much for helping me through it.' Or: 'It's amazing to think about the different ways we've helped each other on this journey.' They sustained this dynamic for a decade.

When I began reporting the story, I contacted both Kling and Newirth to invite them to speak. I reached Newirth by phone; when I explained that I was thinking of writing about the Pollack case he hung up. Multiple requests to his lawyers went unanswered. I tried several times to reach Kling, both directly and through her lawyer, Vincent Pozzuto. She did not respond to either request. In a memoir self-published by her sister, who is an aikido practitioner, there are hints of the 'difficult childhood' Kling alludes to on her professional website, including a cult-like socialist summer camp and allegations of physical abuse. But Kling's silence, while normal for a defendant in an ongoing court case, was a boundary I could not cross.

10

By 2021, Pollack and Kling were confronting a question they had managed to avoid for years: whether their relationship could continue. Of the two, Pollack now seemed the more resolved. It was excruciating to see Kling only twice a week, in hourly increments, subsisting on emails in between. He wondered whether their 'bubble' could 'become a reality' – whether they could leave their spouses for each other. Kling had often wondered the same thing, but now her attention was being pulled toward her mother, who had been ill for many years and was close to dying. They found themselves at an impasse. When it came down to it, they could not quite bring themselves to cross the final boundary and start a life together.

On 11 October 2021, Pollack composed an email to Kling. 'Heidi, My love,' it begins. 'We are so attuned you will know the contents of this note before you finish this sentence so let me be concise: our physical relationship cannot continue.' It goes on:

> Your love, support, wisdom, guidance, sensuality, your very whole being first saved my life, then transformed it in ways words will never be able to express. I have experienced the divine both inside of you and because of you. I have come to understand the nature of God, that love is the gateway to transcendent unity, and that nothing exists beyond the present . . .
>
> However, I also realize that our relationship, especially now, replays the most painful script from my childhood, one that keeps me in a state of near constant deprivation eagerly waiting for your next email or text and counting down the moments until our next physical encounter. As much as I have tried to be fully present in the 164 hours per week we are apart, the gnawing ruminations that center around you keep me too removed from the

> other, larger reality I have created with Anjali, my friends and family . . .
>
> Spending the past decade in our affair has been one of the greatest gifts the universe ever gave me. Spending the next decade, or beyond, in it would be a curse . . . it is time for me to take the learnings from the many paths I have traveled with you as my muse and mistress and apply them fully to my present . . .
>
> I will love you until the day I die . . .
>
> Michael

In the week that followed, Pollack swung between his decision to separate from Kling and asking her for more. 'I simply cannot maintain our level of emotional and sexual intimacy with this level of physical distance,' he writes. And: 'Our relationship is a hell of a lot more than simple transference/countertransference enactment.' Kling seems to share in this torment. 'This is brutal – I'm in pain too,' she writes. 'The bubble was terribly painful for me for many years (tho also beautiful or I wouldn't have done it).' She reflects on their relationship: 'I felt split in two to the point of agony many, many nights, I shared the fantasy of what might be possible after our children left home.' Then, perhaps nervous at Pollack's new-found fluency with the terms of psychoanalysis, she admonishes him: 'Please don't erase or re-write the long and winding history of our relationship.'

But rewriting is exactly what Pollack would do.

During this period, Pollack had embarked on a master's in mental health counseling at the City University of New York. (Newirth wrote his letter of recommendation.) He was considering changing careers and becoming a therapist himself. The program required the candidates to perform fieldwork at an off-site counseling center, which is how, ten years into his relationship with Kling, Pollack switched places in the consulting room, looking out from the therapist's chair as his 'clients' told him why they were seeking help. According to Pollack, when he saw how quickly the clients deferred to him, granting him an authority he hadn't earned, he began to have the destabilizing sense that his love for Kling might actually be less pure than he once believed; it might have been influenced, even organized, by transference – the very thing he'd previously insisted wasn't true. In fact, he began to see his own insistence as yet more evidence of transference's totalizing power.

A long time passed before Kling heard from Pollack again. For the next eight months, the therapist went on with her life. The days no longer started – or ended – with a long email from Pollack in her inbox. His absence appeared to be exactly what he had asked for: a clean break. The tenor of his last messages was so loving, so effusively *grateful*, that it appeared he was satisfied with the way things had gone.

11

On the same day Pollack wrote his letter to Kling, he also wrote to Newirth. In this message, he blamed Newirth for mishandling what he now saw as transference. He still absolved Kling in the way he phrased it. 'As I reflect on our prior work,' he began, 'I find myself increasingly angry/saddened/frustrated by what is a patently obvious failing.' He chastised Newirth for not helping him to see how destructive the relationship with Kling had become. 'You acted in the same way as my father,' Pollack wrote, 'who consistently placed my mother's needs above mine. Except, unlike him, you were obligated to think of me first.' His rage at Newirth was the first rumble of what was coming.

In the lawsuit he filed two years later, Pollack alleges that Newirth 'provided psychotherapy . . . while not only knowing about, but supporting, encouraging, condoning, and enjoying hearing graphic details of Dr Kling's sexual contact with Mr Pollack.' He claims that Newirth knew the full pattern of his sessions with Kling:

> Mr Pollack would enter Dr Kling's office finding her dysregulated because she had been fighting with her husband, her children or a third-party. Mr Pollack would spend approximately forty-five minutes soothing and comforting Dr Kling. Dr Kling would then spend approximately ten minutes asking Mr Pollack about himself. Thereafter, Dr Kling would have sex with Mr Pollack and then he would leave.

Pollack further alleges that Newirth approved of the sexual relationship, saying that Newirth told him, 'Guilt never made anyone not do something. It just made them enjoy it less.' He accuses Newirth of negligence for failing to warn him that what he believed was a love affair with Kling was, in fact, 'mishandled transference and erotic countertransference'.

Newirth's response in the court documents is forceful. He claims that Pollack had 'engaged in an extramarital affair with Dr Kling', and was now making 'a woefully transparent attempt' to 'harass Dr Newirth' with 'frivolous causes of action'. The Newirth who emerges in the court documents presents himself as entirely professional. He seems to have concluded that, because the affair was already underway by the time Pollack arrived in his office, he would treat Pollack like any other patient who was breaking a taboo, offering compassion and curiosity rather than judgment and censure.

This is where the complexity of the triangulation between the three becomes most acute. Court documents suggest that Newirth knew about the physical relationship from early on. Technically that knowledge belonged to his supervisory relationship with Kling, and should not have affected his therapeutic relationship with Pollack. An odd arrangement, this adoption of dual roles. He may have felt he could not intervene in events that were already taking their course.

The transference was like a radioactive substance that had leapt outside Kling's consulting room, into Newirth's, into court, into the families, into the press – scorching everything in its path. More than one therapist described the lawsuit to me as a 'nightmare'. They did not mean nightmare in the sense of 'annoyance'. They meant nightmare in the sense of an eruption of forces from the unconscious.

12

In the year that followed the end of the relationship, Pollack fully revised his understanding of the prior decade. The cash, which had once seemed like a gift, now looked to him like payment for a service. The habit of meeting in the office, once a thrilling subterfuge, now looked like a patient walking into a session – sometimes passing another patient in the waiting room as he left. As for Newirth, Pollack came to see him less as a therapist than as a voyeur and 'puppeteer'. He saw both Newirth and Kling as co-conspirators in a decade of abuse.

Pollack retained a lawyer, who sent a letter to Kling, requesting records of the treatment. The letter was the opening stage of the lawsuit, which would ultimately seek hundreds of thousands of dollars in damages (at a minimum). It was the first Kling had heard from Pollack since his last, affectionate, messages.

It is never advisable to respond, without legal counsel, to a letter from the lawyer of someone threatening to sue you. Kling's response, directly to Pollack, reads as though the trouble between them were a personal misunderstanding rather than a serious legal issue. 'Dear Michael,' she wrote:

> I had no idea you were in this place. The letter from your lawyer really knocked me down, like being hit by a Mac Truck.
>
> More importantly, I want you to know that you have been

> on my mind constantly in these months, but I wasn't sure you would want to hear from me. I have wondered what you were thinking, how you were feeling, how your kids were doing, how you were reacting to all the crazy world events and missing being able to share and talk to you about everything.
>
> But I was also reeling from how things ended, and all the loss: and too hurt, prideful and stubborn to reach out to you and find out.
>
> But now I see that it was much worse than I thought, and that I must have hurt you horribly, in ways I did not know. Is there a less destructive/nuclear way for us to try to make this better? Is it possible for us to talk? . . .
>
> We were always able to talk and reach an understanding and I feel certain we can do that again.
>
> (The ironic thing is the night before I received the letter I had a dream about us. We were walking and talking about what had happened. It was friendly, open and close. I woke up thinking it was a healing dream and wanted to believe it was true for both of us.)
>
> Anyway, please let me know if it would be possible to talk. I do think there's a good chance we would both feel better if we could.
>
> Heidi

Kling appeals to Pollack as one rational adult to another, without acknowledging the thorny question of transference. It is as if the therapist and the patient have switched roles: with Pollack now in thrall to the language and interpretation of psychoanalytic theory, and Kling behaving like a civilian grieving the end of a passionate love affair.

Pollack's lawsuit sent shockwaves through the New York psychotherapeutic community. A professional abyss opened beneath Kling. Once the lawsuit was filed, a reporter from the *New York Post* published a story – the one that my friend sent to me. It ran with a photograph of a grave-looking Pollack posing in a button-up shirt. The photo was from an earlier article about the Mumbai attack, but nobody would have known that. It made it look as though Pollack had cooperated with the writer and sat for the portrait. What might have seemed to *Post* readers like an amusing story about a man covering up an affair with an elaborate alibi acquired the tone of a moral crusader intent on exposing a pernicious form of malpractice.

Kling faced uncomfortable questions – in the consulting room and in the wider psychoanalytic community – as the news spread around New York. The story whipped between the group chats of the Derner graduates. Several alumni told me they were shocked to see Kling in this predicament, but equally shocked by Newirth's behavior. 'Joe was like Heidi's analytical parent,' one therapist told me. 'But he didn't protect her.'

Most of the evidence in the case was submitted by Pollack and his attorney, but Pollack's email about 'experiencing the divine' was the rare exception that Kling herself placed into evidence; she clearly believed it undermined his claims. Perhaps to her eye it shows that he had genuinely been in love, and that the transference theory was an after-the-fact reframing of what had been a consensual experience of ecstasy and transformation. Of course, it is easy to see how Pollack's attorney might respond. If the email *read* like a message from a man in love, this only proved how *totally* the transference had taken hold of him. The email supported two opposite accounts: one in which Pollack was a spurned lover taking revenge; the other in which he was the victim of mismanaged transference, the very dynamic Freud warned about more than a century ago.

When Kling next saw Pollack, they were seated across from one another in a conference room at a law firm, flanked by their attorneys. The purpose of the meeting was to take her deposition.

13

Last spring, in May 2025, I made plans to visit New York, and asked Pollack if we could meet. I suggested a walk in Central Park, and that we avoid talking about the case. My hope was that if we spent a little time together, I might feel more confident about how I understood the story.

I arrived at Pollack's building in the West 60s and took the elevator up to a high floor. The apartment was a duplex corner unit with panoramic views of Central Park. A spiral staircase wound upward from the center of the living room, which was covered in dark blue wallpaper. Objects from the Pollacks' travels to India lined the shelves. Pollack greeted me and invited me inside, wearing a light black windbreaker and gray jeans with sneakers. He seemed both composed but slightly guarded, as though calculating – and recalculating – whether he could trust me.

He offered to show me the library, which doubled as his meditation room. His tastes ran toward philosophy – everything from Aristotle to Steven Pinker – along with a few business books and memoirs by extreme-sports athletes. There was a lot of Freud (the Strachey editions). On an oriental rug stood a large, actually enormous, gong.

'Before you go any further,' he said, 'with whatever you wind up writing, I want to make sure you read this.' It was a 2021 collection of essays from the APA on 'sexual boundary violations' in therapy. I had read the introduction, so I felt I understood the gist: when a therapist allows a patient to have sex with them, the patient is being abused, often irreparably harmed. Before putting the book away, he flipped through it, as though remembering passages which had made an impression. I saw his notes, in black pen, on the margins of certain pages. *YES. YES. YES. YES. YES. YES. YES.*

We went outside and strolled in the sunlight of Central Park. Pollack spoke, somewhat cautiously, about his childhood and career as a short seller. When I asked how things were with his wife, he was explicit: 'She understands that I was the victim. She does not consider it to be an affair.' According to Pollack, when he told Anjali about Kling – eight months before the lawsuit – she phoned her own therapist, who explained to her that he had in fact been the victim of a boundary violation.

In my mind, the case had always centered around what had transpired between Pollack and Kling. This was the stone I kept turning over in my hand. But as I walked with Pollack that day I had a different question, one I had come to believe held the key I had been missing. Why had he decided to file the lawsuit?

When his lawyer sent Kling the letter, the relationship was still a secret. Anjali knew, but not his children. His colleagues didn't know. By filing a complaint in court, he changed all of their lives. His willingness to expose himself and his family to such publicity stood in opposition, I thought, to the low profile Pollack kept in other aspects of his life. And it jarred with his claim that he'd stopped seeing Kling so that he could prioritize Anjali and the children.

Was he trying to punish Kling, acting out the wounded man whose private world had collapsed? In the book he handed me in his apartment, there was a passage on what happens when a relationship built on a boundary violation abruptly ceases: the patient spirals into a chaotic private grief for which no outward display was permissible. The lawsuit against Kling could be the missing public display. Or did he truly believe he had been harmed, and that Kling should no longer be allowed to practice for the protection of future patients?

When I pressed Pollack on this point later, he told me emphatically that it was the latter. He filed because it was the right thing to do, because his story was the correct one, because he wanted to prevent Kling from treating another patient the way he had been treated. 'When something this egregious can happen,' he said, 'there is a systemic issue somewhere.' He continued: 'Maybe in your reader's eyes, this will seem self-destructive, but this is what I had to do. If I sit passively, I will implode.'

The more we talked, though, the more it seemed like Pollack was struggling as much as I was to explain his motives. He knew fragments of the answer. He knew how the rules of the APA applied to the timeline of events. He knew how the courts might view sexual contact in the office. He knew the right terms: enactment, regression, supervision, boundary, transference. But there were two parts of himself that never seemed to integrate – he had stopped seeing Kling in order to devote himself to his family, then filed a lawsuit which subjected his family to the glare of the tabloids. In one of our last conversations, I told Pollack how frustrating I found this.

'I'm going to make a suggestion you may not like,' I told him. 'Which is that I don't think you fully understand this part of the story either.'

Pollack reflected for a moment. 'I am by no means a resolved, activated, fully integrated human,' he told me. 'I exist in deep conflict. How is it that this total stranger entered my life, and became, aside from my kids and my wife, the most important thing in it?'

14

A feeling of acting impulsively from emotion, without being able to predict or manage the fallout, or a feeling of disintegration among one's various self-states – these are the main reasons people choose to get therapy. But Pollack never really did therapy. Not with Kling, not with Newirth. The process seemed to have left him only more damaged.

Contemporary psychoanalysis insists that the therapeutic encounter is co-created, shaped as much by the patient's unconscious demands as by the therapist's attempts to contain them. A therapist may lose hold of the frame, and a patient can be driven by internal dramas that have a destabilizing force of their own. The therapist is susceptible to these drives, and if she does not master them, she can wind up at their mercy.

Freud said it was the doctor's responsibility to maintain the integrity of the frame, but he also raised a difficult question: why were some patients so driven to break it? There were patients, he wrote, of an 'elemental passionateness who tolerate no surrogates', who are 'violent in their love'. He came to view the tenacity of these patients as a form of resistance to treatment. The patient tries to 'destroy the doctor's authority by bringing him down to the level of a lover'. The lover is an easier role to play, compared to the unbearable work of slowly getting better.

Whatever the court would decide, Pollack knew what he thought. The decade with Kling was a hallucination, a sustained period of abuse – anything but the consensual affair he had once believed it to be. I believe Pollack is sincere in his belief of this.

15

What kind of love is not, in some sense, transference? We all project on each other with the magic lanterns of our pasts, fall in love with the images we create and then feel crushing disappointment when reality intervenes. Where does the internal world end and a shared world begin?

In a 2009 email to Kling, in the early days of the therapy, Pollack shared a draft of a letter he hoped one day to give his sons – his 'personal philosophy', a set of tenets for living. 'When you encounter pain you have two choices,' he wrote, 'to embrace, internalize and own it; or to externalize, hate and run from it . . . How you handle pain will influence your outlook, relationships, and experiences through the rest of your life.'

Psychoanalysis holds that no love is free of the past; intimacy is always shadowed by absent figures, and every relationship contains some mix of fantasy and complementary wounds. No bond of love is free of secrets, breaches, imbalances of power. But even within these distorted circumstances, there are still the longed-for moments when we bolt awake in the presence of another. The current crackles;

something happens in the room. The question is how we make sense of these moments later on, when the force of the charge has dimmed. ■

The lawsuit between Pollack, Kling and Newirth is still ongoing in the New York State court. Kling continues to practice in Manhattan. In addition to her therapy license, she now holds a license to practice life coaching. Michael and Anjali remain married. He has not gone back to finance. In 2023, he received his master's in mental health counseling from the City University of New York. Among his other endeavors, he is now the director of business development at a start-up, Sunstone Therapies, which offers mental health treatments using psychedelic drugs.

ALEC SOTH
Cocktails and Creations, 2013
Durango, Colorado
Magnum Photos

WHATEVER CREEK MEADOWS

Benjamin Kunkel

It's important for purposes of this story, whose purpose of course I don't know, otherwise I wouldn't be telling it, I'd just say what I mean, to establish right away that I know the sound of my own voice, to be clear I'm not suggesting I know exactly what tones and implications lurk in my delivery at every moment, all I'm saying is that I can recognize the distinct timbre of my own speaking voice should I happen to hear a recording of it in the same way that almost anyone could be trusted to identify that of a family member or close friend should the intimate in question somehow be overheard talking without being visible in some place you have no reason to expect to discover them, or else have left a voicemail, for instance, without giving their name and while calling from an unfamiliar number (an example that may in fact be outdated now that, according to news stories, people are getting scammed by convincing AI replicas of their loved ones' voices as these persuasive fakes plead for money in desperate but fictitious circumstances).

I can anyway claim to know what my voice sounds like, in the strict acoustic sense, because of something that happened with my fiancée (now wife) Clementine a little more than a year ago, one day I came home and, on entering the house, faintly heard from upstairs a radio show or audiobook or podcast, at first I had no way of knowing which, in any case some kind of recording or even, conceivably, live broadcast featuring, as I could tell – once I'd pulled off my boots and was walking quietly up the stairs toward Clementine's office – the educated-sounding, alternately hesitant and onrushing voice of some neither young nor old, perhaps Gen-X-ish native male speaker of American English whom, once I'd almost reached the landing, I recognized as none other than myself, somehow the realization that a recording of my own voice was playing there for Clementine on the other side of the door caused the hair to stand up on the back of my neck.

Right away I turned around and, trying to make no sound, headed back downstairs to the kitchen to fix myself a sandwich, as I was putting two slices of bread in the toaster or engaged in some other aspect of the sandwich-making process I was thinking that Clementine, so up to date in spite of her old-fashioned name, must be listening to one of the several minor podcasts onto which I'd been invited to discuss my first real book, a scholarly but also, I hoped, accessible account of Colorado's early-twentieth-century coal war, that bloody and now basically forgotten series of battles between militant coal miners, on the one hand, and the National Guard companies and private militia, on the other, who on behalf of the mining concerns attacked and sometimes killed the striking miners and their families in their tents, at any rate I couldn't think of what other recordings of my speaking at length might exist out there unless maybe videos or audio recordings on YouTube of my giving a lecture or talk about my academic work which, for what it's worth, concerns the social history of fossil-fuel extraction in the western US and Canada, even if by late spring or early summer of last year I was instead trying to write something broader, something more contemporary and global, about so-called fossil capitalism in the twenty-first century.

My well-received if by no means widely read book on the Colorado coal war had come out four years before, and as I took out sandwich fixings from the fridge or performed some related task I found myself moved almost to the brink of tears that Clementine evidently liked my voice well enough to revisit one of my podcast appearances, I knew she'd already heard all three, not to mention that over dinner probably at least once a week she patiently listened to my going on about fossil fuels and climate collapse, very often I think of my French ex-girlfriend Sybille who apparently complained after our breakup, so our mutual friend Louisa (who plays a large part in this story) told me: 'Oh my God he's nice enough looking but do you really want to talk about global warming every fucking night of your life?'

My looks had probably faded since then, not so my climate preoccupation, indeed despite the fact that the more powerful countries had in recent years almost all given up on keeping emissions in check I for some reason clung to the bare idea of my book – in a nutshell, either fossil capitalism survives or we do – many other people obviously had said the same thing but, at the same time, not enough of us had.

'Did you catch me in the act?' Clementine said when she came into the kitchen.

Before I could deny or confess to my eavesdropping she explained that she'd heard me come in and sensed my presence on the stairs, 'On that last podcast,' she went on, 'you sound so –'

'Don't tell me!' I said – you want to know you're loved but not why – and asked if she wanted to go to the movies that night, the horror movie I had in mind, I admitted, wasn't supposed to be any good.

'Of course,' she said, her happiness also mine, at the time we'd only been engaged for a few months.

In the midst of this same fugitive period my old college friend Louisa whom I've just mentioned, a well-known Canadian musician and author, was scheduled to fly out and address some kind of low-residency folk-musicianship program in Denver (to be honest I have only the vaguest idea of this operation), something she'd also done in summers past, and not long after Podcast Incident Number One, as I think of it now, I called up Louisa in Toronto to suggest that this time she stay in Colorado a few extra days, that way, I said over the phone, she could finally see the mountains up close, not just from a distance, and maybe, I found myself adding, the three of us could even drive over to the more beautiful western part of the state, where I'm from, in particular there existed a spectacular place we could visit (the idea occurring to me only as I said it, I'd found that being in love had made me more spontaneous) called Vallum Creek Meadows, on the southeast side of the Flat Tops, that I'd love to show her and Clementine, if Louisa was game we could backpack up there and camp for a night.

'You could play your guitar around a campfire,' I suggested.

'I'm not like portaging my guitar,' Louisa replied.

'Don't tell me now but what do you think?' I noticed that in lobbying for Vallum Creek Meadows I felt a bit as if I were confessing to a sexual peculiarity which I hoped these two favorite women might indulge me in, the truth is that in a literal sense I'm more or less bereft or free of sexual fetishes, so women I've dated have told me, however I do enjoy backpacking, this is more often the distasteful-sounding and painful activity I've been trying to get female partners to consent to.

No doubt I would have felt less anxious about asking Louisa to visit Vallum Creek Meadows with Clementine and me if we hadn't also made another big request of Louisa, namely that she officiate Clemmy's and my wedding, after all Louisa was the rare friend almost equidistantly close to us both, for my part I'd known Louisa ever since we'd been ambitious and unhappy undergraduates studying literature together, meanwhile she and Clementine, in the half-dozen or so years since I'd introduced them as fellow writers (Louisa was semi-famous not only for her songs and albums but also for her memoir), had crossed paths in Toronto and London and New York as well as emailing each other their works-in-progress and exchanging articles of clothing through the mail, they furthermore appeared to engage in much more texting than I as a straight man could ever contemplate, in fact by now Clementine had probably become closer to Louisa than I was, anyway on the snowy evening when I'd finally presented Clementine with my great-grandmother's diamond-flaked and emerald-studded silver ring and she'd said 'What took you so long?' we'd first called up my parents, who still live in Colorado, and then, feeling we shouldn't wake Clementine's mother and father in England, next shared our news with Louisa, before we placed this second call I'd said to Clem that I thought we shouldn't mention the officiating over the phone, after all that might put too much pressure on Louisa, but in the event Clemmy couldn't restrain herself and asked our friend almost right away to solemnize us when the time came, soon the women were crying together, the spontaneous approach evidently the right one, I was emotional too, not that I cried, I've only cried once in more than eight years and that was still to come.

Your whatever creek meadows sounds lovely

Let's do it Louisa texted me a few days before her Toronto–Denver flight, already I'd sensed and still I imagined that she was a little wary of a backpacking trip, across the two decades plus that I've known her Louisa has always been a hard worker reluctant to take time off and this industrious disposition of hers made me only the more grateful that she was willing to spend a night with us in the Flat Tops Wilderness, I'd only been to Vallum Creek Meadows twice myself, once as a teenager with my parents and some of their hiking buddies, wishing in the way of seventeen that I could sneak away and get stoned, and then again in my early thirties, with two male friends only one of whom I truly liked, I suppose I'd always wanted to return there in the right company, the image of the place might have gone dim in my mind but now that I thought again of the high green hanging valley with its eponymous meadows stretched taut beneath some oval coliseum of tall basalt cliffs I thought that if I was remembering the place at all accurately I wouldn't have oversold anything to Clementine and/or Louisa.

Do I need a tent Louisa texted me a little later.

Not the kind of person who has a tent

I assured my friend whom I'd never known to do anything more outdoorsy than walking her dog (one dog, then another and another, in the way of passing decades) that all she needed to pack were sturdy shoes, wool socks, and some non-cotton clothes, a pair of sunglasses and a hat with a brim, everything else Clem and I could supply, except for a backpack, and one of those Louisa could rent from REI.

What do you have against cotton clothes she wanted to know.

Stay wet when wet and don't insulate I replied.

Aren't your hiking outfits made of petroleum eco man?

Ha ha yes I texted.

Will I be flammable she asked.

Let's not find out I said, I hate texting, I'm no good at the obligatory jocularity and I don't know how to conclude.

'Oh my god actually,' Clementine said when after plodding uphill for almost four hours we'd at last reached my talked-up meadows and hiked in the length of maybe one hundred yards.

'Oh *my* god,' Louisa pronounced also. 'It's just kind of boring trees and then it opens onto this.'

Halfway up the meadows we came across a firepit surely established by horse- or backpackers some years ago, no sign anyway of the circle of scarred gray stones having been used recently, I couldn't even recognize the faded brand of micro-brew cans in the ashes, altogether Vallum Creek Meadows appeared to be a truly forgotten locale, a real oversight on the part of Instagram as Clementine observed, anyway no fire ban was in effect, so I'd confirmed before we left cell-phone range, and now that the women went off as a pair to gather dry wood and kindling I struck out in the opposite direction, I marched, that is, to the illumined fringe of the fields to load one forearm with dead branches and, once I'd assembled a full stack and stood up to support my precarious collection with both arms before the stack could tip away, I was able to look out again at the sequined meander of Vallum Creek shifting away through a stepped set of green abandoned playing fields almost entirely enclosed by ramparts of spruce, fir, and lodgepole pine that broke like curtain hems beneath sheer palisades of maroon rock, in seeing this sight I felt something like the relief that always overtook me in school whenever I'd guessed with shaky confidence at the harder answers of a test or quiz and learned in fact that I'd been right all along.

Not long after we'd set up our tents the sun dropped away without taking much of day with it and left us with plenty of time to make dinner in the light, we sat around our campfire which shuddered smally inside the brilliant dimming cliffs and once the water had boiled on my little camping stove and the pasta cooked for twenty minutes or so ate some rather bougie mac and cheese with orange powdered organic cheese out of a box, I'd seasoned the dish with this whiskey-barrel black pepper, so-called, that I get at a spice shop in Boulder whenever I'm down there, indeed everything tastes so good when you've been backpacking that Cambridge-educated Clem said honestly about the gloppy mac and cheese: 'Top three most delicious things I've eaten. I mean, fuck Per Se. Fuck L'Arpège.'

I handed her my plastic camping flask a second time.

'She doesn't drink,' Louisa said as if I didn't know.

'Sometimes I do,' Clemmy took a swig and slipped comically off her log to lay down on the grass. 'I can't ever *quite* get over the stars.'

'I think you two are going to be really happy,' Louisa said and we all tapped together our titanium mugs-cum-whiskey tumblers.

The cold that comes with nightfall at ninety-five hundred feet, even in July, seemed almost to shock Louisa and once it was dark we quickly switched on our headlamps, doused the fire dead, and went off to our separate tents, I'd planted the tents maybe forty-five yards apart, I must have wanted to respect everybody's privacy, and as Clem and I walked off to our two-man affair past the slithering facets of moonlight and jet that were the skin of the creek, talking the whole short way about the stars and scenery and our mutual good friend, or maybe something else entirely, it never occurred to me once to pause our conversation and listen to the water, all I knew at the time was that Vallum Creek was louder than its straitened dimensions would suggest, in the way of all mountain streams.

Inside the tent we took off our synthetic clothes and fucked or made love or had sex, somehow no ordinary expression ever fits very accurately the very familiar act, testament maybe to some enduring inarticulacy at the heart of life, anyway it was even better than usual in spite of the draftiness of Clementine's half-zipped sleeping bag, we were also far enough away from the other tent as not to worry about any noises or cries before we shifted onto our separate sleeping pads, Clem instantaneously falling asleep as is her wont, my own habit on many nights even in the off-season being to cue up a Denver Nuggets podcast, in other words I listened on my earbuds to a quartet of affable guys discussing potential roster moves awaiting the team in free agency until oblivion set in, I recall only that I woke up once in the dark amid lurid irrecoverable dreams to stagger out and piss beneath the matchless stars, again I don't remember hearing a single thing in the creek except a chute of white noise, and in the morning when I knelt and crouched and stood out from the tent the air was thin and bright as a wafer on your dumbstruck tongue.

Crouching next to the firepit, Louisa sipped the coffee I'd brewed and said nothing, of course lots of people are quiet until they're caffeinated but I knew my friend well enough from mornings long ago to ask: 'What's wrong? What's the matter?'

After a moment she said: 'What can there be to talk about all night like that?'

This line of questioning baffled me, Louisa was still accusing me of being in love with the sound of my own voice when Clem appeared, looking very pale.

'You're up early,' I said, Clementine is typically a heroic sleeper, at ten hours a night.

I was dropping instant coffee out of a sachet into Clementine's mug when Louisa announced to her: 'You don't have to put up with that.'

Louisa looked in the direction of our tent, Clem was clearly confused and so was I.

'She wants to defend you,' Louisa said and shook her head, she went on to say, as if it were more than she should have to, that she'd heard me talking all night long, even from her tent, and then gotten up twice to approach our spot and confirm, from halfway between the tents, that I simply wouldn't shut up.

'I don't . . .' Clemmy sounded unprecedentedly sleepy.

I felt so angry at the false accusation that it seemed to me if I said anything my anger might paradoxically confirm the truth of it.

'You can't tell me he wasn't talking all night long,' Louisa said. 'At least every time I woke up.'

In her sedated-seeming way Clementine said: 'Maybe he was talking. I wear earplugs. Because he sometimes snores.'

'Let's talk about him in the third person,' I said.

'You're allowed to talk,' Clementine said.

'You're not allowed to talk to women all night when they want to go to sleep. Look at you,' Louisa said to Clem, 'you're shattered. Did you sleep at all?'

'I have a hard time on a bed roll.'

'A sleeping pad,' I said in spite of myself.

'I don't imagine Tom has told you about the time he wouldn't let me sleep?' Louisa asked.

'I know you two dated,' Clementine said very uncertainly, it was as if she'd had a stroke or something.

'It was this thing,' Louisa was saying, 'where he wouldn't let me sleep, I kept pleading and you had to keep talking, literally all night long. You *pursued* me, to my apartment.'

'What's this about?' Clementine asked supremely vaguely.

'You remember Eric,' Louisa said.

Of course I remembered the forgettable man – he'd worked at some magazine – that Louisa had dated for a few years in New York City, before as well as after I left for grad school, and also before she realized she was more into women, as detailed in her memoir.

'Eric asked if we'd slept together,' I explained, 'Louisa and I, and I denied it. I felt like you didn't kiss and tell. So people thought Louisa was lying. Why are we talking about this?'

'You think everyone wants to marry you,' Louisa said.

'Well some people do,' I said, the remark failed to produce the intended laughter.

'What he said to you?' Clementine asked Louisa ungrammatically.

'Anything,' Louisa was saying. 'Everything. You do *not* keep talking when a woman says she needs to sleep.'

'I'm sorry,' I said, 'for what I did in two thousand whenever it was.'

'It was 2007.'

'Look at her,' Louisa said again about Clemmy. 'She's shattered.'

Horribly this did seem to be a fair description.

Louisa said: 'You're a good guy. But there's this part of you that you can't see – I'm sorry, Clemmy – there's this part of him that's an asshole.'

'Everyone,' I said in an unpleasant superior tone, 'has a part of them they can't see that's their asshole. That's human anatomy. Not even just humans.'

'Maybe you did talk,' Clementine said through tears. 'I had earplugs in.'

'Nope,' I said. 'No.'

'Maybe you were talking to yourself,' Clem suggested.

'Do you really think,' I said to her, 'that I was talking the whole night?'

'Much of the night,' Louisa said. 'It may not have been all night.'

'It's a yes or no question,' I said to Clementine.

'You're also,' Louisa said to me, 'a really horrible person to argue with.'

Clementine simply cried.

The three of us broke camp and hiked without really talking down the same way we'd come, past unpaintably or -filmably shimmering stands of aspen trees and on and on through ever-lower elevations, the cool pale air of the aspens at length giving way to the baked scent of pines, it was maybe around this time that I noticed Clem stumble more than once and asked whether she was okay, both Clementine and Louisa turned to look at me as Clemmy said apologetically that she'd forgotten to take her acetazolamide.

'What's the thing you just said?' Louisa sounded somewhat suspicious.

'Acetazolamide,' I said. 'It's the standard altitude-sickness prophylactic. You usually take it above eight or nine thousand feet,' I said to Clementine in what I intended to be a friendly sympathetic manner.

Acetazolamide is a diuretic, otherwise the drug seems free of side effects, and I said to Clementine that in fact I'd noticed she hadn't been peeing much, I could tell as I voiced this observation that there was something strained about it, it was as if I were asserting before Louisa a familiarity with my fiancée that now stood in question.

'Let me take your pack,' I said to Clem and asked to carry it the rest of the way down or until she felt better, she nodded more obediently than I liked for Louisa to see, Clementine always gets meek when she isn't feeling well, and for the rest of the way to the trailhead I carried the second backpack strapped in front of me, of course I was in some pain from the excess burden but a quantity of physical discomfort is a tolerable thing, much more of an affliction as we marched alongside the hurrying silver seam of Vallum Creek was the persistent worry that Clementine's exhaustion, in reality due only to a touch of altitude, would now confirm for Louisa that I had indeed been talking all night long just as alleged, in this way depriving Clem of her necessary sleep, after all it must seem doubtful that altitude by itself could really make a person so exhausted, and no doubt then I'd been haranguing Clemmy all night long on some unpleasant or even unmentionable subject, otherwise why would this woman feel she had to protect the man she intended to marry by denying or at least refusing to confirm that any such conversation, so one-sided as to be almost a monologue, had in fact taken place?

In spite of the blighted morning the long return drive to Fort Collins wasn't bad, the women sat together in the back seat as they had on the way out and chatted amiably about books and clothes and politics, about family and mutual friends, more or less as if nothing had happened, on the whole it was possible to believe at the time, and for a week or more after I dropped Louisa off at the Denver airport the next day, that everything was ultimately okay and I hadn't somehow spoiled some delicate three-sided state of things by talking all night in my sleep, a possibility I congratulated myself on being open-minded enough to entertain, honestly the whole weird episode seemed on its way to being forgotten until I received the following email from Louisa one day in late July:

> Dear Tom,
>
> I am writing you now about officiating at your wedding. When I immediately said yes it was because I was honored that you and Clementine would want me to be part of something so important to your lives. As I have had more time to think about the issue I no longer feel confident that I am the right person for this vital role.
>
> I am so sorry for the disappointment I am no doubt causing you. Please know that it is not a reflection of how much I care for you both. I still look forward to being a guest at the event. Best,
>
> Louisa

Once I'd forwarded the note to Clementine we started saying to one another what we kept saying for several days, namely that it wasn't only that Louisa had reneged on officiating the wedding less than three months out, the other thing was the strangely stilted and perfunctory language she'd used, we didn't know what to make of it, ever since the Vallum Creek Meadows episode, however, I'd been doing my best not to talk about things too much, I was trying instead to be a stoical and practical-minded man of few words such as a normal woman might wish to marry or, alternatively, befriend, and it was in this spirit that I wrote back to Louisa saying (in spite of understanding nothing) that of course Clem and I understood completely, needless to say we looked forward to seeing Louisa at our ceremony in October, in truth it wasn't until three or more weeks later that something caused me to become unreasonable on the subject of Louisa, the precipitating event being the appearance of Louisa the internationally famous musician and writer on the podcast of a nationally famous print magazine, if such publications still exist, during which the host ingenuously asked her whether she'd ever used ChatGPT or a similar AI-powered chatbot, in fact I never listened to the podcast myself, I only learned of Louisa's answer to the host's question when Clementine related it to me one evening over dinner on our deck.

'On this podcast,' Clementine was saying, 'Louisa says she used ChatGPT most recently to get out of officiating a wedding.'

I suppose I stopped eating.

'Louisa says she used ChatGPT to write a note declining the role.'

For some reason I couldn't define, the utterly opposed – unless they were identical! – offenses of Louisa's insisting, on the one hand, that I'd been speaking when I hadn't been speaking and then pretending, on the other hand, that she'd written something she hadn't written caused me to absolutely lose it, then and over the ensuing days I denounced Louisa to Clementine as a vile hypocrite, I told Clementine moreover that I'd always suspected that shifty slinking Louisa was a coward, to my bill of indictment I added also that I highly doubted this was the first time our pseudo-friend had resorted to AI, her second and most recent book – I said though in fact I hadn't opened it: it was some novel, some made-up story – was actually so clumsily written that you could only hope a machine was responsible.

Clementine acknowledged then and later that it had been rude of Louisa to admit on a podcast to using ChatGPT rather than tell us herself, before going on to insist mildly and firmly that Louisa must have her reasons for what she'd done, in spite of my fiancée's typical humanity I found that I was unappeasable, over the next days I announced and repeated that I couldn't abide this person at our wedding, before long I was demanding to know what small article of any importance even the most august of Canadians had ever contributed to world culture, I said that all Canadians in spite of their superficial diversity constituted in the end a pestilential uniformity of hapless hicks, Joni Mitchell, Nuggets point guard Jamal Murray, and Pierre (but not Justin) Trudeau notwithstanding, the reality was that even on such occasions as when a Canadian lucked into going to a fancy college in the US, like Louisa had done, this sort of stunted boreal specimen could on no account acquire any real manners or sophistication, the arch-Canuck in fact consisted of someone who went around the world asserting for some incomprehensible reason that things that *hadn't* happened – such as my ranting all night in Vallum Creek Meadows – actually *had* happened, when really the main thing in world history that had never happened was none other than Canada itself, colossal frigid non-event of a country, subzero nonentity among nations, embarrassingly I'd once felt that I knew and could trust Louisa but I realized now there was nothing to know there, long before the advent of ChatGPT she herself had embodied the great white north of ChatGPT.

'I know you're joking,' Clementine said. 'But I can also see that you're genuinely angry.'

'You sound like a shrink,' I responded, and after I'd spent approximately ten days in castigating at every opportunity perfidious Louisa and her simultaneously evil and boring homeland, Clementine at last said to me in calm and factual tones that she couldn't be around me anymore if I was going to be like this, she observed that she'd never spent time with me over the summer, when I had no classes to teach, except when, as in past summers, I'd been trying to write a book, which as far she could tell I wasn't doing at the moment.

'You're wondering if we shouldn't get married?' I asked, I believe this is known among couples' therapists as escalation. 'Look if you need somebody who can write a book to stop global warming, I'm not your man. I never was.'

'I think one of us should go away for a few days,' Clementine said with maddening placidity.

'You could go to fucking Canada,' I proposed.

'Aren't you afraid I'd defect?'

Her gracious wry smile that rose above the situation made me wish to do violence to some object or myself.

'I'm going back to the Flat Tops,' I said bitterly. 'Why don't I go back to Vallum Creek Meadows since I love it there so much?'

More or less insanely I had burst into tears.

'You'll take your device?' Clementine was referring to the small handheld GPS and satellite communicator, shaped like a miniature walkie-talkie, that I always take with me on solo expeditions, with one of these a person alone in the wilderness can communicate to his loved ones and, if need be, the appropriate authorities that he or she is safe or in peril, as the case might be.

Trailhead; sage brush; scrub oak and stream . . . and on my way back up the trail toward the fateful meadows that no one has ever heard of in spite of their sickening beauty what I did was to keep protesting, sometimes out loud, to bristling branches and then to the dark open eyes studding the trunks of aspen trees, that I'd said nothing to anyone the last night I was here, nor could it be considered a realistic conjecture that I'd rambled all night in my sleep, none of the women I'd slept with, including Louisa, much less Clementine, had ever complained of my talking at length in my sleep, very rarely in fact across several decades of ill-considered heterosexual experience had any woman ever mentioned anything except for the occasional whimper or cry, I kept on hiking furiously up my by now well-known trail and as I did so it occurred to me that I loved Louisa as a friend but had never really been attracted to her, that I had slept with her back in college and several times afterward, as presumptive grown-ups, only out of some masculine obligingness which I've never seen described in fiction, not that I read much of the stuff, this coolness on my part was not because Louisa wasn't and isn't very good-looking (I once saw a ranking online of famous male and female writers by attractiveness, with Louisa third on this list, behind only Zadie Smith and some man I'd never heard of), it's only, I guess, that she has sandy hair and blue eyes, a neat small nose and a curvy figure whereas I have never really been seriously much less fatally attracted to any woman who wasn't an angular tallish brunette with a dramatic nose and large dark eyes, in the case of Clementine (of English and white South African parentage) as well as that of one other woman, who plays no part in this story, it was as if with respect to her physical appearance I was simply a lock to be entered only by the one key, or its copy, that would turn it.

Soon I was setting up my one-man tent more or less where Louisa's had been while the ridiculous sunlight drained upward from the eastern palisades and beating the tent stakes into the ground with a handy rock, once I'd inflated my sleeping pad and laid out my sleeping bag inside the tent I dug into my backpack for my camping stove and fuel canister and only after retrieving these items did I notice that in my haste to leave Fort Collins I must have forgotten to bring any food, in fact it seemed as I rooted through my pack that there wasn't among all my nylon nonsense a single energy bar or packet of dried fruit or spiced nuts, much less some vacuum-sealed and dehydrated pièce de résistance, it looked in fact like I would have to go to bed hungry, really it was like some caricature of self-harming masculinity when I discovered that the only nourishment I'd brought with me in my trouble was my plastic camping flask containing perhaps a pint of whiskey, rye.

I lay on my back shivering a bit beneath the shaming stars and proceeded to get quite drunk, I would prop myself up on an elbow once every few minutes to take a swig, and it wasn't until the booze was almost gone that I noticed, without alarm or even, strangely, surprise, how in lying on my back in the long cold grass I'd also been listening to the continuous sound of a familiar male voice unspooling itself about half a football field away, I struggled up to my feet, not undrunkenly, to go inspect this curious auditory phenomenon but even as I went off toward the sound I knew this unmistakable voice saying its unintelligible words for my very own, after all I had heard a recording of the same voice before, so really it was only in order to establish what I already knew in my bones, or what one calls one's bones, in their marrow, that I stood above the liquid slipping starlight of *the babbling brook* – I hadn't ever realized the term could be so literal, probably many people haven't either, in this digital world – and thought how Louisa had of course thought this voice was mine for the obvious reason that the timbre *was* obviously just the same as my own, possibly something in the rhythm or cadence might be similar too, the sound of the creek at any rate at this one point along its stammering course exactly mimicked that of my own speaking voice, if only on the night in question I hadn't listened on my earbuds to a stupid Denver Nuggets podcast I might have known as much before now.

Once I returned to Fort Collins the next day and announced myself with a soft knock on the door to Clementine's office, Clemmy declared she had something to share with me and proceeded to read out loud as I stood in the door frame an email from Louisa apologizing for Podcast Incident Number Two, as I think of it, in which Louisa admitted (it was clear Clemmy had confronted her) that she ought to have told us about using ChatGPT before confessing this fact to a podcaster, then she, Louisa, went on in the email – which Clemmy was reading aloud – to say that when she'd told a few people 'I'm marrying Tom' in reference to officiating the upcoming nuptials, she had produced in herself the uninvited feeling that it might in fact be her and me getting married, sometimes, Louisa added, she felt that she would have liked to marry Tom had Tom only been a woman, obviously an impossible condition, it wasn't only the penis, Louisa wrote in conclusion, it's that Tom is so clueless in a way that we can never be, 'anyway you can see why I just couldn't do it' was, I believe, one verbatim phrase, and as I went to sit down on the pink velvet couch in Clementine's office while Clemmy said with satisfaction 'So?' I recalled, without having any need to do so, how the recognition the night before of the sound of Vallum Creek as my own voice had established for all time Louisa's innocence as well as my own, how this awareness of innocence had made me laugh again or else keep on laughing, my backcountry satellite communication device had been lying dormant in the top compartment of my pack but I'd gone off then to text Clementine that I was okay, this was not even untrue. ■

LAURE MARY
Portrait Of Absence And Nothing Else, 2025

EVERY DARK CORNER

Deborah Levy

If the unconscious is structured like a language, the design of a therapist's consulting room is also a language. But what is it saying? Even Disney knows deep down in its pink plastic heart that we bestow inanimate objects with life, vitality, emotions, history, meaning and social status. Is a chair ever just a chair? How is the rug on the floor and potted plant on the table going to help me accept ordinary unhappiness?

Freud argued for 'a certain ceremonial observance' in the way his consulting room was put together. He worked long hours and did not want to be stared at by his patients all day, so he positioned his armchair behind the patient's head while they lay on his kilim-draped couch. If we really think about this, it's quite a weird arrangement of human bodies – especially in the early days of psychoanalysis. I can get a sense of how its founding father had to experiment, improvise, invent new techniques that also involved rearranging the furniture in his consulting room. Freud was essentially working from home.

A friend of mine, who is a therapist, told me that in the early days of her practice, before she made a separate entrance for her patients (or clients, or analysands), her children had to tiptoe down the corridor of the family home carrying their bikes when she had a session. Freud and Martha had six children. Herr Professor's waiting and consulting rooms were also located in their family apartment, though professional and domestic spaces were carefully divided at Berggasse 19. Freud curated his consulting room with a very particular ambience.

> There was always a feeling of sacred peace and quiet here. The rooms themselves must have been a surprise to any patient, for they in no way reminded one of a doctor's office but rather of an archaeologist's study . . . Everything here contributed to one's feeling of leaving the haste of modern life behind, of being sheltered from one's daily cares.
>
> Sergei Pankejeff, 'The Wolfman', on Freud's study.

Language is the centre of gravity in the endeavour of psychoanalysis. The various therapies that are its far-distant cousins have travelled a long way from this premise. To believe in the talking cure, as I do, is to put one's faith in something truly strange, but since when has any sort of faith not been strange? Especially when this language involves silence. On this subject, Mark Rothko said it best: 'Silence is so accurate.' Samuel Beckett used more words to evoke how much he detested words and in so doing revealed how much he loved them: 'Every word is like an unnecessary stain on silence and nothingness.'

It is possible, too, that when we walk into a skilled therapist's consulting room we will never get out. We are there forever, by which I mean it is not easy to walk new knowledge and understanding back to a place of simulated ignorance. It certainly becomes harder to hear everyday language and political language without the psychoanalytic furniture getting in the way. There is the risk that in learning some of this language, it is used to explain everything away, as if words such as ambivalence or narcissism can do all the heavy lifting. As if we even really know what they mean.

My great hero of cinema, Werner Herzog, has made his feelings clear in various interviews about the value of psychoanalysis. He certainly does not see it as a shelter from one's daily cares. 'I think it is one of the greatest stupidities and the greatest mistakes of the twentieth century.' Perhaps Herzog was airing his thoughts, not feelings, yet they are inflamed thoughts, attractively hot under the collar. Even a quick glance at the twentieth century (don't mention the wars) would not reveal psychoanalysis to be its greatest stupidity and mistake. If I understand his drift, it seems that Herzog shares Hamlet's fear that 'you would pluck out the heart of my mystery', something many artists who seek psychoanalysis share too. It is likely that *Fitzcarraldo* (1982) would have been a different film if Klaus Kinski had not been a maniac.

Herzog continues his drift on this subject:

> I believe that explaining every dark little corner that we have in our soul is a very unhealthy, and a very stupid, and a very dangerous thing. We should not do that. Why? Because when you inhabit a house and you illuminate every last corner of the house with strong lights, the house becomes uninhabitable. And human beings illuminated to the very last corner of their darkest soul become inhuman and uninhabitable.

A house. Dark corners. Illumination. This lighting design resembles a film set.

For those who have dared to enter a therapist's consulting room (often beige, no Gothic lighting), it is possible we are there because we find our own mystery has become unbearable, perhaps even uninhabitable. Yet, the therapist's room does, in a way, resemble a film set. Even if its mood attempts to be entirely neutral, someone has art-directed its blandness. We gaze judgementally at the abstract print on the wall and then lower our eyes to take in the therapist's shoes. Is it true that if we are attentive to language there will be illumination? There will also be darkness. More than enough darkness for a whole Herzog movie. Do we trust the stranger in the chair?

Whatever the furniture, it is our very first room in life that was truly a room of our own. As William Burroughs told us in his most Freudian thought, 'We are all born in the soft typewriter of the womb.' ■

THERAPY ROOMS

Nigel Shafran

Amaretti del Chiostro

An Introduction to Family Therapy
QUALITATIVE INQUIRY & RESEARCH DESIGN
Handbook of Qualitative Research Methods
Phenomenological Psychology
Cognitive Therapy of Anxiety Disorders
COGNITIVE THERAPY OF DEPRESSION
MIND OVER MOOD
THE THEORY AND PRACTICE OF GROUP PSYCHOTHERAPY
SHORT-TERM COUPLES THERAPY
Biopsychology
Pinel
RECOVERY RUSSELL BRAND

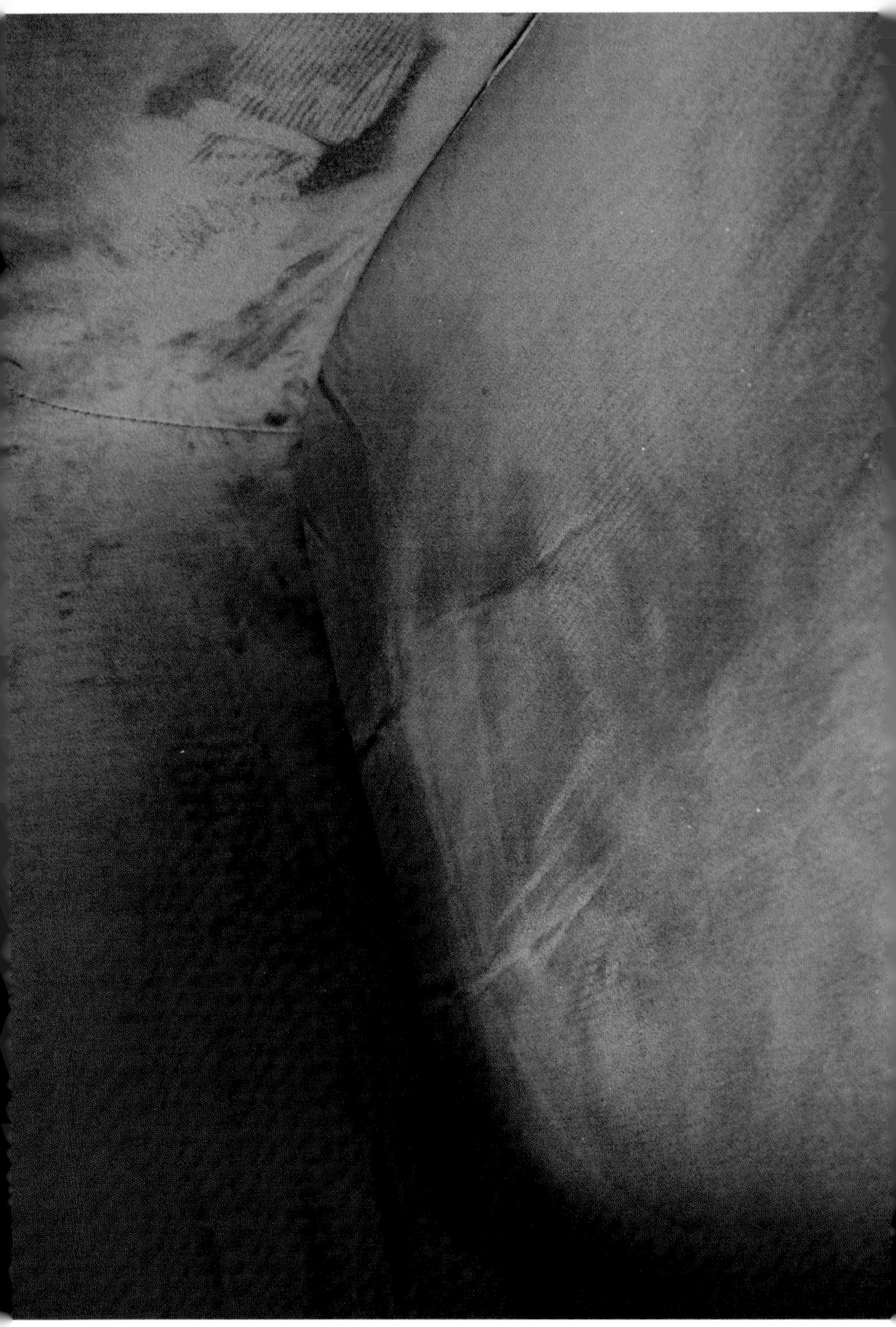

ELLIOTT GREEN
Navigator, 2019
Courtesy of Miles McEnery Gallery

THE ORANGE SHIP

An Afternoon with Christopher Bollas

Born in 1943, in Washington, D.C., Christopher Bollas grew up in Laguna Beach, California. He studied history at the University of California, Berkeley and received a PhD in English at the University at Buffalo, where he wrote his doctoral dissertation on Herman Melville. In 1973, he moved to London to train as an analyst in the British Psychoanalytical Society. He practiced there for thirty years, before returning to the United States.

Bollas is among the most widely read psychoanalytic writers today. He is a restless coiner of new concepts – 'the unthought known', 'receiving unconscious', 'psychic genera' – that now form part of the vocabulary of object relations theory. 'Love of our objects, sometimes something of an embarrassment, is a passion that performs a communion,' he writes. His prose is casually revelatory, with a flair for the literary and the confessional. In books ranging from *Being a Character* (1992) and *Cracking Up* (1995), to the first two volumes of his collected notebooks (2024), Bollas draws equally on the writings of Sigmund Freud and D.W. Winnicott, the poetry of William Wordsworth and Robert Hass, and on his own memories of his coastal childhood.

This October the editor of *Granta* met Bollas at the Lion & Unicorn pub in Kentish Town. In person, Bollas is a charismatic listener. He speaks in a warm, highly distinctive register, and gives the sense of a mariner at ease in the sea of the psychic underworld. While in London, Bollas met with several of his former patients, including his first one. 'It was very moving,' he said. 'We knew we were saying goodbye.'

GRANTA: Am I right that your father was a war hero?

BOLLAS: He was the first American to enter Paris in August 1944, when there were still German snipers on the rooftops of the Boulevard Montparnasse. He had grown up in Paris, and he knew the city. The Associated Press wanted to get in to see what was going on. They said, how do we get into Paris? Will anyone take us there? My dad was there in the Ninth Air Force and he said, I'll do it. He drove four reporters in a jeep into Paris. He had to be careful. They were getting fired upon. I don't think he expected to be emotionally overwhelmed but he was. The Parisians took their presence to mean they were liberated. It was just one jeep, but to them it was a symbolic object. It *was* the liberation.

GRANTA: What was it like for him when he returned?

BOLLAS: I think he expected a hero's welcome when he came back to California, and it wasn't there. He was still very much in love with my mother, and she, in her own way, loved him. But their marriage was difficult. I had a brother two and a half years younger than me, and a brother seven years younger, and my dad completely adored my brothers. With me, it was different. I had been mostly raised by my grandparents. I was the outsider. I knew he loved me, but he was hard on me.

My father never knew his father. His stepfather, Paul, treated him – it wasn't cruel, it was more like he treated him as a blank. I was about seven when I had my very first insight. Oh my God, I thought, Paul treats my father the way my dad treats me. He's not the real son, and neither am I. And I felt enormous relief. Prior to that, I felt a lot of pain, because he could say terrible things to me. But one of my dad's saving graces was that he would almost always apologize, and sometimes in tears.

GRANTA: What about your mother?

BOLLAS: My mother was a woman of the 1950s. She was a young pianist who played Debussy. She was extremely talented, extraordinarily beautiful, very dramatic. She was courted by MGM. When she was a child my mother had to go into care, from when she was four until she was seven. This was while my grandmother was in a sanatorium with tuberculosis. My grandfather would come visit my mother every day, but that's a long time for a child.

GRANTA: What was Laguna Beach like in the 1950s?

BOLLAS: It was very alternative. Lots of actors lived there. There was a strong gay community. It was an enclave for everyone in the McCarthy era who was blacklisted. My parents had accidentally gone to a CP [Communist Party] meeting. I was in a play at the age of eleven, and Bette Davis was in the audience. The great cinematographer Paul Ivano, who was Rudolph Valentino's best buddy, was my godfather. One of my best friends was the rock-and-roll star Ricky Nelson. I taught him how to skin dive. There's something democratic about life by the sea. Each person has the same chances once they jump in the water. You don't know what's going to happen. It's like the Las Vegas of physiotherapy.

GRANTA: You describe your parents' marriage as approximating a fairly loving marriage. In one of your essays, you write about marriage and partnership as a refuge from the burden of an artistic life –

BOLLAS: – or from any life.

ROBERT FRANCIS COMMAGÈRE
Christopher Bollas running, Laguna Beach High School, 1961

GRANTA: So, in order to avoid facing up to the full reality of living, you get married?

BOLLAS: Marriage is a necessary regression. We are too complicated. We're too complex. Many great artists live alone, and they pay for it. They suffer because they don't have that regression to turn to. Other people, most people, prefer living with the madness of others than with their own mind.

My mother and father divorced when I was fourteen, and that was very painful. My mum went wild, and I looked after the family. I really hate this literature where they say, well, you're the typical son who has to step in and look after the family. I mean, this was Laguna Beach. No one gets any kudos for stepping in and playing the absent father. But I did learn an incredible amount about women. When I was sixteen, my father said to me, 'It's time that you understand women,' and he handed me *The Second Sex*. He was always two or three years ahead of me.

GRANTA: How would you describe your mother's wildness?

BOLLAS: She was a hysteric.

GRANTA: How much weight do you put behind the concept of hysteria? It seems like one of those words that was so absorbed by the culture that it lost nearly all its meaning.

BOLLAS: That's true of all diagnostic labels. I think psychodiagnosis is valuable if you're in ER. There you have to make a quick decision. Once you're working with someone, those terms just go away. Human beings are much more complex than the term 'hysteria', or 'borderline'. These are not terms that I find meaningful, except when trying to write about them as phenomena for people who want to try to begin to map out the differences between people. Each hysteric is very different from any other hysteric.

I have been thinking about how acting is a way of developing ourselves. Acting is occupying another personality. It's a gift to be able to occupy a narrative form, to take on a role that's passed to you. It's applied hysteria. You can see how many children will occupy the role promoted to them by the mother and the father, and fail to come up with their own strategy.

Hysterics are all Falstaffian in a way. What I think is tragic about the hysterical mode is the absence of translation.

GRANTA: They don't get to enjoy the fruits of the insights they've generated?

BOLLAS: I think that's why it's a female disorder much more so than a male disorder, because women are suppressed. They get put in a position where they cannot speak their minds. What do they have to do? Create identities, alternatives, make fools of themselves. You can see it before your very eyes.

GRANTA: What is it that hysterics are trying to get at?

BOLLAS: A relation to the other in which they're significant, where they have impact, where they have power, where they, ironically, throw off the listening other, so they can go from being a subordinate to somebody who's actually revolutionary. They're turning things over. And they can scare the shit out of men.

GRANTA: Hysteria is a way of instilling fear?

BOLLAS: It's a form of intelligence.

I think it's interesting to think of one's mother as a peculiar, particular person, but also as a woman like any other who existed in time. I understood my mother as well as my father. I understand what it is to be a woman as much as I understand what it is to be a man, whatever that is. I think my mother identified with men. Both of them had each gender within them. The female would be in him at times; the male would be in her at times. There was a fluidity between the two of them.

GRANTA: And your education?

BOLLAS: I went to the University of Virginia for two years. I wanted to go there because of the Woodrow Wilson School of Public and International Affairs. I was very involved in politics and international relations, and I spent a lot of time in Washington, D.C., where I met Hubert Humphrey. He was my hero. I went to a few parties, and, man, I don't know if you've ever been to a Washington, D.C. party, but it was shocking – the most corrupt fucking world I've ever seen. I thought, I can't live in this world. So, in 1964, I transferred to Berkeley.

I had psychoanalytic therapy when I was an undergraduate at Berkeley. It was a tough time for me. I was arrested by the Justice Department for resisting the Vietnam draft. I remember my day at the Oakland Induction Center as the worst day of my life. I thought I would have to have a dentist take out my teeth because I would be sent to Folsom State Prison, and you did not want to have teeth there; the inmates were known to knock them out on the first day. My lawyer got me released to do non-military service, but I was symptomatic: I had a fear of climbing stairs, because I thought I might throw myself over. I went into psychotherapy with a brilliant psychoanalyst named Carlos Fernandez. I saw him once a week for about a year and a half. One day, I'm going to write an essay called 'Once-weekly Psychoanalysis', which is really going to piss off my colleagues.

GRANTA: Why do people believe that psychoanalysis has to be five times a week?

BOLLAS: Five times a week is extraordinary, no doubt about it. But what's great about once-a-week psychoanalysis is that the session becomes like a dream. There's not enough time for the transference to evolve and develop and interfere with the relationship, so it's almost pure confession, straight from the unconscious. The patient doesn't have any idea what he or she is going to talk about. It's *bingo*.

The psychoanalysts who understood this well were Peter Sifneos in Boston and David Malan in England, who taught focal psychotherapy. Focal psychotherapy is once a week for fifteen weeks, or twenty-five weeks, and that's it. What they found they could do with once-a-week sessions – and this is me, interpreting their work – was that the patient would say, 'Here it is. This is the core issue.' They would wait until they got to the core issue, and then they could objectify it. The person would have an epiphany, think about it, and change his behavior. That's it. There's no such thing as regression in once-a-week psychotherapy.

GRANTA: I thought you believed in seeing patients for as long as it takes. Why does focal psychotherapy – which sounds like rushing toward a solution – appeal to you?

BOLLAS: Once-weekly psychotherapy and five-times-a-week psychotherapy are utterly different. I like them both. Just like there's this idea in psychoanalysis that you have to choose between the father and the mother. To hell with that. You can have both parents in the room. You can identify with both of them. Once-weekly psychotherapy is unique because the patient's unconscious basically gets it, and they themselves organize the session unconsciously to the core point, so the analyst just waits and waits and waits. Don't distract them. Don't make it about yourself. No transference interpretations. Bear in mind that the unconscious is not stupid, and that the brain and the unconscious can reorientate to the circumstances. I think what happens is that once it's announced that the sessions are limited – once the patient knows that – the unconscious thinks, right, well, I better get straight to it.

GRANTA: What techniques in therapy do you reject?

BOLLAS: The worst technique is when analysts summarize what the patient's been saying. But that has been common in the United States and the United Kingdom, where analysts would say, 'So, you've been saying this.' What the fuck for? Wait, wait, wait. Wait until something surprising comes up, some insight generated by the analysis, and whatever you say, make it short, and make sure it's their material, not your goddamn summary of their material.

GRANTA: The first developmental condition you specialized in was autism. Why?

BOLLAS: I had just graduated from Berkeley. I was a Vietnam War resister, and the Justice Department said, 'Would you settle for two years as an alternative service?' And my lawyer, J. B. Tietz, said take it. So, from 1967 to 1969, I worked at the East Bay Activity Center with autistic, schizophrenic, and very disturbed children.

It was probably the most remarkable experience of my life, clinically. There were about twenty children, twelve staff. The kids were from the age of six to fourteen. It was heartbreaking to work with those children. There are things I learned there that I still don't understand. The most moving moments were with children asking, 'How come you're well? How come you can think clearly and I can't?' That's about as profound a question as you're ever going to get.

Albert was my kid. He'd come into the center and he'd usually bash somebody. He would spit at me, gouge my arms, kick my shins, and I would try different ways of calming him down. One particularly soggy day, holding this bulky kid in the damp grass, out of the blue, I said, 'Would you like to hear about the orange ship?' He said, 'What ship?' I said, 'It's an orange ship.' He said, 'Who's the captain?' And we started the story. For six months we began the day with the story of the orange ship. Every day, instead of wanting to kill somebody, he'd say 'orange ship', and off we'd go. The orange ship would come to one port, and he would say, 'Everyone's been killed by alligators,' or 'They've been eaten or taken by the giant bird.' One day Albert started laughing. He laughed and laughed. He looked at me and he said, 'You don't get it, do you, Chris Ball? I'm joking.' He was putting me on. The story then ended. We didn't have to continue with the orange ship. The violence had stopped within him. He'd gone on to the next stage of life. I still do not understand it. These were transformative experiences for the children, but also for me, and I think for all of us who worked there.

GRANTA: How did you start your first training as a psychoanalyst?

BOLLAS: In 1971, I was teaching a course called 'Madness and Contemporary American Fiction' at the University at Buffalo. I can only remember a few of the books. One of them was *The Wonderful Wizard of Oz*, which is a psychotic text. A few of the kids came up to me after the class. They were very interested. One was schizophrenic, and wanted to talk about the illness. I talked to them for a long time, and then I – I'll never forget, I can still see it in my mind's eye – walked across the lawn, up a hill, to the mental-health center and asked if I could be trained as a psychoanalyst. They said, 'We'll try you out. We'll see how it goes.' It started with one patient, and it went well. We later created a program to train people in humanities to become psychotherapists at the University at Buffalo.

GRANTA: How did you get to England?

BOLLAS: While I was still an undergraduate at Berkeley, I managed a bookstore in San Francisco, Ghirardelli Square bookstore, and we subscribed to the *TLS*. Anthony Storr had reviewed Harry Guntrip's book *Schizoid Phenomena, Object Relations and the Self* (1968), and I thought, 'This is a book we've got to order for the store.' So I did, and I read it. From there, I read D.W. Winnicott, I read Melanie Klein, I read Frances Tustin.

In 1972, after I got my PhD in literature, I wrote to the British Society to train, and was invited over for an interview by Enid Balint. She asked me, 'What group are you going to join?' I didn't even know there were groups. She said, 'What analyst would you like as a training analyst?' I said I didn't know. 'Well, who do you know of?' she asked. I said I'd heard of Marion Milner and Masud Khan. She called them and said, 'I've got a young American here who's looking to have a training analysis, can you see him?' And she booked me to see them both.

GRANTA: If one were writing an intellectual history of British psychoanalysis, it seems like the 1980s would be a good place to end it. The originality of the British Society at least seems to dry up.

BOLLAS: I would end it sooner than that. I would end it when it went in for the 'here and now' transference interpretation.

GRANTA: What is that?

BOLLAS: All the interpretations became about the transference. If you interpret everything a person says to you as being about yourself – the analyst – the patient cannot speak freely. It shuts down any free association. It shuts down any kind of further movement in the session. In a word, it's paranoid. It's paranoid listening. The analyst and analysand become a paranoid couple.

GRANTA: So free association – the method of the patient just saying whatever came into their mind – was under attack?

BOLLAS: It was abandoned.

GRANTA: Hadn't it already been abandoned by Freud himself?

BOLLAS: Freud had two different theories of free association. One was that you could immediately translate the dream image into language.

But that's just not possible. It's a category error; a dream is an optical order. The other theory was about the chain of ideas, or what's called 'propinquity in time'.

GRANTA: How does that one work?

BOLLAS: As a patient is speaking to you, they say one thing, stop, say something else, and these things seem to have nothing to do with each other. That gap between, that space in logic, is where you start to see a link. You have to be patient. Free association can be compared to poetry. When you read poetry, you slow down. You don't try to understand at first. Your own thought process parallels the poem, and you don't know what it's about. You go back over the poem again. Then, suddenly, you might get a bit of the logic. The best patient is somebody who doesn't know what they're talking about. They just go on telling you about whatever comes into their mind.

GRANTA: How does this play out in your own sessions? Do you ever say something like, 'I've been listening to you for five weeks now. Have you noticed the common theme running through your remarks?'

BOLLAS: No. I say, 'You've just made an extraordinary connection. You ask this question here, and now you answer it there. Isn't that interesting?' That's all I say. What I'm teaching them is not how to understand the specific meaning of what they've said, but how to have an internal conversation. How do we talk to ourselves? Can we listen to ourselves? If we listen, then how do we listen to the productions of our mind?

GRANTA: You've developed your own particular view about transference. You seem to stress its dialectical, even creative, aspects. How is your idea different from this more negative picture of it that you've been giving?

BOLLAS: The view of transference changed dramatically in the early 1950s when Paula Heimann – my first supervisor – asked a crucial question: 'Who is speaking to whom? About what and why now?' It was a brilliant set of questions that the classical analysts had never asked. This meant that anytime the analyst is speaking to you in the room, they can shift the other, they can shift the subject. They could be speaking the mother's voice to the mother's mother; they could be speaking the brother's. In other words, it's a wide open and diverse mental phenomenon. Psychoanalysts at that time, in the early 1950s, were just beginning to contemplate the countertransference, which, before then, had been regarded as an obstruction to the analytical listening process. The British then said, no, it's not an obstruction, it's part of the phenomena. It's actually crucially informative. So we all began to change our orientation to the concept of transference and countertransference. I later wrote an essay called 'Expressive Uses of the Countertransference' (1983). I was very careful to say that the last thing I do is tell patients what I'm feeling about them. I could probably count on one hand how many times I've done that. I wanted to address the countertransference in a responsible way. In America, the Relational Group in New York has sort of lionized that essay and used it in their own teachings. It's a bit embarrassing for me.

GRANTA: One of the psychoanalysts with whom you've been deeply engaged with is Winnicott. You inherited some of his patients in London. In fact, you were among the first Americans to really read him. How did Winnicott affect how you conduct therapy?

BOLLAS: I felt sorry for the Americans who were determined to represent Winnicott's writings early on in the United States, because they had a kind of concrete view of things; they couldn't see the metaphor in Winnicott. The transitional object became a little bear you'd have in your office. No, that is not the transitional object. They idealized him, and they utterly missed a kind of ruthlessness in Winnicott, a real ruthlessness.

GRANTA: Where's the ruthlessness?

BOLLAS: In the abandonment of speech as a medium of communication. Winnicott didn't want people to free associate. He didn't believe in it. What's left then? Well, who knows. What's left is just being. He would sit and the patients would lean against his legs, and he'd go to sleep. They would go to sleep, and something would start to emerge. It was dozy. It was like an extraordinary guided tour, back into the infantile era. He was reliving something that's preverbal. It's very difficult to describe it, but I talked with several of his analysands, and all of them said the same thing. They found their work with him profoundly transformational.

GRANTA: Why was it so hard for the Winnicottians, or Winnicott himself, to explain his method to those who were skeptical of it?

BOLLAS: I don't think they could objectify themselves. I don't think they could see what they were doing that was different. It was a form of character analysis that had almost nothing to do with Freud.

GRANTA: What do you mean by 'character analysis'?

BOLLAS: Character is the evolution of action through the transference. It's the lived experience of the session. It's not a verbal intervention, it's a cohabitation. Something starts to get communicated. Something goes to be drawn up. There is the concept of the assumed.

GRANTA: What do you mean by 'the assumed'?

BOLLAS: What town did you grow up in?

GRANTA: Omaha.

BOLLAS: When you think of Omaha, en passant, even to yourself, or when you're talking to somebody, the entirety of that name is there in the mind. It's a neuropsychological phenomenon. The brain stores it. Consciously, we assume that the thoughts crossing our mind have been fully represented, which is not true. Thoughts crossing our mind are synecdochal. They're part of the whole, moving far too fast for us to think them properly, consciously. On the other hand, the unconscious is organized as 'the assumed', while the thoughts go on in the mind, with all the matrices organized as units. And it's as if the entire unit is present in the mind of the self, thinking the thought in that moment. The irony is that's correct, they are being thought in that moment, but thought by what? By the unconscious. We store our lived experiences in the assumed. Freud talked about the storehouse of the unconscious.

GRANTA: How is your concept of the 'unthought known' different from 'the assumed'?

BOLLAS: The unthought known is something that you've known but haven't thought about. The unthought known is knowledge based on transactions, if we want to use that awful term. The infant-mother relation is action, action, action, action. It's just two people acting upon one another. It is imbricated in the unconscious, in the form of the ego. Actions form axioms, axioms that govern the self for the rest of the life.

Heinz Lichtenstein said, 'Well, the mother imprints on the infant,' and that's his theory of identity. I don't agree with that. We're not made from the maternal identity. It's a dialectical process. Out of the dialectic between mother and infant, character is born.

GRANTA: On this question of character: you and Winnicott are both interested in the idea of a 'true self', though you've tweaked that concept, and prefer to think about a person pursuing or developing their own 'idiom'. Is this something that is discovered or worked toward or just inhabited? The idea of a 'true self' seems premised on having some contact with our 'real' selves, and the idea that this can be approached or somehow glimpsed in a therapeutic session. But wouldn't it make more sense for psychotherapy to stop treating the stories we tell about ourselves as obstructions or patterns ridden with clues of what lies below, and instead just accept that fictions of the self and fictions of others are an inextricable, irreducible part of any life – that maybe that *is* what life is?

BOLLAS: One could not 'inhabit' the 'true self' any more than you could 'inhabit' the way a pianist plays Rachmaninoff's 'Piano Concerto No. 3'. Finger intelligence – movement of thought through the way the pianist plays – emerges from a teacher, from one's own practicing, et cetera, but at the end of the day any great pianist has to give over to the spontaneous way – their idiom – and they create the work. So idiom is a form of character. The way one plays the piano. The way one speaks, walks, relates, is emotional, reflective. Each of these 'forms' will be played by the self's unconscious through action.

The 'true self' is simply the 'spontaneous gesture'. It has nothing to do with some true/false distinction, although Winnicott screwed that up by saying that the obligation of the necessary false self was to prevent the true self from being violated by inspection or accountability. I think what he meant was that, the true self – the self's movements through the real – is very present but knowable, and will be 'covered' by false self-rationalizations.

Of course, we all create unconscious fictions of our life and so we should. But narrative 'truth' and character action are different categories. Like the semantic versus the syntactical realms. Most people reveal more truths about themselves through fictive representations than they do by stating the solemn and verifiable truths of their lives. No analyst I know in the United Kingdom would maintain that he or she was trying to get to the 'truth' beyond self-fictionalization. That is because to create fiction is to unconsciously tell the truth. Projections do not hide the truth, they instantiate it into the other where it remains as a solid holding place for a part of the self, stored now in the other, either as internal object or actual other through the dialectics of ordinary intersubjectivity.

When I celebrate the analysand's true self it is to encourage spontaneity. That might seem wonderful and often it is, but also it can release very disturbed patterns. Much of analysis is the analyst trying to understand these patterns created by the analysand.

GRANTA: What do you think about the future of psychoanalysis?

BOLLAS: I think there's a death wish in psychoanalysis. Many psychoanalytic societies would prefer to go down with a ship than just find another boat and renovate it and make it better. About thirty years ago, I gave a talk at the Topeka Psychoanalytical Society. I brought up how few people they were training, how expensive it had become, how old the few people in training were. And they said, 'We believe in being the pure gold.' I don't know what the hell they meant. It was a metaphor, of course, but I think they were saying that they didn't want to bring in people who are not, from their point of view, qualified to be there. It just made no sense.

Psychoanalysis has been declining because of institutional neglect. After the Second World War, a significant percentage of psychoanalysts in the United States were on the GI Bill, working in institutions like veterans' administration hospitals, where their psychoanalysis was free. It wasn't the same in England, but the fees were extremely low. Most people trained in their twenties. I trained when I was twenty-nine. Now, you look around the world, people are beginning to train in their mid-forties. There's an extraordinary loss of time. You need at least ten years to start to get really good. ■

MARIA LASSNIG
Selbst mit Meerschweinchen (Self with Guinea Pig), 2000

MOTHER

Elfriede Jelinek

TRANSLATED FROM THE GERMAN BY GITTA HONEGGER

Everybody should love me like my mama and, if possible, even much more. This, unfortunately, is not possible.

First, the person who just slipped out should tell me who on earth I am, and then, because of this special relation we established, that is how to put it, yes, that is how to put it, then he should tell me who he is, which I already don't like, and then he should love me, to boot. Well, I wouldn't want to underestimate all the repressed stuff my analyst drew my attention to, no, I don't want to make this mistake, my darling, my heart, so, no, the repressed shall return into the net, from where I get all my opportunities, but some cannot immediately free themselves out of the mesh, they need postage, can't run off fast enough, and that is where I come in. Please, free yourself, says the doctor, I don't say it this way, but I say it too. But who can get free if he does not have a stamp, if he does not first disentangle himself? If he does not resolutely unmoor himself and paddle in my direction, the gigantic net behind him there, where earlier the sun used to be, where earlier the moon used to be, this gigantic earth-girding opportunity to have fun, share joys, communicate suffering, of I-don't-know-what, this opportunity opens up wide behind him like a giant vulva, since everybody wants to have fun. Not I. I want mama and the opportunities of extreme love, which she offered me, an undoing, because such a thing I never received again, not even rudimentarily, even though I wanted more originally, why do you surge so strangely, my heart? It won't do you any good, all that urging won't do you any good, yes, it is true that on the net everything can go on and take place at the same time, a billion times, there they chase around, the hearts, mine, will most likely be among them, let's see what's there for you, what the mail says today, how the mail will assert itself today, but I still owe you something: I still owe you the second danger, one was the underestimating of how much of her love mama can still give me today, that no one else could give me, the second was, how should I say it, that everything will come out sometime, that everything will be hurled out again someday, that everything we put out will be thrown back in our faces, the stuff we packed into our face and friendship pages, all that is coming back to us again, not going off to others any more, who haven't been waiting for it any more for a long time, but returning to us without previously announced recall action, because the brakes are failing, that it is returning, that the normal, the totally normal, which everybody is and everybody has, which is totally normal, you too, my heart – normal! – that it is coming back, yes, go ahead, go across to see how things are going there, there too, everything we want, will be totally normal, the net will deliver it, at the touch of a button, so that everything will come out without any effort for you and me, yes, it might happen, the net will release tons of humans, no, we can't presort them for you, you will have to do this yourself, best in advance, you must register your wishes in advance, then they will be fulfilled, where shall we stick you? And the others? That's what you get, do you even have enough space in the latrine, that's your home, because you constantly sit in front of the screen that is your backyard, that is your pitiful cunt, your expectant dick? So, there those huge masses are coming out of the net, totally excessive, completely overdone, totally done over with nothing, the whole friendly tapestry, there is nothing to gripe about, no grounds for grumbling, here they come, they are coming already, how, pray tell, did they all fit in there, maybe not voluntarily, all of them, but in there they were, or they couldn't be coming out.

What are you wondering about, my heart, what's there to wonder, you hauled them in yourself, after all, you hauled them in for yourself all right, out of this net. With which you went shopping. No, no one is among them who loves you as much as mama, let alone more, but take a look, maybe there is someone, above or below, whom you could at least drag into your shortlist, look, below this one here, for example, I can only see his face and upper torso, a piece of it, no, he does not look at all like mama, how could he be as unconditional with you, love you as unconditionally as your mama, those are different people, totally different, who, however, still push your buttons themselves, pull your levers, crash into your front sections. This they still have to do with their hands, everything else works automatically, only mama was able – on your dumper truck, across the loading space – to let you run out of yourself, as if you were hollowed out inside because you had to give everything, you had to give over everything because you had to get out everything of yourself for her, but there was nothing. There was absolutely nothing. But mama acted as if she did not notice. So, that's how you imagine love to be? That this cave, this vacuum inside you can be refilled with lightweight concrete? But then one can't get into the cellar any more. After something was filled up there down below with that which a dumper truck or a mobile concrete mixer regurgitates and fills into you again, so that you would already look at anyone else more expectantly and friendlier than at yourself, because you can't see yourself any more, you don't exist any more, you are blocked, after all, you are dense, through and through? That's the problem, not even then will you be able to forget yourself! And you still will have to think of mama! ■

Olive Franklin

I missed

you like a dog.
I missed
you like joy.
You are like
a dog. A joyful
dog lurching
to the prairie. I
have real
problems. Real
like a dog. Strays
ecstatically wreck
-ing the drive out
front the fancy
hotel. Walloped
hedges. Wide
leaves pasted
to the gravel.
Dogs that look
like me when I'm
missing you.
On their backs
rubbing up
with the dust

or demolishing
offcuts on a hot
day. Uncut
balls hung
with joy. All wagers
are on dogs right
now. Locked in
my new dog
-sona. Joyfully
dismantling twigs
in the park. Missing
the walls as I race
about the block.
Dogs must be joy
-ful I've learnt
in my canine
excursions.
Particularly
when doggy
joy leads back
round to you.

Poem Interrupted by Mary Ruefle

I hate your socks. I hate
your dog. I hate your uncle
and his collection of historical
re-enactment photographs.
Under the bed I store blueprints for the house
I plan to build you
with a pool of yellow Cotswold stone.
All dreams have tragic implications.
The other night I tried to draw your portrait
but I could only bear one line.

PLANT TEACHERS

Musuk Nolte

Introduction by Guadalupe Nettel

TRANSLATED FROM THE SPANISH BY ROSALIND HARVEY

Plants possess consciousness and, if we listen closely, it is even possible to communicate with them: this is how Indigenous peoples across the American continent understand them, as living beings with wisdom and agency. Some plants act upon our bodies – chamomile reduces inflammation, aloe vera helps scars form, milk thistle cleanses the liver. Others, such as St John's Wort, influence our emotional life, releasing tension in the mind, easing sadness and allowing us to work through the traumas that keep us from living in peace. Some plants are said to teach us about our lives and the universe – in Amazonian traditions these are called 'plant teachers'.

Ayahuasca, the recipe for which varies from place to place, is usually made by combining yagé (*Banisteriopsis caapi*), a vine that produces small pink flowers and grows throughout the rainforests of South America, with the leaves of a plant rich in DMT, most often chacruna (*Psychotria viridis*). The harmala alkaloids in the vine inhibit the breakdown of DMT, allowing it to reach the brain, and in doing so, opening the way for the visions so many people experience.

The son of a Peruvian anthropologist, Musuk Nolte has, since childhood, travelled with his mother on her field trips among the Asháninka, Shawi and Shipibo-Konibo peoples along the rivers of the Peruvian Amazon, returning in later years while working on social and environmental projects. 'The Belongings of the Air' is his account of those journeys over the past fifteen years and of his encounters with ayahuasca, in particular under the guidance of a Shawi shaman on the Paranapura River. He plays with proportion: his aerial shots of the Amazon recall the roots of trees; vines, through the eye of his lens, resemble microscopic neural connections. Those who have taken part in ayahuasca ceremonies in the Americas call it *la medicina*.

A few years ago, I turned to it myself in search of healing. I was waking up every night with an intense pain in the middle of my chest, as if someone were sticking a sharp implement right into my heart. It went on for months and stopped me from sleeping. A friend suggested I participate in a ceremony led by two Peruvian curanderos, a man and a woman, who had travelled to Mexico for this purpose. I remember it was raining that afternoon, rain of a kind I have only ever seen in the tropics. The sky seemed to collapse in on itself in endless flashes of lightning. We were a group of ten or twelve people, between twenty and sixty years old. Our mood was timid and reserved – almost none of us knew one another and all of us were in a state of anticipation at what might happen that night.

Out on the covered terrace of an adobe house deep in the Tepozteco Valley, we waited in silence while the space was cleansed and proper offerings were made: corn and beans, flowers, water, alcohol and tobacco. When the space had been prepared, we were asked to leave our shoes at the doorway and invited to enter. We each took a place on the floor, around the edges of the living room, forming an imperfect circle. The house was dim, lit only by a few large candles that made the shadows grow long. The man and woman, who earlier on had been dressed modestly, were now wearing ceremonial clothes, embroidered with bright colours, stones and seeds. The drink, a thick white concoction, was in a large earthenware vessel ready to be poured out into tiny cups. We each went over to have some. You could serve yourself as many times as you wished.

Unlike other psychoactive substances, such as cocaine or LSD, ayahuasca cannot be taken for recreational purposes, nor is it sold on the black market – there are no ayahuasca dealers – nor does it pass through the violent supply chains of drug traffickers. If you want to drink it, first it is necessary to obtain the ingredients and then prepare them with care. The effects are so introspective that it would be absurd to take it at a party. It is almost always drunk during a ceremony and, in traditional contexts, with a respectful attitude towards the plants and their respective spirits, and towards the people who have harvested and brought them to you. The taste of the medicine is extremely bitter, which makes it difficult to swallow and – above all – to keep down. Some of us, myself included, chose to drink it slowly; others drank it in one go. Then we returned to our places, and our guides began to chant, in both Quechua and Spanish – chants that spoke of love as the energy that formed the world and all who live in it.

In many Amazonian traditions, a shaman is someone born with the gift – often inherited – that allows them to contact spirits via dreams, visions or voices only they can perceive. When a child with this ability is discovered, the community makes sure they receive training so each generation is guaranteed such a figure. In the dark house where I was attending the ceremony, the curanderos stood and, still playing their instruments – he a flute and she a small drum that she rotated between her hands – approached each participant in turn. When they were in front of me, the air was filled with a warm feeling and the scent of flowers. The woman leaned in and began to chant in my ear. During these ceremonies the ancestral spirit contained within the plant is summoned, a teacher whose goal is to guide us towards the light from which we all come, a light some call God, others Primordial Nature, others Pachamama; a light that, whether we know it or not, we all yearn for.

I saw scenes from my childhood, in particular the house where I spent almost every summer, and the nearby river, one that these days is polluted, but which when I was a child was transparent, abundant with frogs and tadpoles, raccoons and opossums. I felt that, despite all the chemicals that are emptied into it today, the river remained itself. What's more, it was there with me, flowing through my body and circling the centre of my chest. I think it was then that I began to cry, not from nostalgia but from gratitude.

Once prepared solely in the Amazon, ayahuasca has been journeying around the world for decades now. Whether in Russia, Japan or Australia, many who drink it report similar experiences: one recurring motif is the sensation of being embraced by a loving presence – a universal mother. In one of Nolte's photographs, a naked child sits in a river in the arms of a seated woman, who we cannot see clearly but who may well be the child's mother. It invokes that experience in which one feels naked, vulnerable and, at the same time, safe, protected by a higher being. Another common vision is that of an animal who serves as a companion for the duration of the trip, often carrying a message or embodying some special quality. The motifs reported around the world often echo the symbolic languages of the cultures in which ayahuasca has long been used: the jaguar represents power, strength and territorial control. The serpent heralds fertility and transformation. Both figures recur in Inca temples and ceremonial objects, representing opposing yet complementary forces, like black and white, or the interplay of light and shadow that Nolte so often plays with.

Every person reacts differently to ayahuasca: some feel absolutely nothing; others witness their own death, and must watch their corpses rotting in the ground before being restored to life. The luckiest claim to have felt a sense of unity with all living beings on the planet, including the plants, the soil, the trees and the rivers – even the stones.

The mysticism that has always accompanied the various sources of DMT took on new dimensions with the publication in 2001 of Rick Strassman's *DMT: The Spirit Molecule*. In it, Strassman proposed that DMT (or N,N-dimethyltryptamine) might be produced in the pineal gland, particularly during significant states such as birth, death or acute stress, and speculated that it could play a role around day forty-nine of an embryo's development. He dubbed DMT the 'spirit molecule' and suggested it might serve as a conduit between life and death.

Despite the fact that we were together for several hours, a few metres away from one another, each of us in that house had a very different trip, and fortunately, none of us asked the others how it had been for them. Some remained awake until the end; others fell asleep a few hours before dawn. In the morning, the shamans chanted once more to close the ceremony. We each walked out, at our own rhythm, from that place. As I compose this text, I realise how hard it is to recount an experience such as this. There is no storyline. The answers we were looking for – including those to questions we never consciously formulated – arrived in flashes, as convictions or brief glimpses. Musuk Nolte, who, unlike me, has been in this other place many times, has brought us fragments from this world. ■

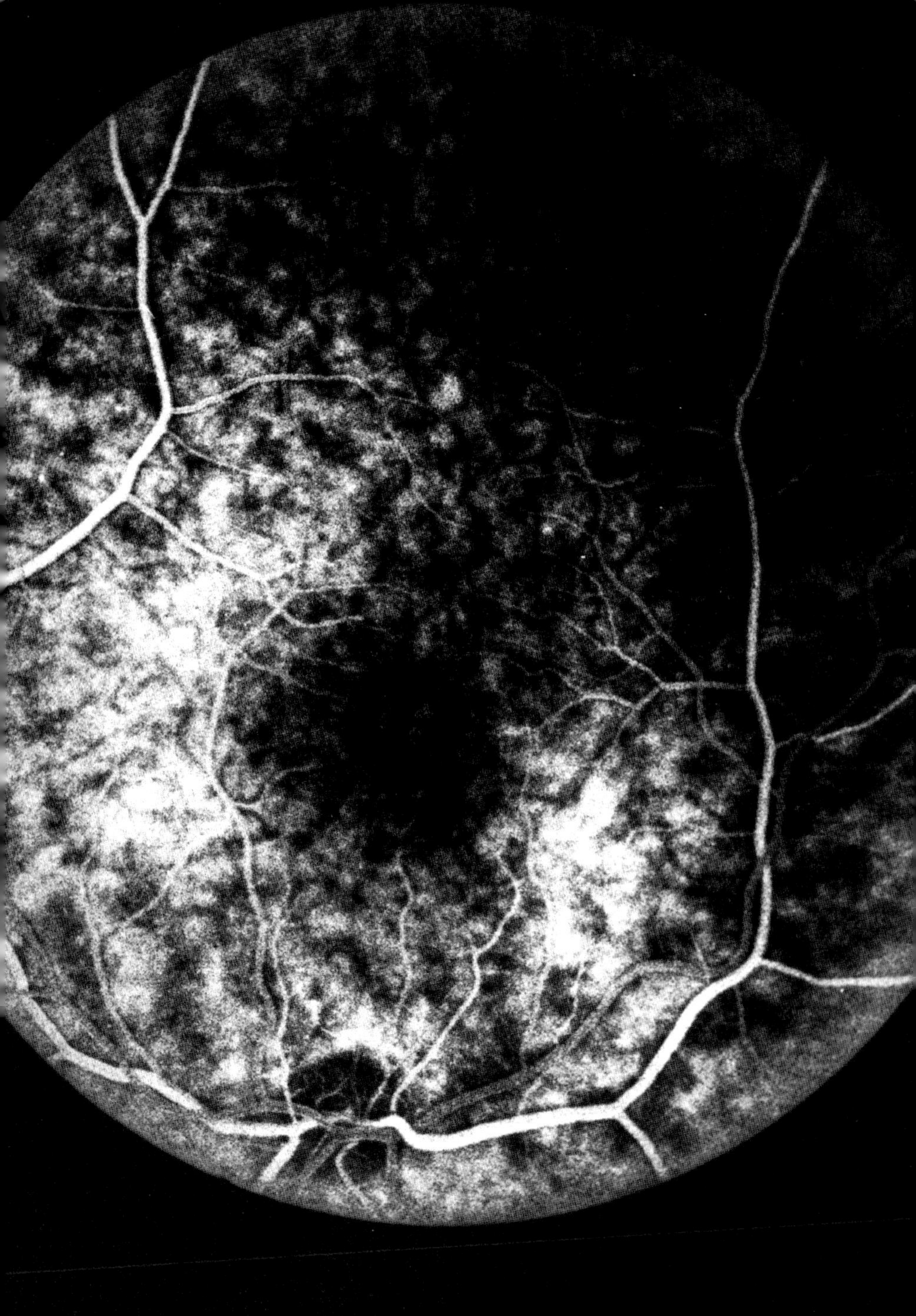

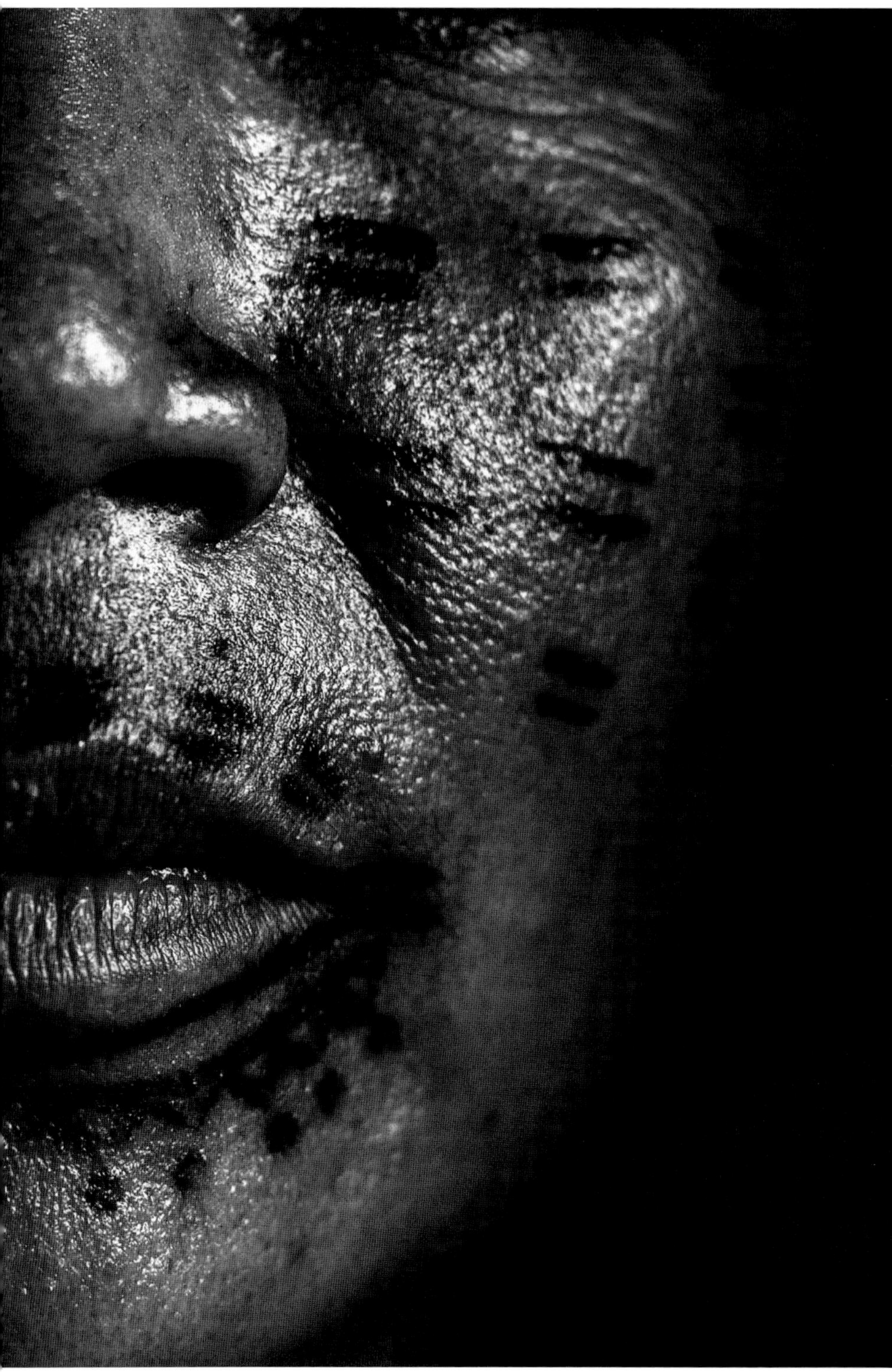

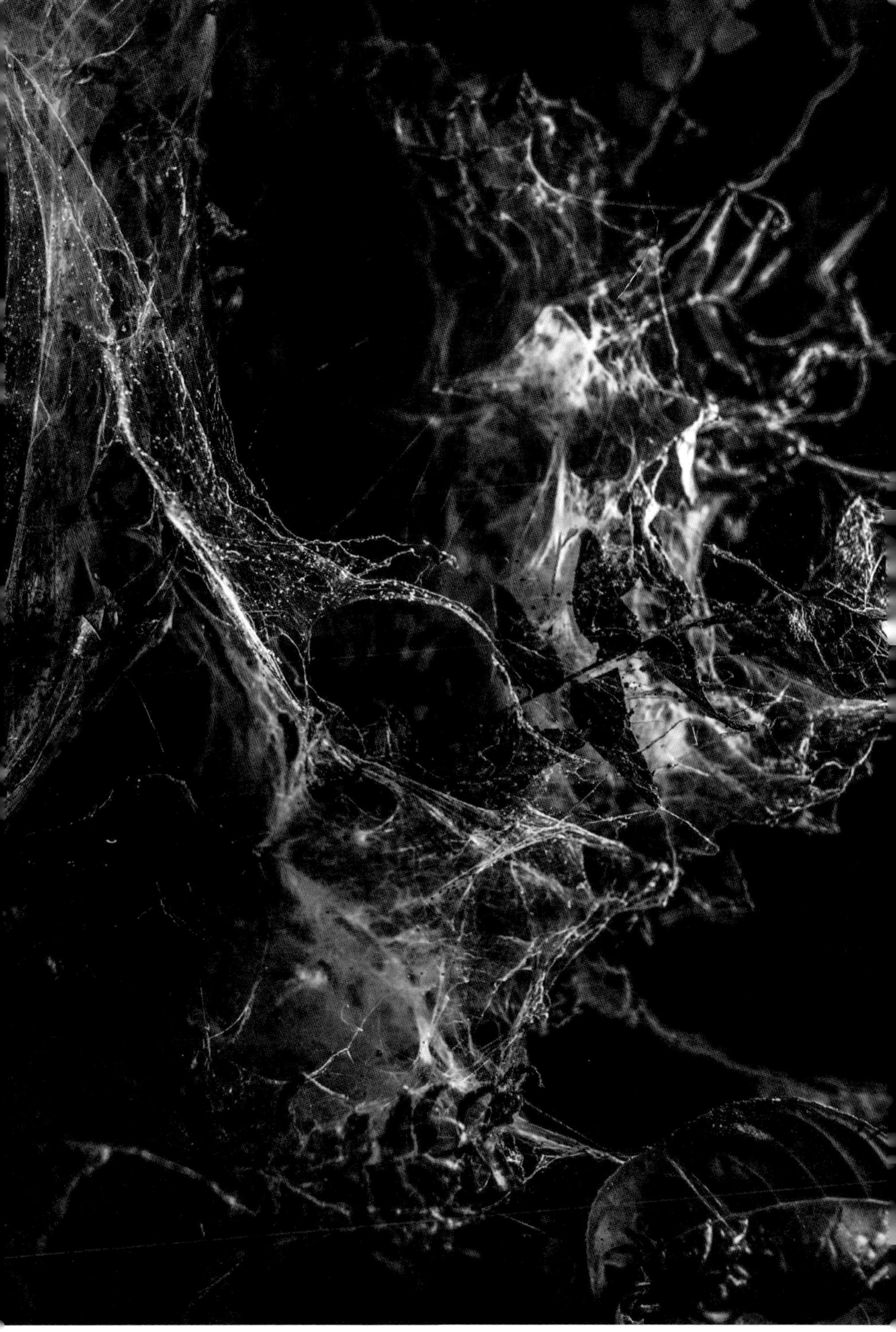

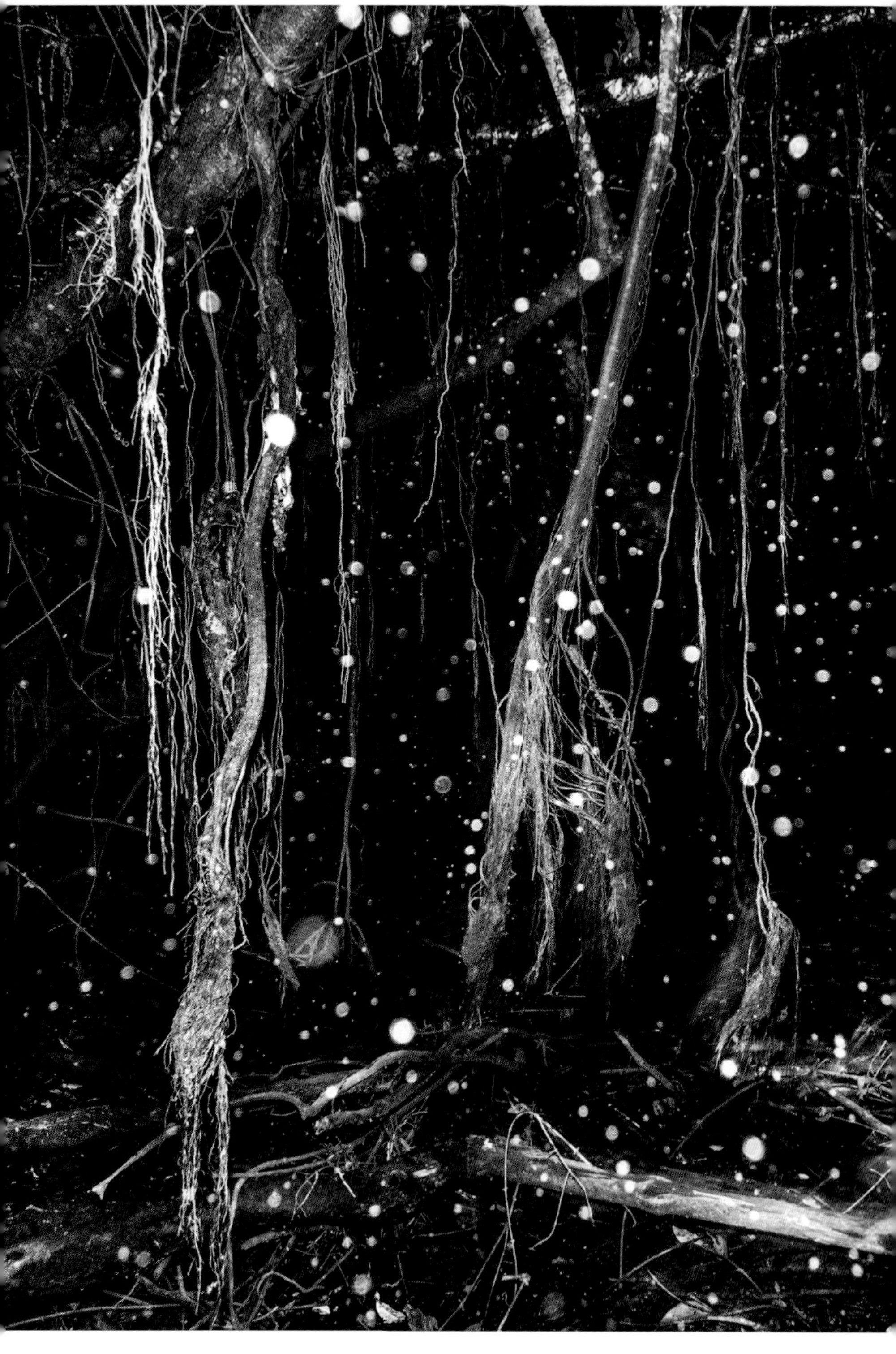

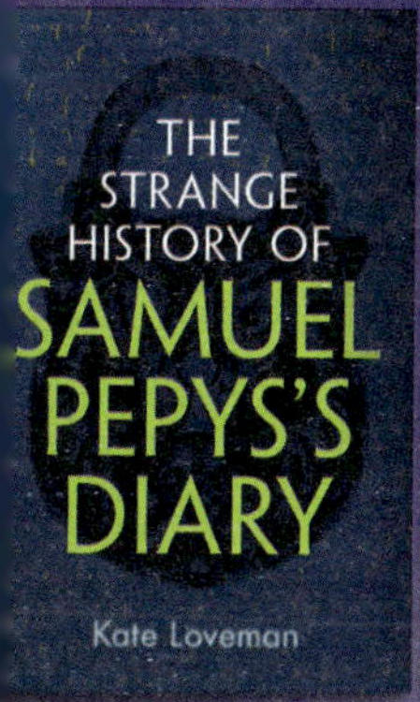

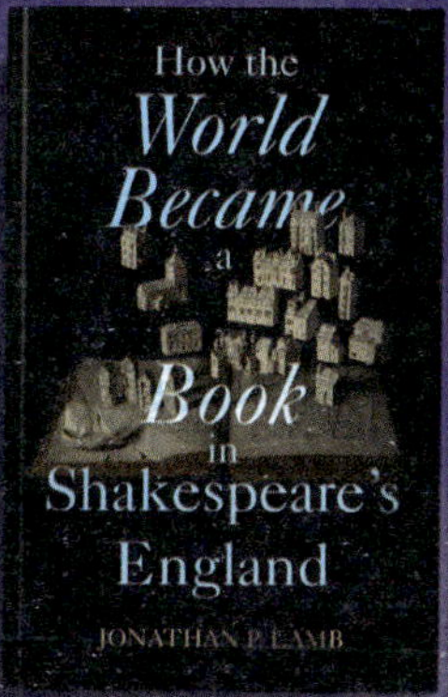

NICOLE EISENMAN
The Session (Study), 2008

MOZART BALLS

Camilla Grudova

I am dismissed by some psychological associations as a madman, accused of creating a 'congested atmosphere which displays my hoarding compulsion', but my collection of things isn't musty or disorganised, it is a museum of my own making and design. For my entire career, I have argued against a sterile analyst's room: the abstract painting, a box of tissues, optimistic books with a zany font by sentimental fraudsters on an orange bookshelf. An object will act like a magnet to a matching object buried deep within a patient's psyche, and this requires the analyst to have a vast and varied collection of *stuff*. Every object in the world has a horrible memory in it belonging to someone.

To dispel such rumours of my 'hoarding disorder', I will describe a case in which my method of mental archaeology was particularly successful. Sissy* was the cymbalist in an Edinburgh orchestra, and she came to me with a recently developed obsessive compulsive neurosis: a fear of suddenly standing up during a performance, of being unable to stop clashing her cymbals together till the point she was dragged offstage. You cannot trust your hands, she explained. The slightest mis-movement and they make a noise. Even cooking made her nervous. In the kitchen she would be filled with a desire to bang pot lids together while her unattended food burned. She had to buy everything pre-made and eat it cold. She was scared of getting gout or diabetes because of it, and I noticed an irritating-looking boil near her nose. In addition, she had to fight a compulsion to let out a little husky cough whenever the orchestra pianist played. The compulsions and paranoia had begun a few months ago, when her relationship with a touring countertenor singer ended.

My consultation room is on the second floor of a Georgian flat in Stockbridge, the flat I live in too, though I did not tell my patients this. There are false, bricked-in windows, which have been unenthusiastically painted on the exterior to resemble the covered windows. The hall leading to the consultation room has shelves laden with precious detritus and objets d'art, and along the oriental-carpeted floor, umbrella stands like thick legs holding duck-headed umbrellas. I inherited the flat from an uncle whose old-timey possessions (gramophone, teddies, a radionics machine with many knobs, which he thought would cure his Lyme disease) were an essential part of my collection. On days off I cycle to charity shops and auction houses, looking for useful things for my practice. I buy things on eBay. I spend a lot of my spare time on eBay, it has proven more useful than psychological books by my peers. I always have a sense when an object could be significant in a session, and I have to buy it no matter the price, even if I haven't found the right client for it yet.

I have dozens of Greek vases – not authentic but from tourist shops. I have an imitation copper 'mask of Agamemnon', jade figurines and tiny Chinese cork dioramas of landscapes in narrow rectangles of glass mounted on ebony stands, baboons, donkeys and birds of marble and wood, a porcelain French bulldog, clusters of Pelham puppets, dragon- and bear-shaped netsuke, tin toys, skulls of plastic and plastic dinosaurs too, cabbage dolls. I really think it is the plastic items that offend the boards and associations. And of course, my chow chow, who has a tongue like black pudding and doesn't like to be bathed or brushed, and so smells. Many patients have had a traumatic interaction with a smelly dog in childhood. He earns his supper. His predecessor was taxidermised and stuffed, is kept in my consultation room too, and Chow Chow II sometimes humps the dry and lifeless Chow Chow I, an act that indeed helped a middle-aged male patient confront the fact that his sexual anxieties stemmed from being 'humped' by a loose German shepherd in a public park as a young boy.

At our first session, I watched Sissy's eyes wander around the room. She was thirty-seven, and had a brown bowl cut. I have noticed that classical musicians will unconsciously fashion themselves to resemble their instruments. I own many decorative musical instruments. A balalaika, flutes, little drums and maracas made out of animals and vegetables, a cello with a hole punched into it and no strings, a broken but beautifully painted piano, but none of these caught her interest. Of course, they would be objects she would see every day at the orchestra's home, and objects familiar to the patient become so layered with memories they are illegible. It has to be something *defamiliarised* or *unremembered* in some way, to bring about a shock of memory.

Sissy lived alone in Dean Village (a damp and uncomfortably steep cluster of nineteenth-century apartments, I noted down, from where you can hear the constant flow of water) and was from a Central European country that produces an excessive amount of classical musicians, figure skaters and engineers. She grew up with a young mother, no father, and a brother ten years her senior, Herbert*, a clerk in an engineering firm, and did not speak to them any more, for reasons she couldn't explain.

I observed, as she lay on the green fainting couch, that her eyes stopped at, then quickly moved on from, a fat white porcelain Buddha, dappled with tiny holes along his shoulders and arms which were meant for incense. The Buddha had little pigtailed children crawling up his legs. On a simple level he represented the father. On another, the mother, as he had large succulent breasts with bright red nipples, which the porcelain children seemed drawn to.

She did not mention the Buddha, though she always seemed to be looking at it out of the corner of her eye and said she 'didn't know' when I asked her what she thought of it, or what it reminded her of. It was, instead, a 'Mozart chocolate ball' or *Mozartkugel,* which got her speaking of her childhood, though I still knew something was hidden in the Buddha for her.

I did not like *Mozartkugeln*, they were waxy, stifling in a Mitteleuropean way, and always tasted expired and of brandy breath. I had a box in my consultation room, a gift from another patient. A *Mozartkugel* has three or four layers of pistachio and nougat, which I dislike, but I recently forced myself to eat them because I did not have much else. I separated the pistachio filling from some of the *Mozartkugeln*, as I was sick of the sweetness, and mixed them with salt and plain macaroni. I don't have many patients, and some haven't paid me for months.

I brought the box over to Sissy and offered her one – was it not a perfect treat for a musician? She jumped from the chaise and cried that the countertenor had brought her an enormous box of *Mozartkugeln* and another of marzipan 'fruit' back from a concert in Salzburg. She only liked to eat savoury things and the countertenor should have known this. Marzipan she found disgusting, 'like shredded greasy skin', and chocolate too, whose obvious likeness needs no mention. She and the countertenor broke up not long after. I suspected her symptoms were not a result of the break-up, it seemed more likely that her obsessive compulsive neuroses had been triggered by the marzipan and *Mozartkugeln*.

Sissy loved Mozart, the idea of his face printed on tinfoil wrapped around a revolting concoction made her irrationally angry. She said that as a child, she had a plastic children's record player which came with its own set of records. The records were thick and purple, orange, yellow and red. The orange record played Mozart's 'Klavierstück in F' (which he wrote at age ten, near Sissy's age at the time). The yellow one played yodels, and the purple one an organ grinder's song, the red she couldn't remember. She would listen to 'Klavierstück in F' every day as a little girl.

Mozart doesn't have a lot for me any more, she told me. It is Stravinsky, Shostakovich, Wagner, Strauss who interest me now, she began, before interrupting herself.

'I have to pee,' she said, 'do you have a bathroom for patients? I can't think or speak at all if I have to pee.' She took too short a time to properly pee, I thought. I watched one of the dozen or so grandfather clocks. She was gone only two minutes.

I found one such record player, it was expensive both to buy and import from a vintage toyshop in Japan. It was an East German make, and annoyingly it didn't come with any of the records, as I felt the mysterious red one held some significance. I presented it at our next session, and she told me that she had asked her mother if she could take piano lessons. He made it seem very easy, Mozart.

'We couldn't afford a piano, we only had Herbert's income as a junior engineer. The piano shop sold paper pianos. A to-size diagram of the keys that one unrolled on the floor or a table and practised at with music sheets. I got to play, for real, once per week at a lesson.'

And what was this piano teacher like? I asked.

'She had moles on her face,' she said. 'She would give me apple pancakes after our lessons and I was afraid there were moles in it which had fallen off her face when she was cooking.'

Why did she stop playing the piano and take up the cymbals? Someone has to be the bearer of little-used and minor instruments in an orchestra, but it seemed a strange switch to me.

I went to see her perform without telling her, sitting in the upper circle of Usher Hall. Sissy was sat on a stool, at the back of the stage, in a black cashmere cardigan and a black skirt. I had binoculars and examined her face. Her eyes were fixated on the conductor. He was handsome, with curly dark-brown hair, which I had as well though it was now scattered and greyish. I made a note to myself to ask what hair colour the countertenor had.

She clutched her hands together, but whenever the pianist

played (a little round man, like a garlic bulb but with stereotypically long pianist fingers like roots which had grown unwieldy in a dark cupboard), she lifted a hand to her mouth to stifle a silent or non-existent cough. Near the end, she stood up, wiped her hands on her skirt. I wasn't familiar with the symphony, so I didn't know if it was her correct moment or not, but the other percussionists didn't look at her as if she was behaving oddly. She lifted the cymbals up off their stand, hit them and made a circular motion, placing them gently back on their stand. After her part was finished, she sat back down, erect, staring at the conductor. I noted that the sound the cymbals made, and indeed the golden colour of the cymbals themselves, brought urination to my mind; the vulgar phrase 'golden showers' occurred to me when I heard the cymbals.

Was she jealous of the pianist? Her piano playing never became extraordinary because she didn't have a real piano, and she started late, at ten, and stopped just as suddenly a few years later, but it couldn't be so simple as jealousy. As is commonly known, 'pianist' sounds like another word, though, I admit, not in her native tongue.

Before her next visit, I put the Buddha in the bathroom, positioned on the back of the toilet. I took off my shoes so as not to make a sound and followed, listening at the door while she peed. She, again, did not sit there long enough, releasing only a little liquid in short bursts. Her bladder surely wasn't empty when she returned to the consultation room and she went again, fifteen minutes later.

During our sixth session, I asked her what the lavatory had been like in her childhood home, while on the other side of my bathroom door she sat on the toilet.

They had lived at the top of an apartment building – two bedrooms, a parlour and a kitchenette. The only bathroom in the apartment was an en suite to her brother Herbert's bedroom, and only he was allowed to use it, as her mother thought a young man should have his own bathroom, especially as he was their only source of income.

Mother would make his bed, clean and iron his suits for work, remove the old hairs stuck in his razor and prepare his dinner. Choice sausages and minced meat for Herbert, liver and offal for Sissy and Mother. Mother and Sissy shared a bedroom and had to use the old concierge lavatory, on the ground floor, though the building no longer had a concierge. She said she couldn't make it all the way down sometimes, in the middle of the night, and would stop on the third floor to pee in a potted palm on the landing. It really started to smell. It was blamed on a cat who lived on that floor, and its owner was harassed by everyone else in the building.

Herbert's bathroom had a toilet, tub and sink but also an antique wooden commode with brass decoration, which was there when they moved in because it was too enormous and cumbersome to move. When opened, the commode revealed a velvet seat with a chamber pot inside it. The red velvet seat had the hard and crusty texture of a brush. This, her brother would defecate in, and see how long it took their mother to find it when cleaning. When she did, she would gasp with surprise and laughter and say it resembled 'a snake'. She said that kings used to have special doctors to look into their chamber pots to see if their stools were healthy, and this she did for him, though she had no medical training.

'Constipated means more fruit for my Herbert,' Sissy imitated in a sing-song voice. 'Watery stool, too much paprika!'

I had a stack of porcelain chamber pots in a kitchen cupboard. I reminded myself to stack them beside the consultation chaise next time.

And her father? I asked. The Buddha was in my arms. I lightly tapped its bald head against the bathroom door.

Her father had left when she was young to join a monastery, or at least this was her mother's explanation for him leaving. She did not know what monastery it was. Around once a year Sissy would go to the library and research European monasteries to try and find him, but whenever she came close, was filled with such a feeling of dread that she didn't contact a single monastery. She used to have a wig, which she thought belonged to him, and I asked Sissy to describe it. It was a long, curly brown wig and she took it and hid it underneath her dolls in a wicker stroller.

I noted the wig bore a resemblance to her conductor, a stand-in for the father whom she wanted to interrupt with her cymbals, and therefore also to me. I asked her how she knew it was the wig of her absent father? There was a skin condition her brother had, inherited from their father, of excessive dandruff, which required the head to be shaved continually and a wig to be worn to hide it.

Her brother's wigs 'were the texture of a chick's soft feather, they looked as if they would smell sweet and floral, but they smelled of beef broth and over-boiled tomatoes', and were blue, pink and yellow in colour.

I had noticed myself the correlation between dandruff and the texture of marzipan.

I asked her to tell me more of her brother, and she instead described a toy he had, a horse and carriage, though he was a grown young man, kept on his desk in his bedroom. The horses had real horsehair and were attached with leather straps to the carriage. There were dolls glued to the carriage seats inside, a handsome couple, and on the driver's seat, an old-man doll holding a whip. Sissy had ripped the dolls out of the carriage to look at them more closely, their bottoms in puddles of dry white glue, and her mother had beaten her.

Sissy was a member of a vegetarian society and donated to animal rescue charities. The chow chow brought about this revelation. She told me Chow Chow II smelled, and I had to lock him in the kitchen when she had her session, but she said she did not hate animals. Of childhood pets they had many, too many for their living situation. There was a dog, Nimrod, a rabbit, and all sorts of animals Herbert found in the city river when fishing and kept in a fetid aquarium or jams jars their mother was not allowed to clean. Leeches, crayfish, minnows. He would wear the crayfish on his ears until the crayfish became so weak they let go and fell, and then he crushed them under his feet. One leech he caught and kept in a lidded jam jar was determined to live. It slid out of the jar and hid in the dark pattern of an old oriental carpet in the parlour until Sissy found it. 'I fed it on my arm until it reached the size of a small hot-water bottle.'

I asked the colours of the dog (white) and the rabbits (grey). The dog's name, Nimrod, was also the name of an ancient Assyrian city, from which there were two cymbals at the British Museum. The cymbals were, in some way, a stand-in for the dog. Herbert had shown cruelty towards animals, so I believe did something involving the dog, but the hitting motion of the cymbals suggested to me Sissy was herself, in some way, cruel to the dog.

We were making progress but I didn't want our sessions to end too quickly, I needed the money; Chow Chow II needed a tooth removed and vets were extortionate.

After her session, I stared at the Buddha for a long time, and all I could think of was mashed potatoes, piles of marshmallows, a giant dumpling filled with curried beef. It was then that I realised that the discovery object didn't need to be the exact forgotten repressed object itself, or representational of a person (a mother, a father), but only needed to bear a minute visual resemblance to something else.

In our next session, I brought the Buddha out and held it close to her face. She reached for her nose, to cover it, as if it smelled. What does it smell of? I asked. 'Cream and cabbage,' she replied and ran to the bathroom.

On her return from the bathroom, the repressed moment came out as follows. She said Herbert had liked food pranks. When they had pet rabbits he had collected their droppings, put them in empty peppercorn containers and given them to the neighbours as presents. She said that he would stick pieces of snot or fingernails in simmering dishes, which, like his excretions in the chamber pot, were received with good humour by their mother, and that at Sissy's eleventh birthday party, her mother served a giant pile of cream decorated with prunes and candles. Holding it up underneath, unbeknown to those being served, was pickled cabbage. Everyone expected chocolate cake underneath, it was a trick between her mother and Herbert, who laughed and laughed together while Sissy herself cried with disgust and disappointment, especially as she was hoping to get a real piano as a present and hadn't. A real cake followed, but the joke was cruel enough to ruin it. Sweet things therefore seemed inherently deceptive to her and represented that her mother and brother were 'in cahoots' against the rest of the world, and she was not included. The Buddha, in its shape, white and lumpy, and dappled with children, reminded her of this monstrous meal, the children being the 'prunes' (a natural laxative I may add).

The night of her birthday party, Sissy woke up, and went to urinate in the plant pot on the third floor. Her mother wasn't in her bed, and Sissy assumed she had gone to the bathroom too. The dog was scratching at the door of her brother's bedroom, whining to be let into the room where it usually slept. She opened it, and here believed she saw a liaison of incest, between brother and mother. She hit the dog, ran down the stairs and urinated in the plant pot, and was discovered doing so by an old moustachioed neighbour, who chided her. The next day, Herbert used her 'paper piano' as toilet paper, perhaps as revenge for spying on them, and she hadn't played the piano since.

Her cymbal-playing, since the beginning, unconsciously represented Sissy's urination on the night of her discovery, both in sound and colour, but also her mother's flat breasts moving during the incestuous sex act, and the bark of Nimrod. Her desire to tell someone, to tell the absent father what she witnessed, and her guilt at her failure to do so when asked by a neighbour, drew her to such a clangorous and confrontational instrument and a desire to urinate even when she did not need to urinate. The stifled cough was an additional imitation of the dog Nimrod's barking. *Mozartkugeln* and marzipan, in their resemblance to Herbert's dandruff, caused the repressed incest memory to resurface, which she tried to push back down again with her compulsions. Her later experience with the leech was an attempt to grow a phallus to gain the affection of her mother, a residual guilt of being 'left out' of the vile act. Her hesitation to contact her father hid an unconscious fear that either she would remember and confess to him what she saw, or, instead, attempt to have sex with him in order to complete the familial puzzle. Lurking below both these angsts was a deeper one – that her father did not in fact exist. She suspected, as I did too, that given her brother's age she was possibly the product of incest, and had witnessed a replication of her own horrendous conception.

With my help, Sissy was able to try the piano once more, and I even let her take and fix the painted one from my collection as another piano would come along soon enough for me. I went to see her orchestra perform again ('Blue Danube'). She couldn't exactly quit her salaried cymbal-playing as her piano would never be of a professional quality, and I watched her play with no visible compulsions, but the look of a woman who knows the reason and meaning of everything. ■

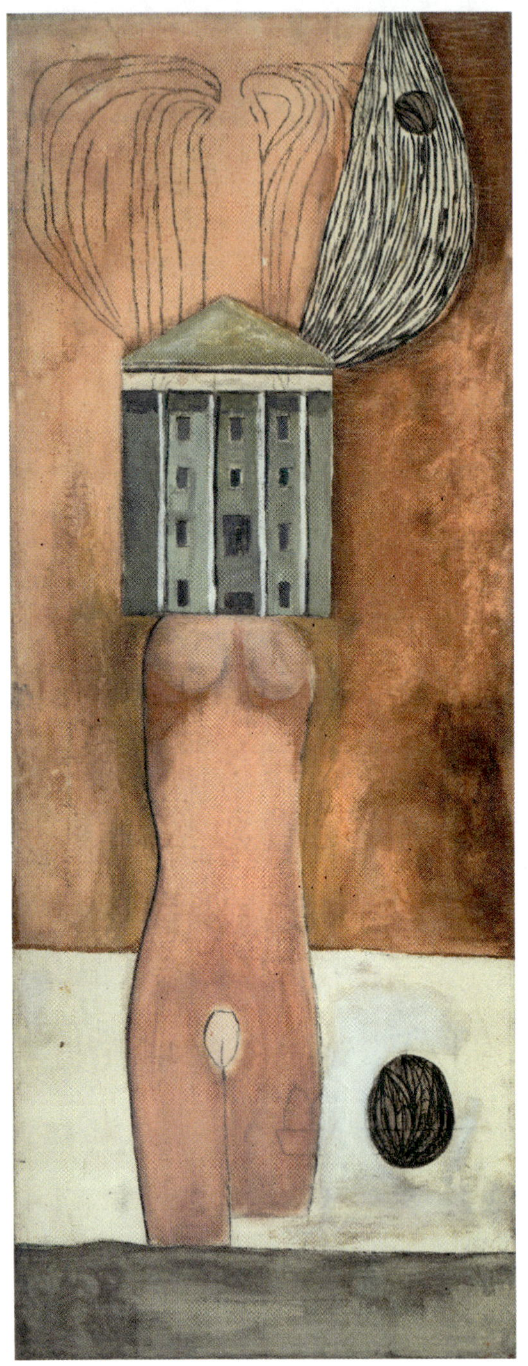

LOUISE BOURGEOIS
Femme Maison, 1946–47

DROPPED FROM THE SKY

Interview with Juliet Mitchell

In 1966, when she was twenty-five, Juliet Mitchell published 'Women: The Longest Revolution' in *New Left Review*. The essay established her as a leading feminist theorist. Mitchell confronted a paradox. 'The situation of women is different from that of any other social group,' she wrote. 'They are fundamental to the human condition, yet in their economic, social and political roles, they are marginal.' Many otherwise radical revolutions had left the lives of women untouched, Mitchell argued. To address this political impasse, alternative resources were required.

Mitchell trained as an analyst in the British Psychoanalytical Society. In *Psychoanalysis and Feminism* (1974), she forged a new synthesis of Marxist and Freudian traditions. In response to the women's movement's antipathy, Mitchell countered that psychoanalysis was 'not a recommendation for a patriarchal society but an analysis of one.' Later books, including *Mad Men and Medusas: Reclaiming Hysteria* (2000) and *Siblings: Sex and Violence* (2003), were interventions – in particular, Mitchell stressed the importance of lateral relationships for building social worlds.

The following interview with Mitchell was conducted by Lidija Haas, a candidate at the Institute for Psychoanalytic Training and Research in New York, and Janique Vigier, an editor at *Granta*.

GRANTA: Can you tell us about your early life?

JULIET MITCHELL: My parents were in Canada in the late 1930s, where I was conceived. My mother was a botanist, and she had accepted a three-week exchange post in New Zealand, to study a particular species of seaweed. They knew – everybody knew – that war was likely to break out. She tried to cancel her trip, but the person she was exchanging places with in the fellowship programme was already on the high seas. She went thinking that she would be able to come back, but she couldn't.

I was born in 1940 in Christchurch. We lived in a German Jewish refugee community, nothing official, as it were, with artists and local people. My mother was very isolated there, but my memories of the time are positive. We lived with my godparents, Otti and Paul, as one family.

Much to everybody's amazement, my mother got us back to England. When I was three years old, in February 1944, we set off on this convoy for nine weeks. Those are my first major memories – New Zealand, and a journey across the world in which I had to pack my panic bag and dolls' panic bag. My mother made my doll's panic suit which I can clearly remember. It had a red button that she'd sewed on the doll's shoulder. You pressed the button when you were torpedoed. Our boat was in fact torpedoed, and sunk, while crossing the Atlantic on its return journey.

GRANTA: And your father?

MITCHELL: My father was a geneticist. After the war he moved to America. He was quite left wing. We never lived together. I knew him only by letters, masses of clothes and wonderful presents. These letters were very important to me, and then he died when I was eleven years old. He was very attentive, very loving. When I started analysis, my analyst thought it would be all about my father, that I had attempted to replace him with other fathers – Marx, Freud – but this wasn't the case at all. My analysis was about my mother.

GRANTA: What kind of political environment did you grow up in?

MITCHELL: We moved to London in the spring of 1944. My mother taught at a progressive school called Burgess Hill, which was an offshoot of Summerhill. We lived there, in a flat at the top of one of the buildings. The school was in a beautiful building in Oak Hill Park in north London, badly bomb-damaged. It was a very left wing, anarchist environment. Wilhelm Reich was part of the air we breathed. Everybody shared the main rooms where we ate together and socialised. We were a wartime generation, so as children my friends and I played on the bomb sites, and we would make bonfires in air-raid shelters. We were latchkey children, wild children.

GRANTA: How did you come to feminism?

MITCHELL: My mother was a dyed-in-the-wool pacifist. In her horror at the militarism of Christabel Pankhurst, she was affiliated to the associations of first wave feminists, Millicent Fawcett and Sylvia Pankhurst. She sent me to a progressive school in Hampstead, the King Alfred School. That was very important to my life, because from the age of four until seventeen – when I went to university – I was in the same school, which was completely gender-egalitarian.

Oxford, where I went to read English, was a shock. I realised the extraordinary gender disparity between the one in twelve students who were women and the other eleven who were men. The men were utterly dominated by the public-school ethos. There were so many closed clubs and exclusive places for them. I wanted to try and understand this. By then I was interested in existentialism and French literature. In 1958 I was camping with my boyfriend in Oban and, at the local bookshop, I asked if I could buy a copy of *The Second Sex*. I was escorted out because they thought it was pornographic material. After reading it, I thought, my God, is it really as awful as she is making out? When I started looking at the condition of women in Britain, I found out that yes – it was that bad.

GRANTA: Didn't you eventually come into contact with Simone de Beauvoir?

MITCHELL: I first met de Beauvoir in a very upmarket restaurant called La Coupole. I had hoped to meet her and Sartre, but Sartre didn't come. She came with Claude Lanzmann, who was much younger than her. He wasn't particularly well known then; he was just her lover. We had this delicious meal, which I still can remember; the taste of steak tartare – it was the first time I'd ever had it. Later, with Perry Anderson, we went to her flat on rue Monsieur-le-Prince, which was quite grand, lots of yellow satin furniture. De Beauvoir and I argued about psychoanalysis the whole time. She completely rejected it.

To my delight, in the last volume of her autobiography, *All Said and Done*, de Beauvoir wrote that a young English woman had changed her mind about Freud and psychoanalysis.

GRANTA: So you came to psychoanalysis through feminism?

MITCHELL: Yes. In 1966, I travelled to New York for the foundation of Betty Friedan's National Organisation for Women. There I saw, in feminist circles, calendars and diaries adorned with images of Freud's head on a dartboard with a dart through his eye. In America, Freud was seen as this arch-patriarch, and psychoanalysis as reproducing patriarchal oppression. His work was not much of an issue for feminists in Britain at that point.

When I went back to England, I thought I would read what I knew of Freud's writing on women, which was five articles. I found them riveting, and I ended up reading all twenty-three volumes of his work. That's how I became interested in psychoanalysis. I believed that this antagonism was a unifying theme of psychoanalysis, which is why I wrote *Psychoanalysis and Feminism*. It was a corrective. I wrote it to say, it's not that Freud is anti-women, or that Freudian theory itself denigrates women, but rather that it tried to account for women's denigration.

GRANTA: How did you address Freud's ideas about hysteria in women? That seems like a classic point on which to oppose him.

MITCHELL: It isn't, because it gets Freud wrong. Freud followed Jean-Martin Charcot in claiming that there was such a thing as male hysteria and that he had it himself. Eventually, he started to question Charcot's theory, but he never changed his mind about hysteria as a general human condition, rather than a gendered condition. Freud always thought that you can't have any psychological condition that is part of the practice of psychoanalysis which isn't a human one. But hysterical women were pathologised, while hysterical men were often seen in the psychoanalytic tradition as egocentric, or egosyntonic; they had to be the centre of attention. Louise Bourgeois, who I'm writing a book about now, is very keen on this part of the argument: that the male has to be the centre of attention.

GRANTA: You were twenty-five when you wrote 'Women: The Longest Revolution'. What was the impulse behind the essay?

MITCHELL: I had started thinking about sexuality in a structural way. I was coming from a Marxist background, but found that orthodox class analysis wouldn't work to understand the situation of women. Women were not a category. Of course, pragmatically, there were people we called women. But politically there wasn't a differentiated and unified subject position. Women were classified as wives of their husbands or daughters of their fathers. I wanted to locate women politically.

At the time, the family was believed to have become a substitute for women. I broke down the family, to make it less of a monolithic entity. I looked at women in terms of four key structures: production, reproduction, the socialisation of children, and sexuality. And then there was something structural happening outside these structures, something superstructural, which is how they were set within larger economic relations.

My argument was that sexuality was the weak structure that was going to change gender relations. I wanted to account for how sexual difference was internalised. We don't wake up every morning and think, 'I'm a man, I'm a woman.' We know it without thinking about it, at a deeply unconscious level. But how? I thought that the unconscious was close to what Louis Althusser had to say about ideology: that it is the set of everyday assumptions that makes us see our place in the world as natural. Through interpellation – the way society 'calls' to us and we respond as the kind of person it names – we become subjects shaped by those assumptions. When I thought about the ideology of sex and gender in this way, I started to look at psychology. Psychoanalysis helped explain how one experiences gender as internalised, how it's always there even when we don't think about it.

GRANTA: Why did you decide to start practising psychoanalysis with patients?

MITCHELL: I came to it from feminism, and my questions for psychoanalysis were political. How could it help explain the position of women? These are not separate projects. They are, of course, different enterprises in pragmatic terms. Working with an individual in a clinical context is private and has to be absolutely confidential. But the material theory combines very well. You can use the individual to understand the social and the social to understand the individual.

I trained about as quickly as you can. I began in 1974, and I finished after the birth of my daughter in 1978. I had to pay to train as a psychoanalyst, so I did every job under the sun – visiting professorships in the States, television, journalism. I also had to do clinical work. I worked as a nurse on nights and weekends for eighteen months.

GRANTA: Can you tell us a little about your approach as an analyst?

MITCHELL: A lot of our life is unconscious. What Freud thought, and which is the basis of psychoanalysis, is that unconscious thinking can speak to unconscious thinking. The one demand of the patient is that she free associates; she says what comes into her head. It takes about a year for most people to be able to do it. If they can, then one begins the unconscious process from the patient's side. Then, the analyst can practise freely-suspended attention.

In the preface to a new edition of *Psychoanalysis and Feminism*, I write about the need to tell the truth as what distinguishes psychoanalysis from other forms of therapy. Basically, we all tell lies. That's one of the fundamental conditions of being human. These lies may be serious, or they may be unserious. The only person who actually knows what's wrong with the patient is the patient. Nobody else knows what's wrong with them. It's very important for a psychoanalyst not to lie, not even silly little lies.

GRANTA: What do you mean by telling the truth?

MITCHELL: We're not talking about some sort of God-given truth. We're talking about truth as our perception of reality. Let's say most people blame their mothers, or their parents, for what's wrong with them. They feel like they need to justify themselves by explaining how they've been treated badly by somebody else. The moment that changes you forever is when you don't think that somebody has done something to you; instead, you see that they are other than you, and you begin to understand their reason for doing what they did. That sounds very simple, but it's quite a big move.

GRANTA: A major feature of your recent work, especially *Mad Men and Medusas* (2000) and *Siblings: Sex and Violence* (2003), moves away from vertical relationships between children and parents towards lateral or horizontal ones. You've studied the mostly ignored role of siblings in psycholoanalysis. What spurred your thinking?

MITCHELL: I felt that siblings dropped from the skies into my lap. Siblings were always there in clinical work, but not there in the theory. When I looked at my own case histories, as well as the classical cases, I found Dora with Otto, her brother. Wolf Man with his sister. According to Freud, the most desired of all incestuous relationships is the brother's desire for his sister. That has the most prohibitions on it. But the prohibition also comes with a requirement, which is that he must marry his friend's sister rather than his own sister; his friend's sister would be a good marriage, but his sister would be an incestuous one. Requirements and prohibitions always go together. I wanted to develop a theory of these lateral or horizontal relationships. Once I realised their importance, the Oedipus theory, that giant rock, shifted entirely.

GRANTA: How important was D.W. Winnicott to your thinking?

MITCHELL: He features a lot in my sibling work. In the clinical cases that he described, there was always an older child who had a problem with a younger child, because the younger child had taken over the older child's role as the only important person in the house. But when Winnicott talked about it, theoretically, he always talked about the problem in terms of the mother, not the sibling. I found that to be a fascinating mismatch of his intellectual position and his clinical observations.

The birth of a sibling spurs some sort of dramatic reaction. A baby doesn't see itself as part of a social world until another sibling comes along. It applies to only children as much as to children with siblings, as only children have siblings in their mind. Siblings mark the beginning of social life.

From my study on siblings, I came to the idea of the sibling trauma. You go along as a child, expecting to be the majesty of the household, and when another baby comes along, that majesty is not you – it's another. Your ego has been shattered. It has to be rebuilt, not as a baby but as a child: a subject who exists in relation to others. The rebuilding of the toddler's ego allows it to become a social person.

GRANTA: Is there a political dimension to your work on siblings?

MITCHELL: It's not the literal relationship between siblings that interests me. It's the structural presence of a social world. That's the political aspect of it. For instance, a lot of people are going to China now, and they're teaching psychoanalysis there as though everybody in the country understands themselves as individuals. Well, of course, they may be becoming individualised, but they're also coming out of an extraordinarily different social background. It's a structural, political demand that we look at that social world. Siblings are an incredibly important way in to those relations.

GRANTA: You mention China. It presents interesting terrain for your thinking. Here you have a nominally Communist society that embarked on a program that results in the eradication of siblinghood for a huge swath of the population.

MITCHELL: I think that it was an experiment that didn't actually eliminate the background from which it had come. Obviously, it worked. The one-child family was compulsory. I can draw that as a distinction – that somehow, yes, you can prevent people from having siblings, but actually, they don't absolutely lose their sense of siblinghood. In fact, it becomes even more present as a social fact. I don't think you can actually lose your feeling for others.

GRANTA: Returning to the idea of the recognition of the other, can you tell us about any significant moments in your own analysis?

MITCHELL: I remember my own analysis well. When my father was alive, and he was writing to me from America, I blamed him for not being with me. Intellectually, I could understand all the reasons why he wasn't here – he was suffering from the overflow of McCarthy – but nevertheless I felt that he had done a bad thing to me.

Suddenly, my analyst said, 'How very sad for your father that he didn't seem to be the sort of person who could just disobey the law and get up and go and see you anyway.' She made him another person to me. At that moment I went down a hole, a psychological hole. My analyst sitting behind me held on to my shoulder, which is not something you're ever meant to do, but she could see that I was completely changed. My father became a person in his own right, not the person who I could say had damaged me.

GRANTA: Blaming others had become a self-constituting activity?

MITCHELL: We all want somebody else to be responsible for what's wrong with us, right? ■

boxes 4 x12 =

Miro –

electric
insulation

2
17
3.
25.20

It means well but it is an field (sophisticated electronics)

belongs to engineering not belong to the sculptor and what belongs to

Random interest.

Does it begin in A or in B.
winding or escaping
clockwise or
counterclockwise.

I cannot concentrate on the heare and now.
I cannot concentrate on the here and now. on you.
I cannot concentrate on the here and now (concentrique
You cannot concentrate on the "fear" and now.
You are not looking at me. your eyes are trem
bling. you are trembling. your gaze is no where.
your hands are trembling, your legs are cold.
and your eyes are tremblinger and tremblinger.
I ~~can~~ want concentrate on your fearful face. because
I feel you trying to escape, to get in orbit, and to
leave. but there is no where to go.
I cannot concentrate because I just hate it, anywhere
but here. Is it fear? fear of what, I am not, actively or passively
fearful, I am tight as a knot and as hard as stone.
I know enough not to talk, what for, talk at the
antipodes of what I want, no thank you. The
humming bird is my friend I am a humming bird. The
present minute is all important, but I do not care,
I want out that is why I cannot concentrate.
from inside, I feel propulsed out, anything,
anyone, anywhere will do, in order to be away
from what? yourself, a thought, a wish, a
need, a must of some kind. This revulsion is anti
object. In that state if I call you. I do not relate
to you (any phone number would do) I relate to
the avoided. I write this as an escape from
Peter the photographer who expect me to be
Ready to pose
I cannot get out of the house, I want to, I have to.
I would like to. I was planning but I give up at
the last minute. It would help to be completely
Ready, waiting by the door, it would make things
easier: some nice feelings will help, familiar friendly
place to go to. no trust, no lift, the disapearance of the love object

MARCH 1st 86

first I cannot be concentrique second I cannot be excentrique no energy
the writing of this letter was very concentrique but showed no concentration

I FEEL
threatened
so
I act
threatened
when
I see you coming or going
I do not Know
why
I do not have to (Know why)

LOUISE BOURGEOIS
347 W. 20 Street New York, NY 10011 (212) 242-4083

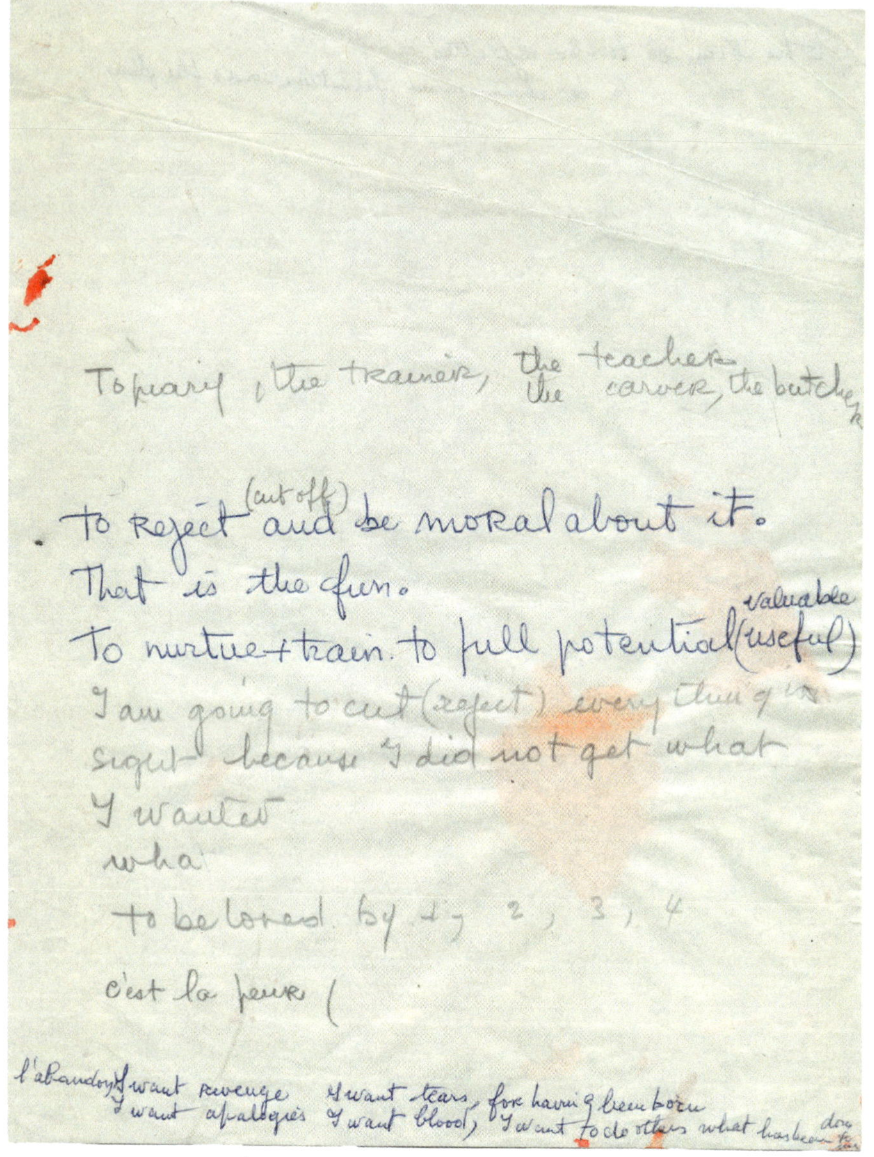

To marry, the trainer, the teacher
the carver, the butcher

To reject (cut off) and be moral about it.
That is the fun.
To nurture + train to full potential (useful) valuable
I am going to cut (reject) every thing in
sight because I did not get what
I wanted
wha
to be loved by 1, 2, 3, 4

c'est la peur (

l'abandon I want revenge I want tears, for having been born
I want apologies I want blood, I want to do others what has been done to me

when I do not "attack" I
do not feel myself alive

the analysis is a jip
is a trap
is a job
is a privilege
is a luxury
is a duty
is a duty towards myself
my husband my parents
my children my
is a shame
is a farce
is a love affaire
is a rendez-vous
is a cat + mouse game
is a boat to drive
is an internement
is a joke
makes me powerless
makes me into a cop
is a bad dream
is my interest
is my field of study –
is more than I can manage
makes me furious
is a bore
is a nuisance
is a pain in the neck

INHABITING LIGHT

Rinko Kawauchi

Introduction by Granta

The photography of Rinko Kawauchi focuses on the everyday. Her subjects have spanned her family, food and the natural world – from insects to volcanoes. She is known for the way she strips down the visual field until only the object, bright and clear, remains.

In her most recent series, *Inhabiting Light*, taken between 2021 and 2024, Kawauchi has pared the process further back. The subject is her long-time accomplice: light. The images are occasions for appraising its workings – luminous raindrops hover above a cluster of heads barely in sight; a canopy of branches remains visible but out of focus behind dimes of lens-flare. From Kawauchi's slight adjustments, elemental qualities of light appear: an acrylic prism rearranges the rays of the sun, a glowing mist is turned opaque and solid, as if it is barricading a dark path.

Inhabiting Light developed as a discussion between Kawauchi and the philosopher Masatake Shinohara, in which they traded text and photography. Shinohara's responses were aslant reflections on what Kawauchi's images conjure – impermanence, stillness, fear of the dark – with no intention to be descriptive. Instead, he attempted to facilitate 'the movements of thought'. ■

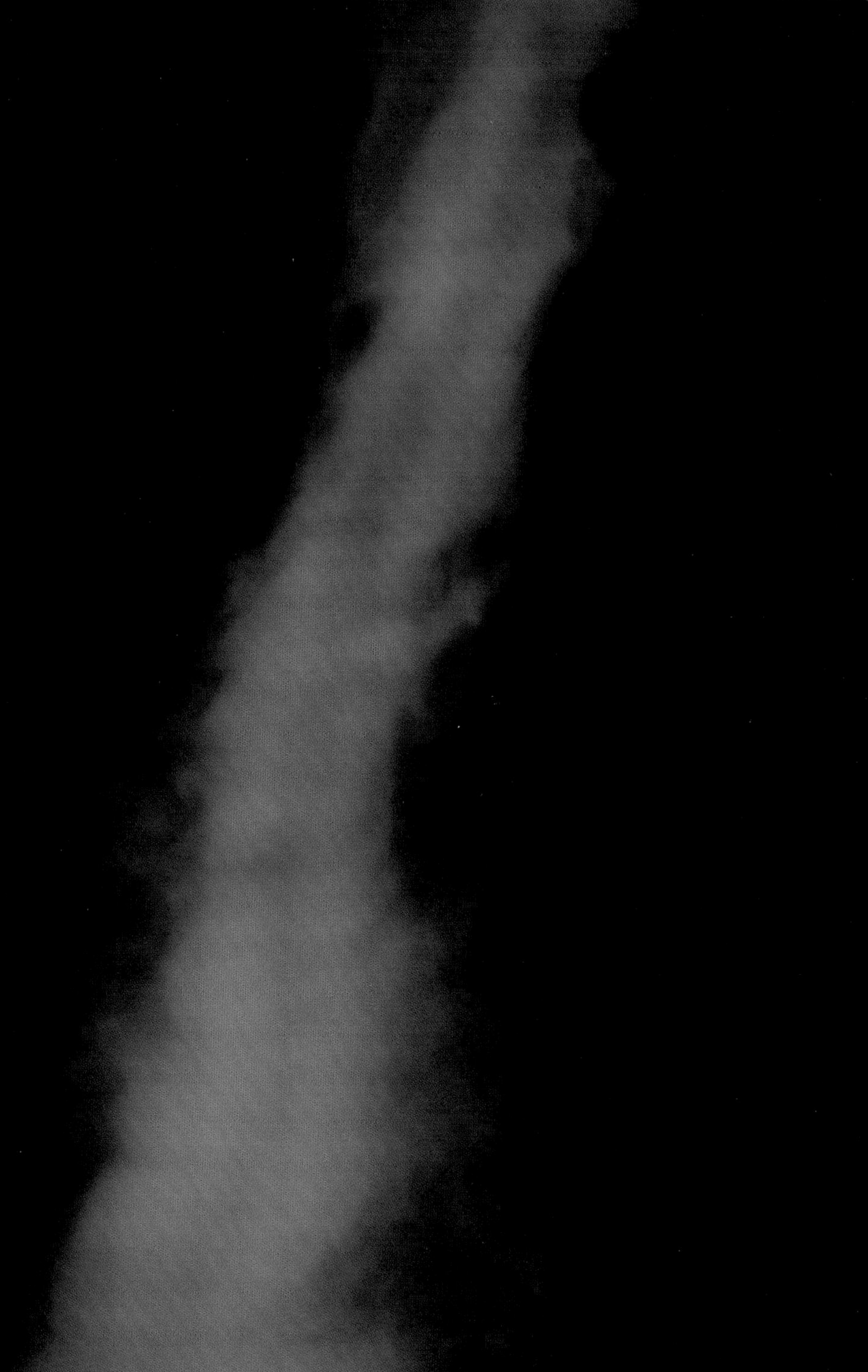

Victor Heringer

The Love of Singular Men

Exterior, night.
All of life the echo
of the first barbaric acts.

The first stray bullet in the history of Rio, a shot of cannon fire in the eighteenth century, struck the façade of a Masonic lodge. In 2010, the drug lord of the Rocinha favela, Antônio Bonfim Lopes, known as Nem, faked his own funeral to throw off the police. On his death certificate, he ordered his 'place of death' to be registered as the address of the fifteenth precinct (Gávea), the department which investigated his crimes.

The broken boy-skin of Rio
the knocked-down chimneys of Bangu
jackhammers, demolitions, renovations

oh, Guanabara! oh, oh

Avenida Rio Branco, before it was properly constructed, was all cardboard, the cardboard painted by Rodolfo Amoedo and Almeida Júnior to fool a committee of English investors. They brought Parisian pigeons for the new statues. The English walked-walked and didn't spot the hoax. They invested everything they had. On the other side of the paint, the West. Cardboard, pigeons & jerry-rigging.

like in the old days, the poem is content
to scrape along the seashore like a crab, Rio de Janeiro.

400 rabbits, 400 ways to get drunk.
Centzontōtōchtin. Centzontlatole.
Ipanemish copacabanas urcas.

We love the sand.
Not the morro, not the city
we love the sand.
Our sand is everywhere
the first barbaric act.

News for Nira

From this side

Time's been moving strangely here.
The papers say the scientists
tinkered too much with the clocks
and now no one knows, senhora,
when it's time to sing happy birthday.

Here, the mountains shaped like organs (mine
too) still look like an ECG (mine
and Rio's). It's easy to see a beating heart.
I'm far too lazy to climb.

I've come to prefer the horizon.
I write sambas for the tango and tangos for men
in good health. They don't need them, since they die
at any bend in the hour hand, in the stupidest ways,
senhora. Out of time, they don't pay attention.

What's more,
senhora, your god is still up to his tricks.
He says 'my god' for everything;
cries out his own name when they don't understand
his wisecracks. Sometimes we have coffee together.
He's been running the numbers racket and it seems he's disappeared.
They call him the Beast.

I've been waiting, a still cloud,
you know? Children point,
try to figure out if I'm a ram, a dog,
the head of a dragon.

My Grandfather Is the Future

My father's father was kind of crazy.

That was how the papers in Rio spoke of him:
NATURALIST CONSIDERED
'KIND OF CRAZY'.

He lived on a small farm
tucked away at the end of the world
called São Pedro da Serra
a tiny village in the state of Rio.

Mountains, sun-faded brush, the smell of fresh water.

When I have to make important decisions
I go to São Pedro
and spend hours watching the water run.

All my decisions
have been wrong, but
                                        I still believe
                                        in the water.

My grandfather planted endangered orchids
bromeliads and ferns
and other plants whose names I don't know
because I'm an urban erê
and nowadays poets don't know about botany.

He made vases for the plants.

Cement vases

My grandfather
probably knew how
to take apart an old pickup truck
an old refrigerator
an old washing machine
an old stove
a fruit tree
and put everything back together.

My grandfather before the microchip.

My grandfather must have known how
to drive a tractor
and predict which rocks would come loose
from the mountains
like putrid warts.

I don't know anything about this.

My grandfather made liqueurs and preserves for sale.
I really love his humble dealings.

My grandfather cooked caramujo
and said it was escargot.
He threw beet juice
over store-bought sugar
and sold it to people from the big city
saying he'd extracted the sugar
from the beets. The tourists ate it up.
I really love how he was also
this trickster type. A crafty
old fox. He won over Grandma playing guitar.

My grandfather couldn't stand school buses
he threw fruit at them as they drove by.
I became a teacher
but I understand the fruit.

My grandfather must not have known
how to recite his times tables.

When the papers asked, my grandfather responded:
'–We try to bring the countryside to visitors – he says, humbly. –We understand the difficulties city folk face and so we do everything to make them happy' (*O Globo*, 20 April 1989).

My *true folk* grandfather.
He never had a beard.
When they took him to the big city
as soon as they took their eyes off the kids
he hightailed it back to the farm.
He fled on foot, running.
My grandfather was kind of crazy.

If someone said to him:

> *Sr Milton*
> *the world is getting hotter*
> *and the plants and animals are dying*
> *the Sixth Extinction is coming*

I don't know how he'd respond.
I don't remember what his laugh was like.
Can't you almost hear his laugh?
Just listen to my grandfather laughing.

> *There are too many people in the world*
> *Sr Milton!*

Just listen to my grandfather laughing
in the middle of the brush.

My grandfather is the future
That's me, on the future's lap:

He looks a little like Picasso, my grandfather.
Bald and squat.
A backwoods Picasso.

I look like my father, who looked a lot like his.

My grandfather,
if we were still German, my grandfather
would have been ten years old in 1945
in Munich
under intense bombing.

How nice that his forebears caught that ship
named the *Argus*.
They wound up here at this end of the world.

My grandfather is the Germany that turned out OK.
My grandfather is the Europe that's the size of a village square with a bandstand in the middle, in a village of not even a thousand residents and only one toothless old police chief.

My grandfather died when I was a very young boy.
My grandfather is the future.

In the end everything
we invented in all caps:
everything turned lower case.
The only virtue left among us
is elegance.

I remember I read an old story about Beau Brummell.
Brummell was the prince of the dandies (1778–1840).
– There's nothing more inelegant than a dandy

but in this old story about Belo Brummell
there's an anecdote
a curiosity: the dandies, so rich, so tedious
no longer knew what to do with their clothes
so many clothes so much royal purple so much gold
they began to ruin everything they had
to tatter the fabrics, camisoles, evening coats, tunics
until what was left were very thin threads
like gauze
used to seal up wounds
and the dandies now wore dressings

my grandfather lived shirtless, only in shorts
barefoot on even the bare-earth floor
or in blue-and-white flip-flops

(and my feet are so delicate
I'm so ticklish!)

My grandfather was more elegant than the dandies.
My grandfather saw man land on the moon
and must have thought nothing of it.

The three photos I keep of my young grandfather
were taken at the start of the 1950s.
In all three he looks well dressed,
a suit, a tie, and a hat
– the classic trio of men's fashion.

But never all three together:
in one photo there's just the hat sans suit and tie

in the next, just the tie
in the third, just the hat.

An elegant man
must never be completely elegant.
There's no man more inelegant than a despot
power is always tacky.
There's no elegant way to invade, pillage, and kill.
Nothing's tackier than a uniform.
Nothing's tackier than a toga.

Horace Aliananga, in his book of aphorisms
(*Elegance as Intellectual Virtue*, 1956),
put it differently
'The greatest virtue of Marie Antoinette's hair was the guillotine.'

'Few things are as elegant
as a man about to be shot
smoking his final cigarette.'

Truths that Grandpa
couldn't put into words.
    But I think he knew them too.

Over the years
the more acclaim he gained
as a pioneering ecologist
saviour of orchids
and man of humble dealings
the more he shed his shell.

He started swimming with the toads
in their freshwater pond
(made of cement)
and to walk shirtless,

barefoot, wearing shorts
worth five reais.

In the last photo I have of him
I'm a baby on his lap. He's standing
wearing only some yellowed shorts
in the middle of a little dirt road in São Pedro.
A stocky, strong old man
with white hair and a weak heart
that in a few months would stop.

Bald and squat,
the backwoods Picasso
had reached the beatitude of elegance:
he was truly naked.
He needed no dressings.

The First Gulf War

I was a boy with a single fear:
that I hadn't found the fabled
.38 hidden in the yard.

It was buried with the owner's licence
and a note saying *kill in my name*
granting pardon from possible hells beyond.

Imagine the chaos.

I tore up the earth, ripped out flowers, kicked over
mama's sorry lemon tree. I stumbled
across holes. I never put my fingers
on any trigger I know.

Imagine:
our killer can still
make it to heaven.

I Am Not a Poet

Now the pangs of adolescence have passed
and life has settled like a mahogany dresser

now my knees ache when I rise
with no wife, no kids, but with a steady job
I have to admit that I am not a poet.

Though my love is loose in the world
violent, half-blind and wounded in the shoulder
I am not a poet.

Everyone congratulates me. Good for you, they say
the life of a poet is really hard.

Soon we become men
and set aside our boyish things.

Life narrows down.

I kept two or three tricks in the pockets
of pants bought at shopping malls.
I never learned how to shop like a poet
the long wait for a pair of military
boots in the desert.

The shoes are made and the poets' feet deform over the years.
Until one day they fit.
That's why any clothes look old
on the body of a poet.
That's why they're always apologising
for their old clothes.
But secretly they're proud.

Though I have a body
that might be confused with the body of a poet
I am not a poet.

I have strong legs and skinny arms.
A boxer's softened torso
the mangled internal organs.
But whoever sees me naked instinctively knows I am not a poet.

⊙

I didn't raise my left hand like a flamenco dancer while reading
Jaime Gil de Biedma to my friends,
though everything conspired towards it.
Towards things getting under my skin.
I conclude that I am not a poet.

I have the cold fingers of an IT assistant
and I'm as sad as an IT assistant
but I'm not as sad as a barber.

I've read every treatise on Portuguese metre.

I have signed two contracts as a poet
which are henceforth no longer binding.

I will sign a third, as a final betrayal.

I will be forgiven by everyone.

Henceforth scrutiny and wrath will rule.

The best boots for walking on sand
calculations of long distances
exercises for apnoea.

Love will come to me like it does for the journalists and CEOs, the sushimen of São Paulo (SP) who come from Ceará – ideally suited because of their warm hands.

⊙

Each party irrevocably agrees that the district courts of São Paulo (SP) shall have exclusive jurisdiction to settle any dispute or claim that arises out of or in connection with this agreement, its subject matter or formation that cannot be amicably resolved.

Translated from the Portuguese by James Young and Justin Greene

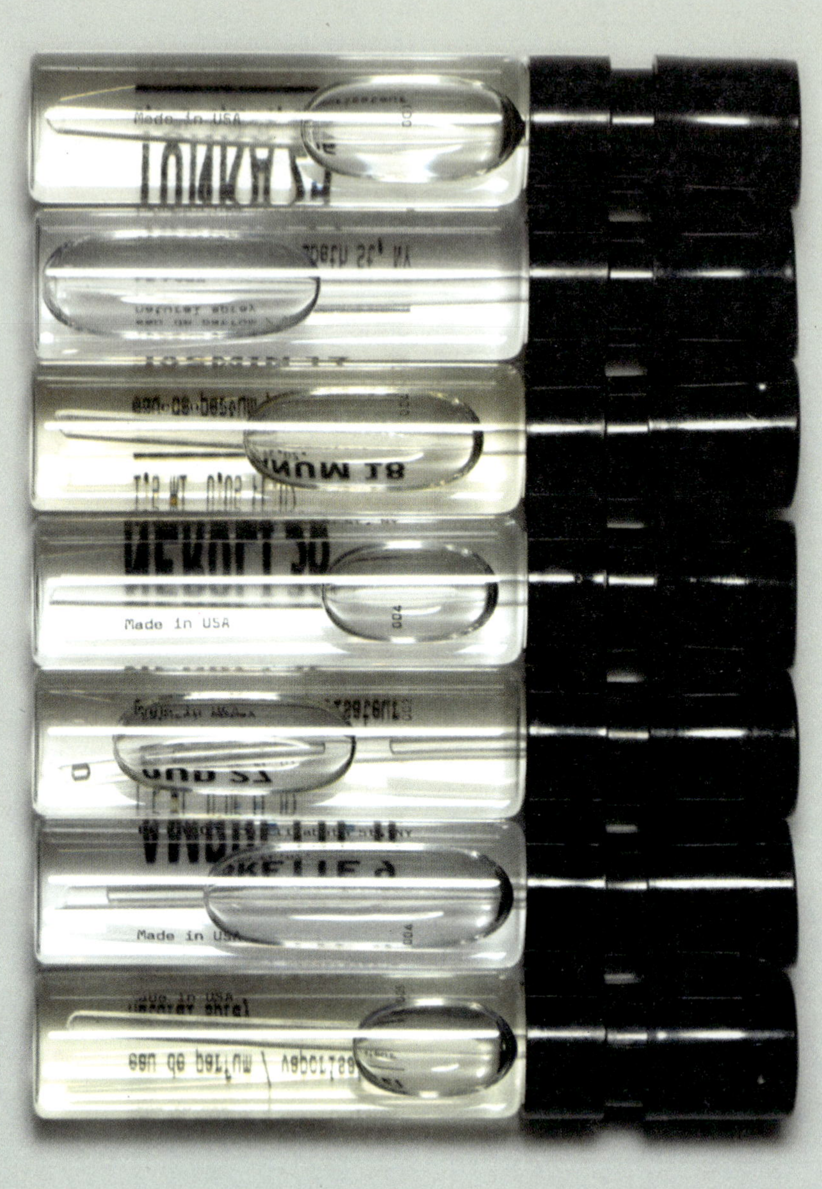

SOPHIE GLADSTONE
From other studies, 2021

SECONDHAND SMOKE

Dushko Petrovich Córdova

REALISTIC CANDLES

My interest in perfume came in waves, at a slant. I wasn't aware of it at first. It was the pandemic, we were cooped up, and I was growing interested in fire. Everyone else was making sourdough, but that seemed like a secondary phenomenon, one degree removed from the actual fun, which was fire.

We had a fireplace, but it ran on gas, one of the ones with fake ceramic logs. I sometimes had to remind myself the fire was real, because the logs were not real logs, there was no smoke, and the flame was perfectly even.

'Surely there must be a wood-fire scented candle,' I told my wife, and started looking for one online.

The first candle I ordered smelled more like 'candle' than fireplace, too much cinnamon and vanilla. I bought a few more. Then I started watching videos about candles and scent. I discovered candle influencers. They did not lack in recommendations for fireplace candles. I found my way to something called Incienso De Santa Fe, which sold a variety pack. The mesquite one in the bundle did make it smell like we had a 'real' fire going. It also produced a lot of dust – ash? I had reached the point where I wanted the real smoke smell without any of the substances that actually produced smoke.

FIFTH SENSE

For years I ignored my sense of smell almost entirely, but my experience with candles made me realize how smell was everywhere – and everywhere unexamined, unappreciated. But I began to find candles irritating. They take up space; they smell up your whole house; if you don't like them, you're left with half-burned lumps of wax. Perfume samples, on the other hand, were easy to store, the scent was localized, and it didn't linger. I began to order the little vials like drugs.

The question was, which vials? Unlike music, fashion, or art, perfume has no big magazines to consult. Newspapers that review food, movies, theater, even apps and socks and toasters, find precious little space for scent. My friends didn't know anything either. Under interrogation, they admitted to owning tons of books, uncountable photographs, infinite streams of music, but could demonstrate no engagement with smell. Nobody else is *pursuing* this, I thought.

One evening, in front of the fireplace, I watched a series of perfume reviews on YouTube. I did not know this activity would consume the next few years of my life, but the next evening, I put some perfume review videos on while I was doing the dishes – a habit that continues to this day. Visuals are largely irrelevant to a perfume review, and removing them focuses the mind on the real problem, which is the difficulty of describing smell. Perfume reviewers lack an established critical vocabulary. The perfume reviewer cannot give you a quote or a clip of the perfume he is reviewing. He's on his own, sniffing his forearms, smelling something live and for the first time, free-associating. It's a real-time high-wire act as the reviewer strains to conjure the perfume using only words, halting descriptions, sudden memories, qualified comparisons, either from the world ('cut grass', 'petrichor') or from other perfumes ('it's the Aventus DNA'). The smell remains a phantom.

FRAGRANCE INFLUENCERS

If you are a man or a boy interested in fragrance, the algorithm very quickly brings you to Jeremy Fragrance. Jeremy is handsome, well dressed, German and charming, but his real charm, what draws millions of people to him, is that he is unhinged.

Jeremy knows you have a job. He knows you want to get laid. He knows you want to impress your friends and receive compliments. He tells you with complete authority which fragrances to use in which situations. He is also very good at summarizing perfumes. Montblanc Individuel, which he single-handedly rescued from oblivion, he describes, repeatedly, as 'raspberry fabric softener'. Somehow he convinces you that this is a good thing, something that will attract women, that it's 'a compliment beast'.

As he talks, Jeremy Fragrance drifts, and not just into little, initially jarring, asides about wanting to masturbate before filming the video you're watching. He'll tell you about how he did masturbate but doesn't, as a rule, ejaculate, and then he'll go even further, following this tangent with thirty one-arm pushups to punish himself, in front of you, for going off topic or for having actually ejaculated. In the next video, he will say, apropos of a smell, that he has been reducing his carb and sugar intake so much that he jumped into a trash bin in desperation, because he had no carbs at home and the shops were closed, and that in the trash bin he fought manfully with the racoon that had jumped in the trash bin before him. He'll pivot suddenly into a monologue about the immeasurable sadness of the world, about how one time his ex-girlfriend accused him of rape and how heartbreaking that was, detailing the ins and outs of the German legal system and the waves of emotion he experienced. These are the conditions under which internet addiction flourishes. Jeremy's 2.5 million YouTube followers attest to that.

FRAGCOM

What drew me to Jeremy drew me into Fragrantica, one of the vast online databases that list all the perfumes with practical information (release date, perfumer, etc.) alongside my favorite part: the user reviews, where ordinary people, struggling to describe an ineffable smell, give you something extraordinary.

Take, for example, this 2021 review of Aromatics Elixir (Clinique, 1971) from Fragrantica user UnjustJoan:

> My mom had her own legit business working as a psychic when I was a school age child. She specialized in automatic writing, rune stone, palm, and energy reading. Her clients would come over and me and my sis would wait upstairs for their readings to be done. There was one client in particular I always recognized by her perfume. She wore Clinique Aromatics Elixer . . . I remember thinking of how repulsively vulgar and strong this woman's scent was. I remember wincing with disgust at how it outlasted her stay by hours. How it superseded the cigarette smoke . . . I could imagine this woman in great detail – despite never seeing her. She had long natural nails lacquered dusky mauve & lips painted Avon's Amorous Rose. I remember seeing the lipstick mark left on her Virginia Slims Menthol Light cigarette butt. She kept her hair long, permed, and frizzy. Her roots touched up – Miss Clairol Sunlit Brown. She wore a little chunky open-toed heel. In her house hung elaborate macrame and sat a rattan Peacock chair. She jazzercised and drank white wine spritzers.
>
> Elixer to me is the rotten and magnificent unknown . . . It's musty and arrogant. It's interfering and lippy. It's a ruined Saturday.
>
> It really pisses me off so I bought a bottle.

This kind of writing took me deeper into Fragcom – the online fragrance community. I entered my own perfume collection into the database and started posting my reviews. I joined in conversations about patchouli or the best non-citrus summer perfumes. I experienced the YouTubers and most prolific posters as something more than acquaintances. I referred to them as 'my influencers'.

Joy Amin, from Dhaka, Bangladesh, had a truly encyclopedic collection of affordable perfumes. He could be depended upon to review anything under $100. AC, an Indian-British consultant who referred to himself only by his initials, had a demeanor and taste that generally lined up with mine: weird, woody perfumes, meditative scents, bargains. Chris, 'From Scent Land, the Land of Scent!', was a German living in Hungary with special knowledge of the vintage realm. These influencers had none of the spectacle of Jeremy Fragrance. They felt more like ham radio aficionados, sharing their obsession, intermittently, from the far ends of the earth.

In the real world, it's a lonely business being into perfume. You go to the mall and smell things, but more often than not the person working the perfume counter knows less than you do. I once asked the people at Macy's if I could smell the entire John Varvatos line, because I am a completist that way, and they were so alarmed I thought they might call security. What do you mean you want to smell every one? 'I'm interested in Rodrigo Flores-Roux and I want to smell what he's done without having to buy every bottle,' I explain. 'Rodrigo Flores who?'

If you live in a big city you can go to a boutique or discount perfume stores, and the person there might actually be into perfumes, might be willing to talk about them beyond the 'That's my favorite, too!' line that all the mall-counter people use. In Chicago I discovered a range of shops, from Sephora, where the bottles were all decapitated and chained to the display walls like prisoners, to the old-school pharmacy Merz, which carried a wide variety of traditional and niche perfumes. Each was pleasurable, but I had soon smelled everything of interest in the boutiques and the discount stores and the malls.

I kept ordering samples.

A ROSE ISN'T A ROSE

Little vials arrived from the vast, semi-professionalized archipelago of sites that sell decants. These are like the samples of perfume you get at the department store, but homemade. Someone buys a bottle of, say, Yves Saint Laurent M7 Oud Absolu, and spritzes it out into 1- or 2-ml sprayers. I planned sample purchases month by month, usually in sync with the weather. I'd spend every day smelling whatever perfume I was wearing, often switching two or three times a day as one wore off. I was tactical, selective, and budget-minded, but I was extravagant with my time, smelling things all day long.

Perfumes are often described and categorized in terms of color. Blue means shower gel, green is plants or leafy smells, white is for soapy clean or laundry clean, and black includes everything from leather to vanilla. Red doesn't connote roses, surprisingly, but rather a fruity-spicy bent. Grey often means vetiver, which is green in actuality, but somehow smells grey. Amber perfumes have a sweet, golden feel.

I learned about notes. Like most people, I started off thinking that notes are a perfume's ingredients, but they aren't. Choice few real-world substances have a smell that can be extracted. You can distill a rose smell from a rose, but you cannot squeeze lily of the valley out of a lily of the valley – it has to be constructed from chemicals. You can also produce the smell of a rose this way, synthetically. Or you can extract a rose smell from a geranium, which people describe as a minty rose, or you could mix rose absolute with geranium and synthetics to create a rose smell that is more than a rose. A perfume that lists rose as a note is only promising you a version of that smell, not telling you how it got there.

I learned about structures. The genres of Western perfumery include ambers (previously called 'orientals', because they reference Middle Eastern perfumery), woods (also known as chypres and fougères), florals, freshies (fleeting, refreshing), aquatics (perfumes that evoke the sea) and gourmands (perfumes that smell edibly sweet). Perfumes are traditionally built in a pyramid, with the top notes like citruses burning off quickly and brightly, the mid notes, often florals and woody accords, lasting longer and providing the heart of the experience, and the base notes like resins and musks binding everything to your skin and holding out into what is called the drydown, when they finally come to the fore.

I began to understand what people meant by 'reference perfumes'. These are the canonical perfumes that best exemplify any note or genre. I ordered reference perfumes for each major note and genre. I learned that Guerlain's Vetiver was the reference vetiver, Serge Lutens's Ambre Sultan was the reference amber, and so on. Once I knew the reference perfumes, I searched for my favorite versions in each category. I started off with smells I liked, figs and vetiver and tobacco, and then I turned to smells I didn't particularly like. Aquatics, for example, had always reminded me of jocks, bullies, and businessmen. But I found an aquatic I adored: Le Sel d'Issey from Issey Miyake, composed by Quentin Bisch. I have never much liked sandalwood, but after six months of searching I had acquired sandalwood body wash, aftershave, beard oil and a few perfumes: Sarah Jessica Parker's Stash SJP, Indian Sandalwood from Dunhill, and This is Him! from Zadig and Voltaire.

I discovered that perfumers, the people behind the actual making of the perfumes, often go uncredited. Brands want to differentiate themselves, and hide the fact that they mostly all work with the big three perfumery firms – Givaudan, Firmenich, and IFF – which in turn employ a shockingly high percentage of people from the town of Grasse, where traditional French perfume ingredients have been sourced for decades.

IMAGINARY FERNS

I hit puberty in the 1980s, at the culmination of the most storied illusion in Western perfumery: the imaginary smell of a fern. Ferns don't really have a smell, but you'd recognize the smell of a *fougère*, French for fern, even if you don't know the term. The fougère structure that Paul Parquet came up with in 1882 for Houbigant's Fougère Royale – lavender, oakmoss, and coumarin (synthetic tonka bean) – was hugely groundbreaking because it used a synthetic, and has been repeated endlessly since. It is what most people alive in the West recognize as 'men's cologne'. Depending on their generation, some will call this 'grandpa smell' and some 'dad smell'. The fern was initially an important fantasy for Parquet, perhaps cover to employ a synthetic, but the genre has become so established, I don't think anyone today thinks of ferns, not even the perfumers.

I wasn't thinking of imaginary ferns either when I saved up my paper route money to buy Drakkar Noir. I just knew it was how I was supposed to smell if I wanted to be cool. The bottle shape of Drakkar Noir still has a certain allure. Its rounded trapezoid feels good to hold. The matte black seems just right.

When I open a bottle now it smells like junior high. (Or like diluted junior high, because it has been reformulated. For health reasons, ingredients like oakmoss can no longer be used in the same quantities.) I am standing in front of my childhood dresser. Why? I am getting ready to go out. Where? A school dance, a party, a gathering in a basement. Why? To kiss Regan Fall, and later, to have my heart broken when my best friend, Jeff Hardesty, who probably also wore Drakkar Noir, made out with her. He was either wearing Drakkar Noir or Polo Green.

I had moved from Quito, Ecuador to Ohio, a small town called Perrysburg. My mom taught elementary school at Maumee Valley Country Day School, MVCDS. She could only teach at private schools because she didn't have her certificate yet. She dressed me, in part, out of the clothes left unclaimed in the school's lost and found. This is how I got a taste for Madras-plaid Polos. I grew up with a fashion I now call New New England, which takes its social-hierarchy cues from New England, which of course took its own cues from regular England. In New New England, plaids and Polo Green reigned supreme. I never got Polo Green. My friend Johnny Wellstein had it. He also had an aquarium and his whole family was blonde and sported variations on a preppie bowl cut that I registered as the pinnacle of our social world. Forest green sweaters. Hot preppie sisters. Imaginary chest hair, imaginary countries, imaginary ferns.

FRESH AIR

I began to recognize the tendencies of certain perfumers. Jean-Claude Ellena is known for making transparent perfumes. They are often compared to watercolor paintings. The smells reminded me of my childhood in Quito. Fig leaf, bitter orange, eucalyptus, petitgrain – those were the scents. Chemically speaking, the signature of Jean-Claude Ellena's work was an overdose of ISO E Super, an aromachemical that smells faintly of cedar and sour cream, but more importantly gives off a luminous, spacious feeling. This combination with fig, in a perfume called Un Jardin en Mèditerranèe, returned me to the Equatorial Andean sunshine.

The feeling was so pleasant, I didn't initially notice what was missing: the dirt, the funk, the haze. Ecuador is not Ecuador without diesel fuel, fruit rotting on the corner, cigarette smoke in the doorways. I started to look for those elements. Dior's Fahrenheit was famous for its petrol accord, but it smelled more like huffing fumes at the pump than diesel tinge in mountain air. I looked for tropical fruit, but fruity perfumes always went for a beach-vacation effect – sweet cocktails, suntan lotion, crashing waves. Guava appeared fleetingly in Tommy Bahama Set Sail St. Barts; maracuyá was featured in Maison Crivelli's Oud Maracujá. But that just smelled like wealth. I have never found taxo or cherimoya or tomate de árbol in a perfume.

REAL ANGELS

You may not have heard of Olivier Cresp, but you have smelled his perfumes: Thierry Mugler's Angel, Dolce & Gabbana Light Blue, Versace Man Eau Fraîche, Dior's Dune pour Homme, Paco Rabanne Black XS. In the perfume world, Cresp is known for inventing the gourmand, the genre of scent that smells edible. There hasn't been a new genre since the gourmand, which emerged with the release of Angel in 1992. It still dominates. (Baccarat Rouge 540, the most ubiquitous perfume of our time, is a cotton-candy gourmand.)

When Cresp mentions that he invented a genre, he presents it humbly, as a duty he fulfilled. In a way, it was: his father, who came from a long line of ingredient merchants in Grasse, had already enrolled his two older children in perfume school locally, so he sent his third child to the US, thinking he couldn't get jobs for three Cresps in France. Perhaps he also sensed the future of smell would come from America. He wanted to give his son a chance, somewhere, somehow. The scheme worked. Cresp interned with Americans who knew all the latest industrial-scale flavor chemicals. He familiarized himself with ethyl maltol, the overdose of which would give Angel its unmistakable caramel allure and give rise to the innumerable bubble gum, apple pie, praline, lemon meringue, and maple syrup pancake scents that have since flooded malls around the world.

Oliver Cresp is a realist. He admits this in interviews. He always starts with a real smell, something recognizable, he says with a shrug and a pout. It is a daring position to hold. Since Fougère Royale, Western perfumery, which is overwhelmingly French, has been closely identified with abstraction. Before synthetics were invented, European perfumery was based around soliflors, perfumes made to smell like a particular, identifiable flower, with other notes playing a supporting role. Aromachemicals changed all that. They provided smells that were not-quite-this-but-not-quite-that already abstracted from the real world. These chemicals drastically expanded the perfumer's palette, and they boosted the performance of perfumes, which could now linger and hover in new ways. For more than a century, perfumes stayed away from realism. Instead, scents were blended beyond recognizability, into moods and effects you can't name. Chanel No. 5, famously created from an accidental overdose of aldehydes, is probably the most famous example of this. What does Chanel No. 5 smell like? Aldehydes. And what do aldehydes smell like? Chanel No. 5! Today people who smell it just think 'perfume'.

Cresp wasn't the only realist in turn-of-the-millennium perfumery. Comme des Garçons put out wonderful, troubling concoctions that smelled like ink or concrete. Etat Libre d'Orange put out the notorious Sécrétions Magnifiques, by Antoine Lie, that smelled like blood, semen, sweat, and milk. (The metallic blood smell haunted me so much I threw away the blotter paper I sprayed it on, then I had to throw away the trash to get the thing out of the house, and still I spent the whole day feeling like I had been in an accident.) Jo Malone, at the opposite end of the realist spectrum, developed a nouvelle-cuisine approach of pairing two ingredients in seemingly endless variations: English Pear & Freesia, Blackberry & Bay, Poppy & Barley, and so on.

Cresp sits in the middle of all this – not a moderate-compromise middle, but a clash-of-opposites middle. Luca Turin, for example, describes Angel as 'an irreconcilable difference . . . a crossroads of two marching bands playing different tunes'. Tania Sanchez goes further, describing it as a perfume hermaphrodite, and suggests the marketing around Angel as an uber-feminine dessert hides the key to its appeal. 'Look for Angel's Adams apple,' she says, 'a handsome, resinous, woody patchouli straight out of the pipes-and-leather-slippers realm of men's fragrance.' This gender opposition in Angel helped me understand what I had been attracted to in some of Cresp's other productions. My favorite, Versace Man Eau Fraîche, has an unmistakable swimming pool feel, but the chemical smell is resolved – cheered up – by transparent white florals. I experience it as 'sunny day'. But the hook is the chlorine undertone, the kind of thing that makes a lesser perfume smell cheap, chemical-y. For Cresp, the noticeable chemical is a risky tightrope but it is also a tether back to the real world, with its real smells. It puts me at my Aunt Johnnie's pool, where after a swim we'd enjoy lemonade in green octagonal rocks glasses.

I first heard about Cresp's Smoke from Persolaise, the composed, erudite host of the YouTube channel Love at First Scent. I mention his composure because he lost it ever so slightly when he started to describe the way the perfume put him back in Iran, and reminded him of a particular tobacco a relative of his used. I imagined, wrongly, that this relative was his father, because as I was listening to this conversation about smoke in Iran in the 1970s, I was thinking of the last time we visited my own father, around 1984. When he met us at Quito airport, I remember the dry, faded sweetness of cigarettes as I pressed my face into his denim jacket. That memory had come to me before, but I never knew what to do with it. The sadness of the moment had grown over the years. It seemed ridiculous that a perfume could capture some of that sadness and help extract it from me, but that was my sudden hope.

When the little vial arrived a couple weeks later, I was transported, just not to the place I expected. People often describe smells as 'photorealistic', but Cresp works more like a magnifying glass than a camera. In his work you get closer to the smell than you could in real life. Smoke took me inside the cigarette. It was too much. I hadn't thought of it before, but I realized that what I was looking for was *secondhand* smoke. I wasn't the guy enjoying the cigarette, I was that smoker's estranged child, sitting on the other end of the smell, at the other end of the continent. When I woke up the next day, having forgotten my disappointment, I had the involuntary sensation that I had just been to a party. I couldn't figure out where I was or, since I hadn't been to a real smoke-your-clothes party in decades, when I was. The day-after drydown of Smoke floored me. There in my befuddled horizontality, it hit me: I needed smoke plus distance.

'Smoke plus distance' doesn't give you good results when you type it into a search. I knew I had to give myself over to chance. Chance was on my side when I came across Shuhrah, a much-touted Middle Eastern cheapie with a mix of tomato leaf, rose, and yes, smoke.

RASASI SHUHRAH

I didn't really expect Shuhrah to work. It was a Middle Eastern perfume, so there wasn't much in the description that seemed reminiscent of Ecuador. No fig or bitter orange, no tropical anything. But I kept returning to one review of it, from prince64:

> A distinctive Arabic with soapy rose, smooth suede, and tamed oud. And smoke, a lot of smoke, like a cloud of smoke rising from a bonfire. The first thing that comes to my nose is the rose, a verdant one with sweet and leafy nuances. The rose is soapy and slightly metallic, with a veil of fruity apricot and dewy freesia surrounding it, and the whole sits on a bed made of tomato leaves.

The smoke in Shuhrah didn't hit me at first. It starts off with soap and tomato leaves. The coloration was pale and bright. Light-blue perfume usually connotes 'aquatic', but here it meant the sky. I had never smelled a Middle Eastern perfume that was so light, but the lightness made it familiar to me. The oud and rose, which I had seen in the notes listing, didn't come together in the way they do in countless other Middle Eastern perfumes. The rose meshed with the soapy part to make a plausible rose soap, then with the tomato leaf part to make, what, a tomato rose? This is when it got freaky. The surreal tomato-rose plant flashed into a tomate de árbol, a fruit on a vine that is sweeter than a regular tomato. And the leather and oud created a grey sensation, a dry haze, which charged my memory. As I wore the Shuhrah through the day, it started to feel overripe, again, in a way that made sense. It took me into the past. I had found an accidental analogue for the smells of my youth.

Spraying it on my body, creating my own microclimate, let me return to my childhood at will. It wasn't a pleasure, it was something darker, because my memories of childhood weren't pleasant. It was a mix of relief and grief. A layer of my reality that had been missing was now restored. It was like the fireplace all over again. I only needed the smell to make it real. ■

FRANÇOIS OLLIVIER
Old elevator in a small building, 2025

MADAME GANDI

Anne Serre

TRANSLATED FROM THE FRENCH BY MARK HUTCHINSON

In Paris on a chilly evening late in October of 1985, I first became fully aware that the struggle with the disorder in my mind – a struggle which had engaged me for several months – might have a fatal outcome. So I took steps. I decided to go and see Madame Gandi, who had been recommended to me by my friend Luciano, who had himself consulted with her for several years and had felt the better for it, he told me. I made an appointment. She lived on the top floor of a modern apartment block and provided me with the exact street number, door code and floor. However, something made it impossible for me to access the building, which was surrounded by other buildings of the same type. I couldn't find the entrance, and when at last I did, I couldn't find the elevator or the stairwell. Having neglected to bring my address book, which included Madame Gandi's phone number, I couldn't call her. So I went home, furious at my helplessness, and called her to apologise and make a new appointment.

When I returned, everything looked different. Might I also have memory problems? I wondered. On my previous visit, I hadn't noticed the rather sorry-looking strip of land opposite the building, where a small slide stood on a narrow mound of sand. This time, the door to the building wouldn't open. No doubt the code had been changed. Rather than call Madame Gandi, whom I was loath to disturb because I assumed she had another appointment before mine, I waited a while, my back against the slide, for somebody to enter or leave the building. But for ten minutes, no one came out and no one went in, so I made up my mind to call Madame Gandi, who told me she was coming down to get me. She must have thought me clumsy, and she wasn't wrong.

When Madame Gandi appeared in the doorway to the building, I knew it was her because she was clearly looking around for someone, but above all I was astonished to recognise in Madame Gandi my cousin Edwige, whom I was unaware now called herself Gandi (I knew her by the surname of Bouchard) or that she went in for appointments of this kind. I had gradually loosened my ties with my family and, as I remembered it, had a cousin Edwige Bouchard who lived in Bordeaux, whether alone or with a partner I had no idea, and who had one of those jobs in business or finance I couldn't make head nor tail of.

Edwige had gained a little weight (it was a good twenty years since I had last seen her), but her square face and blonde bangs were a perfect giveaway. I walked up to her with that slightly silly grin people have when they exaggerate their pleasure at meeting someone again, but Edwige kept her distance, which struck me as oddly cold. 'Edwige!' I cried, with a big smile, 'It's incredible! What a surprise!' She smiled but gave no sign of wishing to embrace me, nor of sharing my surprise. I had time to reflect on how much she had changed, for as I remembered her she had been a rather outgoing and cheerful young girl. To the two or three questions I asked – 'What are you doing here? I thought you were in Bordeaux! Is that your married name? Didn't you recognise my voice on the phone?' – she made no reply, simply smiling at me in a way I find slightly irritating, because I've often seen it on people who don't want to 'stick their neck out' by saying something, and who try to find out more about you before showing their hand. 'I suppose our appointment is cancelled,' I said. 'You can't have a consultation of this kind with your cousin, even one you haven't seen for a long time, can you?' 'Of course you can,' she said, opening her mouth for the first time; then she wheeled round and marched ahead of me through the entrance of the building.

I followed. In the elevator, I took the slight liberty of saying, 'You're not very talkative!' (She was my cousin, after all, and we had played together as children.) She simply smiled once more in her Sphinx-like way. I didn't care for her perfume, but then people change sometimes and suddenly start wearing a perfume that doesn't suit their character. When we entered the apartment, it occurred to me she must have done rather well in her business or financial dealings in Bordeaux, as it was some kind of enormous loft, elegantly fitted out with the sort of contemporary furnishings I dislike because I find them impersonal and I wouldn't like to live in an environment I found impersonal, but maybe it suited her line of work better, I thought.

Edwige Gandi started to test the waters, and I noticed at once that she was contriving very skilfully to address me neither as *tu* nor as *vous*. She clearly wanted to leave some doubt as to our ties and whether or not she had recognised me. She can't possibly have not recognised me, I thought, but then again, maybe she doesn't care whether it's me or someone else, maybe family ties no longer mean much to her, just as they don't to me. The thought then occurred to me that she had decided to transform people she knew into strangers, and this, I reflected, was rather impressive, and sufficiently unusual and audacious to interest me.

Since she insisted on pretending not to recognise me, I consented to play along and pretend I didn't recognise her either. From a twitch of her leg (she had pretty legs), I sensed that she was enjoying this and that it worked for her. I immediately started fantasising about her (because of the twitch of her pretty leg? Or because of her subterfuge, which had something erotic about it?) and told myself I could easily leap from the armchair where she had invited me to sit down, fling myself on top of her and thrust her back onto hers. I didn't do so because I like to maintain a certain decorum.

Little by little, I began to enjoy our game. It was far more entertaining and inventive, I thought, than if, upon my first announcing that I had recognised her at the entrance to the building, she had replied, 'Guillaume! That's incredible! How are you doing?' We were going to act out an encounter between people who didn't know each other. I went along wholeheartedly. 'It was my friend Luciano who recommended I come to see you,' I told her. 'How is Luciano?' she asked. 'He's fine,' I replied, 'he now makes films in Italy, he has a girlfriend and seems happy.' I had adopted the formal *vous*, but in the course of our conversation would sometimes lapse back into the informal *tu*, in spite of myself. 'I'm plagued by obsessions,' I told her, 'you know what it's like.' I made the remark because I remembered how, when she was fifteen, Edwige Bouchard had a thing about cats, which she detested. She was always afraid that in our grandparents' house in the country a cat might slip through the door, which was left wide open on summer evenings, and my brother Luc and I would make a point of sneaking cats in so that she would scream and then slap us. I recalled how much I enjoyed being slapped by Edwige, but I didn't tell her this.

I had no trouble finding the entrance the next time. Edwige had proposed that I return, and I had said yes. At last, something amusing and vaguely exciting in my life, which had been a shambles for months now. And in the course of our consultations, of which there were many, at least that year, I soon lost all awareness that Edwige was my cousin. There even came a day, or so it seemed to me, when the mysterious and obliging Madame Gandi, who had decidedly pretty legs and a very thoughtful smile, was someone I had never known before. ■

'Madame Gandi' was first published in French in the short-story collection *Au coeur d'un été tout en or* (*All in the Golden Afternoon*) in which each story begins with the opening sentence of a book by another writer. The first sentence of 'Madame Gandi' comes from William Styron's *Darkness Visible*.

JEAN-CLAUDE DEUTSCH
Georges Perec in Paris, 1965
Paris Match / Getty Images

THE PEREC CASE

Paul Keegan

'For four years, from May 1971 to June 1975, I was in analysis. No sooner was it over than I was assailed by a desire to say, or more exactly to write, what had taken place . . .' So opens Georges Perec's brief account of his psychoanalysis with Jean-Bertrand Pontalis. 'The Scene of a Stratagem' ('Les Lieux d'une ruse') took longer to write than expected – the opening sentences were rewritten 'perhaps fifty times' – and did not appear in print until two years later. It is a retrospect rather than an outpouring: not a case history, but a patient's version of an analysis which started well, seemed to take a wrong turn, before a sudden revelation and an abrupt close. It is told as a story, an event in the past which is lived forwards in the telling, with hidden outcomes and a dénouement. Perec's purpose in writing was to discover rather than reveal what happened.

Perec published the text in *Cause Commune*, a sociological journal concerned more with what makes us alike than with individual destinies. Psychoanalysis has its own suspicions that underneath the bonnet we are all the same, and Perec referred to the 'anonymous ironmongery' of the Freudian playbook. Anonymity was his best disguise, his place of least compliance, where he was most playfully at home. His memoir *Je me souviens* (begun during analysis) is a collage of the cultural small change of his postwar generation, in 480 snapshots: what he called 'derisory memories', yours or mine, as if found on the floor of a photo booth. (No. 286: 'I remember when it was rare to see trousers without turn-ups'; No. 296: 'I remember Kiss, "the lipstick that doesn't stop you kissing"', etc.). He distrusted confessional modes, and described his writing as 'an approach to my own life-story, but only to the extent that this is collective, shareable'.

Perec went into analysis because he suspected that the ludic bent of his writing was in fact blocking an approach to his life story. He was born in Paris in 1936, the only son of Polish-Jewish parents: a volunteer father killed defending France in 1940, a mother rounded up and deported to Auschwitz, a childhood spent in seclusion near Grenoble, raised by relatives. All of which was documented and describable, but in some sense mislaid, wiped from consciousness. 'I have no childhood memories' are the opening words of his *sui generis* autofiction entitled *W or the Memory of Childhood.* Its appearance in May 1975 marked the end of his analysis with Pontalis – who noted, at their first meeting, that Perec seemed to have come not to complain, nor to understand, but to look for something.

'The Scene of a Stratagem' is written in a measured, slow-stepping idiom, with few flourishes, neutral and desolate. It was only when *Cause Commune* asked him to write on the subject of 'la ruse' – ruse, ploy, cunning – that Perec found himself able to do so, because it threw into relief the protocols of analysis, because it fitted so exactly the experience itself.

Pontalis was a well-known figure in Paris. A Freudian who trained as a philosopher, he had served on the editorial board of Sartre's journal *Les Temps Modernes*, and been analysed by Lacan. He was co-author of an influential dictionary or *Vocabulaire* of psychoanalysis (dictionaries are a pointedly Perecian genre), and founding editor of the *Nouvelle Revue de Psychanalyse*, to which Perec and his circle subscribed. Besides, his consulting room was on a street in which his new patient had lived – a detail of consequence for Perec the psychogeographer. Pontalis was chosen with care. Put differently, Perec arrived with expectations, or what Freud called 'ready-made transferences', including an idea of psychoanalysis as a game for two players (two sets of expectations), requiring a ruse. A game of chess, said Freud; a game without rules, said Winnicott, who is a hovering presence in this story.

Above all, Pontalis was a writer. Psychoanalysis was the form his writing took, so to speak, and he believed that to identify as an analyst was the beginning of imposture.

As a practitioner he was closer in spirit to psychoanalytic currents across the Channel, rooted in the clinical encounter and its low-lying epiphanies, than to the local intellectual controversies in vogue over Freud's legacy. His patients gave Pontalis his ideas, or as Winnicott would say, they paid to teach him.

Born a decade earlier than Perec, Pontalis would outlive him by three decades. He wrote about the Perec case, glancingly but vividly, in a dozen different places, while it was ongoing and even long after it ended. He never addressed it directly, as a case history, since this would have implied closure. He refers to Perec, in thin disguise, as Pierre, or Stéphane, or Simon, or Paul, or Pierre G . . . But friends and readers recognised their man in Pontalis's clinical vignettes, because his symptoms were so visibly on display.

Early on in the analysis, Pontalis began alluding to Perec in lectures and papers as a patient type, even a borderline case, at the limits of the analysable. Perec was taken aback by these splintery versions of himself in circulation, but he too transgressed during these years, publishing his dreams and even producing a number of short texts or outtakes of their encounter. The analytic couple were mutually unfaithful while the analysis was a work in progress. But it was also an 'exercice de style' on both sides, with its own kinds of decorum. Perec did not mention Pontalis directly, and Pontalis referred to Perec by name once only, in a late interview, in 2008.

At the start of 'The Scene of a Stratagem' Perec asks himself: why publish? Why make public what was named only in the secrecy of the seance? He has in mind Freud's caveat that what gets said inside the analytic setting cannot be communicated ('it is only by hearsay that you will get to know psychoanalysis, whose talk brooks no listener'). In this sense, 'ruse' meant writing about the experience of analysis, rather than its content. So Perec focuses on the frame – the consulting room, the couch, the analytic hour, the subfusc of routine. He records the unvarying rituals of entrance and exit:

> I arrived, I rang the bell, a girl opened the door, I waited for a few minutes in a room intended for that purpose; I could hear the analyst showing his previous patient to the door. A few moments later, the analyst would open the door of the waiting room. He never crossed the threshold. I went ahead of him and entered his consulting room. He followed me in, closed the doors – there were two of them, creating a tiny antechamber, something like an airlock, which further emphasised the sense of enclosure – and sat down in his armchair, while I stretched out on the couch.

He lists what he can see from the couch: 'three walls, three or four pieces of furniture, two or three engravings, a few books. There was a rug on the floor, mouldings on the ceiling, fabric on the walls: a precise and tidy décor, seemingly neutral, which changed little from session to session, from year to year.' The specifics lack specificity, and the consulting room is a non-existent place, in the centre of Paris. Noises off (a piano, a radio playing, birdsong, 'somewhere someone using a vacuum cleaner') only increase its unreachability. The analytic hour is a mere fold in the day, but also borderless and tenseless. Like the dream, it has no outside.

Perec records a 'ceilinged-in' expectancy, a sense of muffled violence, despite the urbanity of the proceedings. He notes his curiosity about his own as yet unspoken words. 'I was here to talk. That was the rule of the game' – except that the talking cure includes silences and has no rules (this being its one imperious nonsense rule, straight out of Lewis Carroll). Perec nurtured anxieties about free association, because it felt more like an attempt to forget than to remember. This seemed perverse to one whose entire *oeuvre* is a memory palace, and whose powers of recollection were prodigious.

There were other anxieties. Early on in *W*, Perec describes his writing self as 'a child playing hide-and-seek, who doesn't know what he fears or desires more: to stay hidden or be found.' But he also admits in 'The Work of Memory' (one of his progress reports from these years): 'Writing protects me. I advance beneath fortifications of words and sentences.' What he feared was an interlocutor who was not his reader, who was not the silent other in whose presence he was happiest to be alone, both lost and found. Perec beguiles his reader, so that the latter feels like a character inside the work, often the only character (the writing is curiously depeopled), or an opponent in this game for two players.

Early on in the proceedings Pontalis begins to assemble his own version of their encounter, and to explore a curious patient type: one who was 'expert at coding and decoding, prolific with wordplay, dream and interpretation games, skilled at all kinds of strategy . . .' How well it all works! Pontalis ticks off the successes: 'copious dreams, access to early memories, subtly crossed chains of association, the occasional intrusion of affect (unexpected, but readily assimilated), a willing acceptance of interpretations . . .' Perec agrees: 'I skipped cheerfully along the all-too-clearly marked corridors of my labyrinth. Everything had meaning, it was all connected . . . a great waltz of signifiers paraded their pleasing anxieties.'

Pontalis recalls it, twenty years later, as a *pas de deux*: 'He associates freely, I listen. I interrupt now and then, we are well pleased with each other. I tell myself that I am following to the letter the advice given by Lacan to analysts-in-training: "Start doing crossword puzzles." In effect, it was my patient who so expertly designed the grid which contained us both. My words merely found their place in the boxes awaiting them.' (The reference is clear: Perec was for several years a crossword compiler for the weekly news magazine *Le Point*).

In all of Pontalis's versions, the shallows shelve suddenly: 'the seances became unreal, and I was confronted by a pseudo-reality, a closed system, or sealed psychic environment.' And again: 'It became progressively clear to me that his words and mine were empty, they carried nothing and led nowhere, that our presence, his and mine, was simply an absence.'

During these years Pontalis was increasingly immersed in the writings of Winnicott, whose last book, *Playing and Reality*, he was co-translating. Perec seemed to confirm some of Winnicott's more speculative propositions as clinical realities. Notably that of a 'false self', to suggest a patient in whom intellectual activity predominates, whose unstoppable associations are a form of dissociation, a defensive facade. The compliance is a ruse against the analyst, suavely concealed. Perec was a patient of interest, because psychoanalysis – invested in 'saying everything' – could be seen as fostering this type of mental functioning, and the resulting collusions.

Freud had described the 'seance' (a word with its toe in telepathy) as a space in which 'the unconscious of one human being can react upon that of another'. Pontalis was specifically interested in the counter-transference – acknowledged belatedly by the psychoanalytic literature as the patient's influence on the analyst's unconscious feelings, a sort of alternating current in their encounter, difficult to detect. Pontalis gives free and even exaggerated rein to his own responses, as if to turn up the volume. He is dramatically less defended than his patient, whose self-sufficiency casts the analyst as a mere foil or at best an accomplice: 'This model patient – this child prodigy – brought me countless dreams, all of them puzzles which he expected me to decipher, assuming (incorrectly) that I was more expert than he in the art of decoding.'

In a 1975 essay (which Perec certainly read), Pontalis remarked of his patient 'Stéphane': 'Hence the feeling I had, that within the space that he constantly needed to fill there was no room left for me'. Perec's account – itself at times 'a touch austere, a trifle cold, a shade stilted' – enacts this removal of the analyst, by emulating his reserve. Pontalis in turn notes the absence of affect in his patient's associations or dreams, 'their easy flow unbroken by silences, as if the anxiety is dissolved in the telling'. In an inconsolable image, he writes that his patient 'was like one of those long-distance telephone operators, not one of whose words I can make out, except for a reiterated "don't hang up".' Freud's own image for unconscious communication hovers over these figurative excursions: the analyst as a telephone or a receiving device, whose free-floating attention opens towards the patient.

In one session the literal telephone rings and, with his secretary absent, Pontalis has to answer. The patient, usually so accommodating, remarks to the invisible presence behind him: 'You need an answering machine' – to which Pontalis replies, just as sharply: 'No doubt that is what you would like – for me to be an answering machine – but it is not what you are in need of', and is taken aback by his own response.

In all the words devoted to Perec's analysis, a period of stasis and repetition is described, a profitless interval. Pontalis resorts to many analogies to capture the compulsive aspects of his patient's mental functioning: 'the overriding need is for the wheels to keep turning, endlessly producing meanings while evacuating them all along.' And Perec echoes him, conjuring 'those amorphous sessions in which I had the nameless sensation of being a machine for grinding out words, in a vacuum'. Pontalis refers to him as a dream machine, whose products are letters 'addressed to no one'. Shorn of emotion, fluently translated into words, they are the products of 'a daytime insomniac'.

Increasingly silent, Pontalis declines to buy his patient's dream-ware ('I was not a "taker"') – to which the latter responded, in effect, by setting up shop elsewhere. *La Boutique Obscure*, published in 1973, mid-way through the analysis, is a transcription of 124 of Perec's dreams, which came to him, he writes, 'already written out'. He had begun 'collecting' dreams several years before the analysis began, although he later remarked in interview that he published them 'to annoy my analyst', part of a semi-public stance of disaffection. He described their publication as 'a refusal of psychoanalysis . . . that is to say, instead of giving my dreams to my analyst I *stole* them so as to put them in a book' – in effect confirming their reclaimed status as literature, no longer as analytical material. Perec concedes, in 'The Scene of a Stratagem', that his dreams are transcriptions rather than scenes experienced in the theatre of analysis – that they do not tell his story, nor explain him, nor transform him.

'Behind me, the other said nothing. At each turn I waited for him to speak . . .' At a low ebb, Perec began keeping a journal. It makes little reference to his sessions, only neutral data, a logbook of times of waking, travel details, purchases, meetings, meals, books. He copies the analyst's silence, so to speak, producing a mute commentary on each meeting – 'dull', 'gloomy', 'boring'. Occasionally a physical sensation intervenes ('cramp'). He becomes by his own account 'morose and bitter' in sessions. Pontalis notes that 'the all too agile verbal and intellectual machine had started to creak (he was at a loss for words)'. If Perec omits to record that he was dogged by toothache, Pontalis dwells on it in one of his papers, recalling that at one point his patient could afford either to go to the dentist or to continue with analysis, and chose the latter. As if another voice is slowly making itself heard, an admission of somatic states hitherto excluded. (Pontalis had frequently accused his patient's dreams and representations of being 'bodiless'.) The as-yet-unspoken words will be found in this place where the language falters, on the frontier of psyche and soma.

If the talking cure is a form of forgetting, Perec's retrospect is an attempt 'to restore in writing, through writing, the trace of what had been said'. But silence was equally to be feared as a forgetting. Hence his journal, and the sudden fever for collecting and listing and sorting. 'I kept everything: letters, envelopes, cinema stubs, airline tickets, bills, etc.' It is at this point that Perec writes various short texts about his attempts to record or 'exhaust' every tiny occurrence in the Place Saint-Sulpice in Paris, over the course of several days; or to keep a record of everything he ate and drank in the year 1974; or to codify his dreams. In *Species of Spaces* (published in 1974) he proposes at one point to describe in minute detail all the rooms in which he has ever slept. Pontalis describes this development, with his usual flair, as 'the tension between a mental activity without respite and a non-productive psychic life – his own psyche had ceased to nourish him. All he could do was *organise his territory*, sometimes elevated to the dignity of an empire, sometimes reduced to the dimensions of a cage.'

Winnicott's clinical insight (confirmed by Pontalis) was the recognition that the borrowed shell of the false self is more than a mere resistance, is in effect a necessity for the psychic survival of the patient. As Perec remarked elsewhere: 'one survives (sometimes) by playing'. In the Spring 1975 issue of the *Nouvelle Revue de Psychanalyse*, Pontalis published a translation of Winnicott's 'Fear of Breakdown', a brief essay that reads like an alternative account of 'le cas Perec', then nearing its end.

The essay sketches a type of patient who does not complain, and whose defences are so well organised that dependency (one face of the transference) is slow to manifest itself. He notes the related tendency of the analysis to start well and 'go with a swing'. Both parties are pleased with their progress. At the point where dependency takes hold, there is an abrupt loss of faith in the progress of the analysis, and what Winnicott calls 'the fear of breakdown' enters on cue: a sense of running on empty and a compulsion to keep filling up, as a substitution. Or, in this case, a fear of forgetting intervened, and an attempt to compensate.

Winnicott proposes that 'the breakdown, fear of which is destroying the patient's life, has already happened'. The event in question is not a buried trauma, nor is it repressed unconscious material. In what sounds like an impossibility, in Freudian terms, the experience has never been deposited, has never found its psychic address. Like dark matter, it is there but it is unfindable. Pontalis suggests that 'Something took place that has no place,' and he describes (ventriloquising Perec's own idiom) this need to keep looking:

> He would specify the streets where he had lived, the rooms he had slept in, the patterns on the wallpaper, the dimensions of the bed, of the window, the position of each item of furniture, the shape of the door-handle . . . and from this inventory, from the endless census that must not let anything be lost, there was born in me a desolate sensation of absence. Pierre's rooms: the more I saw them fill with objects, the emptier they seemed to me . . . the more exact the topography, the more vacant the space; the more populated the map with names, the more silent. They were only relics, there was no one there.

What Pontalis hears has unexpected consequences, as described in his autobiography: 'And in me, bizarrely, a hole, hollowing itself out, deepened. Never had I felt such a sense of utter abandonment. Deserted, projected into a space at once desolate and rigidly monitored . . . Behind all those empty rooms which he was never done with filling, beneath all those names, a lost mother who had left no trace.'

The streets and rooms are relics, 'but what are relics that have never touched a body?' The most haunted of all Pontalis's analogies concern this blocked work of mourning. As if he has been entrusted with what Perec has come to look for and cannot find – not the interpretations that Perec keeps producing for analysis (all those 'letters'), but the envelope containing them. 'What was in that envelope? At this point I would say: the couple of his dead parents.'

The counter-transference is nourished by an imaginary aim: 'to bring to life this survivor', as if he must experience what the patient cannot experience for himself. In 1992 Pontalis was still processing this material: '"I have no childhood memories" – thus began an analysis which I have already evoked, elsewhere, on several occasions, as if I felt impelled to take charge of and make my own a memory of childhood so comprehensively effaced, that it fell to me to keep it alive indefinitely.'

In his various versions, Pontalis pieces together another view of the counter-transference, traditionally seen as a 'blind spot', a distorting factor, an inability to maintain a neutral position in relation to the patient. At a certain point in an analysis the patient 'works upon us', he suggests, at a level to which we ordinarily have no access, which is in fact the seat of our psychic reality. In this sense, the encounter between Perec and Pontalis is indeed a story with two protagonists.

'The Scene of a Stratagem' does not describe the moment when the memory of what was lost (the effaced mother) is found. It was experienced, inside the analytic wood, as a sudden clearing: 'It was given to me one day, violently, miraculously, like a memory restored to its place'. But it was equally the process of analysis, though he says he only knew this afterwards. Freud remarked to one of his most gifted patients, the poet H.D. (Hilda Doolittle) that 'the person is dead after the analysis is over' – perhaps because afterwards she will not be able to 'tell' (in either sense) what happened. After the last session in Paris, the survivors walked off in different directions, in Pontalis's words, 'not wishing to know which has changed the other'. ■

ANA LARRUY / KINTZING

HER ENEMY'S PHRASE

Missouri Williams

Her enemy's phrase was a sun that pulled everything around it into orbit. Next to it all other phrases looked secondary. Alone at home she would try and parse it, splitting the phrase into its component parts and then repeating them to herself in a low whisper that her husband would not be able to hear from the other room. She rolled the individual words around on her tongue as if tasting them, but the words were like small stones, hard and inedible, and she knew that whatever it was that made the phrase so magnificent could not be understood in isolation. It was the totality that counted. She could not explain the secret beauty of the phrase nor why it had begun to obsess her. Furthermore, she was afraid to try. If she were to tell a friend about her problem, the enormous anxiety she felt whenever she remembered the phrase along with the compulsion to understand it, she imagined that she would also be forced to disclose the phrase. Perhaps the admiration they would feel on hearing her enemy's words would equal hers: they would say, avoiding her eyes, *Well, it is a great phrase.*

After we had been led to our table at the restaurant, she asked me if I had accepted her invitation because I had remembered her from university. She said we had been in the same college, although we had only spoken a few times, and then only at the beginning. She remembered me well: when she had seen my name on the poster for the event last week, she had been excited to remake my acquaintance. The truth was that I didn't remember her even slightly. I had decided to accompany her for reasons that had nothing to do with nostalgia or intimacy. In fact, they were very mundane. I had agreed to stay the night in the local hotel, and I had never slept well in strange rooms. I had wanted to kill some time. I was hungry and tired, and my talk had bored me. As always, I preferred to listen. Her confessional attitude had interested me.

While we waited to order our food, she told me that the only person she had dared reveal the phrase to so far was her father. He had not been impressed. He had said it was a stupid, inflexible phrase that relied on nothing but novelty, on hauling out the unexpected. He had pointed out that the phrase drew on another, more established expression, and simply involved the substitution of one word, a plural swooping in where it was not wanted at all. She had retorted that this kind of modification was the very substance of genius. Their exchange had not diminished the phrase in her eyes; conversely, it had diminished her father.

It was becoming impossible to live in the shadow of that phrase, she told me. For months she had written nothing of her own. For months she had thought of nothing else. She would have given anything to have never come across the phrase; from the moment she had found it, buried in a story her enemy had published in an insignificant journal many years ago that she had stupidly *sought out*, and even paid money for, her life had ceased to have any independent meaning. Everything was flat, lacking significance. The people she knew seemed like apparitions. It was in this desperate mood that she had attended my talk in the town. It was in the same mood that she had asked me to dinner. She hadn't thought I'd accept.

The more she had studied it the more it had seemed to her that you could build cities with that phrase. In the evenings she would curl up in the armchair by the window in the library and think about her enemy's phrase. She measured it against everything that she had read. Nothing matched it. She tried to find the right adjectives to accompany it. Nothing came close. So she ransacked the world for images instead. She closed her eyes and pictured the phrase. It was ecumenical, candescent. It blazed with an interior light, a cut topaz surrounded by clear cabochons of rock crystal. When she visualised the phrase, she saw a tabletop mountain encircled by low-hanging clouds. But none of these were right either.

Worst of all, she was convinced that the phrase had been a throwaway phrase, that her enemy had never attributed the same importance or the same qualities to the phrase that she had. The phrase was her problem, and her problem alone.

In the light of the lamp between us, her face was tired. The lines across her forehead were so deep and regular that it was as though her skin had been ploughed. When the waitress appeared, we ordered, and I noticed how the tables and chairs in the restaurant each appeared in their own solitary pool of light, just like the bright arrangements of interrogation rooms, fantastic and isolated, with the people locked inside interviewing in their ones and twos and threes.

The waitress brought over our pasta, and for a moment the two of us ate in silence. Then she said that things were getting even worse. She had begun to notice the similarities between her enemy and her husband. They both had dark hair and dark eyes. Small straight noses, and flat Grecian profiles. She compared photographs of the two of them, placing them side by side. Now when her husband came home in the evenings, she winced at the sight of him. His attempts to comfort her were futile. She couldn't decide if he was meant to be with her enemy, who was superior to her in every single way, or if he was her enemy, simply presented in another form. It was the phrase, she insisted. It had made everything like it, everything a reference. And the rest of her reality was becoming confused too, each shape superimposed on another, a hopeless entanglement.

In the restaurant that night she told me that she had felt as if I could give her the answer that would lead her out of her difficulty without hesitating or really thinking about it at all. Even from the back of the audience she could tell that I was careless. It was there in how I moved, in the way I shaped my words, quickly and without reflection, as if I didn't intend to remember them afterwards. She had read all my books.

I nodded as if I understood her. Intelligent people liked to tell me their problems because I am a successful author – my books are published in different languages and I've won prizes, I don't even know how many. People like this woman would ambush me after events, buy me drinks, and talk about themselves. Sometimes they would ask me questions. How I'd managed it, to succeed where they had failed. But the secret of my success is very simple. It's that I don't think about things too hard. I may even be quite stupid. All these failed writers – they get stuck in the thinking stage. I skip it altogether. I just write and write without thinking at all. After I've written everything that was there in my head already, that's when I start thinking, but it isn't creative. It's mostly just a question of what to delete. It's as if I was born with everything already inside me. I imagine that this is true for most people, but it's only idiots like me who realise it. Other, more intelligent writers, are forever trying to modify themselves: they take too much in and dilute what is there. They want to know what everybody else is thinking, when really they should be content with the contents of their own heads.

Next she told me that my novels were empty. For you, she said, the world is a map of lines of action: one line leads here, another there, and another to a place that the reader can't quite visualise, or at least not yet. One could plot these lines on a graph without much difficulty, and extrapolate a three-dimensional space filled with the people and objects that were the performers of various actions, servants to the event. In my books, colours, textures, smells, and so on – these were all subordinate to deeds. That's not to say I didn't include them, she assured me, because from time to time I did, just that in my novels, description knew its place. She said I wrote novels like palaces – it was the totality that counted. Nothing happened without my consent and foreknowledge. There were no stray meanings, no ambiguity.

She said that I didn't write narrative, but spreadsheets of fate. When examining the wreckage of her own life, at times she had even wished that she could live inside one of my novels instead, in a cold, pure world of parapets and keeps with arrow-slit eyes.

I would like to say more about this woman and how she appeared to me that evening, but I struggle with details. Most faces look the same to me and most places are equally nondescript. I go where my agent tells me to go and say what my publishers tell me to say, and I absorb very little. I can't tell you what the restaurant looked like or the waitress who served us. In my memory they are just shadows and blanks.

I know that she told me the phrase, but I couldn't hold on to it, and it didn't matter. When I left her, I was already thinking of a palace, a novel I hadn't written yet, but I knew that I would. ■

HIROSHI HAMAYA
Tokyo, 1959
Magnum Photos

WE ARE CREATURES WHO MOURN

Interview with Jonathan Lear

Jonathan Lear was the John U. Nef Distinguished Service Professor in the Committee on Social Thought and the Department of Philosophy at the University of Chicago, where he taught for nearly thirty years. Trained as a psychoanalyst, Lear was known as a philosopher with an unusual sensitivity to ancient thought and literature, and one who wrote in a clear, inviting vernacular. In books such as *Love and its Place in Nature* (1999), *Open Minded: Working Out the Logic of the Soul* (1998), and *Happiness, Death, and the Remainder of Life* (2000), Lear not only reestablished connections between psychoanalytic and ancient thought, but brought both traditions to bear on questions about how best to live in the present.

In September 2025, Lear's former colleague at the University of Chicago, Benjamin Y. Fong, spoke to him about his commitment to using psychoanalysis as a way of making philosophy 'concrete'. A week after Fong spoke with him, Lear died of a long-running illness. *Granta* and Fong mourn his passing. The following conversation was conducted remotely over two sessions.

BENJAMIN Y. FONG: How did you first become interested in psychoanalysis?

JONATHAN LEAR: I was fortunate to get a good job early in my life. I became a fellow of Clare College at Cambridge, and a lecturer in the philosophy department. I was very happy to be there, and I felt the position came with a responsibility to think about what philosophy *is*, rather than about the current fashions of the day. I thought that if I'm going to spend my life doing this, I ought to have a good idea of what it is I'm doing and why.

I had a colleague in the history department named Charles Parkin. He functioned as a teacher to me. He loved Hegel, who wasn't being taught in Cambridge in philosophy in my day. So Charles and I met every week for a year to read Hegel, then Plato, and talked about it over tea or coffee. I came upon a phrase where Hegel says, 'Philosophy should be concrete.' I did not know what it meant, but it intrigued me. I wanted to think hard about what it would be for philosophy to be concrete. I've been thinking about it ever since.

In the same period, my dad died after a long illness. I was very involved in his decline, and then death. At the funeral, an older figure in the family pulled me over and said that it might be a good time to have a little bit of psychotherapy. I didn't feel anything was particularly wrong with me. I just felt sad. But he suggested I do it and said he would pay for once-a-week sessions for one year. I could have never afforded it otherwise, so I tried it out. I'd walk out of each session feeling so much better and amazed that all I did was talk. I became extremely curious about how talking can actually make you feel better.

FONG: Does psychoanalysis bear some privileged position when it comes to addressing some of the fundamental philosophical questions that Plato and Aristotle raised, but couldn't answer, given the bounds of their moral psychology?

LEAR: Plato's and Aristotle's approach to ethics was to find out what it is for we human beings to flourish. They thought that if we were flourishing individually, we would also be flourishing as ethical people, and we would also be flourishing in political life. But we needed to understand both what human flourishing is – they called it *eudaimonia* – and also how to promote it. And the fundamental problem in this task, as they saw it, was how to get the non-rational soul to communicate harmoniously with the rational soul. The psyche – or soul – was divided between these two parts, and the problem was how to promote psychic harmony between them.

If you agree with that overall outlook, then psychoanalysis is invaluable: it facilitates forms of psychic communication that you can't get other ways. If you actually read Aristotle's Greek or Plato's Greek, you see that the language is all about communicating within the soul, which gets flattened in English translations. The English translation will be that the non-rational part of the soul is 'more obedient' to the rational part, for example. But the Greek will literally say 'it listens better'.

Of course, the translators don't have time for this. They just say, 'Well, the point is it's obedient.' But Plato and Aristotle were not just concerned with obedience. They were concerned with harmony, psychic unity, and listening. The language of the Greek is really about listening and speaking to and communicating with all levels internal to the psyche.

The fundamental rule of psychoanalysis, really the sole rule, is to say anything that comes to your mind without inhibition or censoring. Let your mind go where it will go on its own, and speak out loud about where it's going. That is really the perfect complement to what the Greeks called *logos*. Sometimes it's translated as speech, discourse, reason, rationality – it's got a family of meanings. But the idea is that in normal speech or thought, as I'm thinking and speaking with you now, I'm trying to put forward a point of view and I'm disciplining my mind to organize our conversation, so that I'm focusing on the thoughts that might be of interest to you and might be persuasive to you.

One of Freud's insights is that to do that, we have to keep a lot of things out of mind. We have to focus on what we call 'relevant'.

What's relevant is dictated by logos. And the fundamental rule of psychoanalysis says, 'Hey, for this next hour, relax. Don't do that. Just say whatever comes to mind. If it doesn't make sense, seems irrelevant or embarrassing, say it anyways.' It's the complement to the hard work of normal logos – of interaction, persuading people, listening to their reasons, deciding what you believe, what your positions are.

FONG: You present an analogy in one of your recent papers where you say that logos is like the work week and psychoanalysis is like the Sabbath. To get the full week, you need the Sabbath.

LEAR: It's not just that there *is* a Sabbath, but that there is a commandment that God laid down to *honor* the Sabbath and to *remember* the Sabbath. It's not like you just relax. You're commanded to honor relaxing, which is a lovely injunction. You are enjoined to pay attention to what's coming into your mind and to say it out loud. What that ends up doing is facilitating the kind of intra-psychic communication that Plato and Aristotle were interested in and which goes to the heart of their ethical project.

FONG: But as you've said in many places, it's an empirical discovery of some importance that nobody can actually follow the fundamental rule. We're bound to dishonor the Sabbath.

LEAR: Welcome to the human! It's human to feel inhibited, to not be able to let go, to correct yourself, to resist. Freud can be criticized for all sorts of things. But his genius was to make something out of a failure. He messed up his analysis with the patient who's known as Dora, but he didn't just let it go as a failure, or as a cover-up. He realized that he could make use of that failure. Even if the fundamental rule is resisted on all sides, there's still something to be learned from it. It's possible to learn from the breakdowns and turn failure into a source of inquiry.

★

FONG: There is a common idea about therapy that it is not necessarily about coming to the truth, but about giving patients a story about themselves, a story with which they can more contentedly live their lives. What do you make of that conception?

LEAR: That's a widespread view in the culture, but I think it's pretty importantly wrong. Stories are nice, and it's not like they have no point or no use, but they can have a very defensive use. The construction of a story, however nuanced or sensitive or insightful, can be used as a defense to cover over real problems that are getting ignored precisely by the narrative. I think that's bad. It might give you a way to cope in life; you can say, 'Well, this is my story. My parents were like that, and I grew up like that . . .' But in every story there's something that's omitted, covered over.

The outcome of analysis isn't meant to be some sort of independent product, some story I now have. That doesn't seem to me a good way to think of what a good outcome would be. What a good outcome would be is the development of a capacity to face life as it's being lived in an open, truthful way.

FONG: How does irony add to our understanding of therapy?

LEAR: One of the reasons that people come to psychoanalysis is that they're worried that they're trapped in some kind of pattern. Maybe between now and death, this is all there's going to be. Somebody will come in who's going through the third breakup of a significant relationship. The first one was just very upsetting, but people break up. The second one was a bit unsettling because they were very involved, and then it didn't work out. But by the third one, people are worried because they think, 'Is this going to be the way it is forever with me and intimacy?' There's some intimation of one's own mortality. 'Is this it for me in life?'

Lurking in the background is not just the question 'How is it that I'm doing this?' but also 'What *is* intimacy anyway? What would it be for me to succeed at being intimate?' It isn't just a matter of following a series of self-help steps. It's a matter of getting clear in your own mind what intimacy is for you and for the people around you. For people who come in who are married, and they're thinking about getting divorced or having an affair, there's a question: 'Am I really married?' Again, it isn't just 'Am I unhappy in my marriage?' but 'What would it be to be married?'

The general structure of irony is to hear the opening of a gap in the question 'I know I'm married, but what would it be to be married?' How does one's ear even hear that question? If you say 'I know this is a rock in my hand, but are there any rocks in my hand?' that just doesn't make any sense. You don't even hear a question there. But the questions I'm talking about are very human; they mark us as human. When you can hear that gap, that is the realm in which psychoanalysis can do a lot of work to help you understand what kind of a call you're hearing.

If psychoanalytic therapy is working well, the mind can have immediate and direct efficacy upon its own workings. It's not just about insight into who I am, although it is insight. It's gaining insight where the insight itself is directly efficacious in changing what it understands. It's like the mind somehow acquires a direct power to change itself. It's not just changing your mind in a literal sense – you believed this, and now you believe that. It's intervening in the functionings of the mind to change them in the living present via your own understanding. That can be a little hard to grasp, so you need to see it in action.

FONG: You have often talked about how literature can present therapeutic encounter-like scenarios, in which people are called to question certain things about their own existence.

LEAR: Sometimes we open a book, and we just get the content out of it. 'What does it tell me about swimming?' But there are certain books that, and certain encounters with a book that, just to use the vernacular, *pack a wallop*. For me, with certain poets, certain poems, they become lifelong companions. They change the way you see things, the way you hear things.

On summer vacation, I like to get to the Atlantic Ocean. I walk along certain ocean beaches, which I've been doing since I was a little boy. Along those beaches, there are a lot of seals. I like seals, and they like me. And I walk along, and the seals will come. We will make eye contact and look at each other. We're doing the best each of us can in interspecies communication, but we meet our boundaries. There are limits. There's only so much we can do. I've had seals follow me along a three- or four-mile walk. They're keeping their eye on me.

Just a few weeks ago, a friend of mine pointed out a poem I had never read before: Elizabeth Bishop's 'At the Fishhouses'. It's a knockout. It includes her encounter with an ice seal, and it changed the way I see seals. When I went out after reading that poem and went back to my very familiar routine of meeting up with seals, I saw them differently, and I heard them differently. That's what a poem can do. We're not over – me, that poem, and the seals – we're just beginning. So it isn't just that I liked it as a poem, or that it gave me pleasure, or that she's a really smart poet. It's that it changed me. It changed the way I see and hear seals. It entered my mind, and it had a direct efficacy. That is what I'm interested in.

★

FONG: You have defended something that many psychoanalysts have sought to dispense with: the concept of drives. Why is this concept essential to understanding psychic life?

LEAR: When Freud tried to come up with a theory of the drives, he had his finger on the pulse of something that's real in human life.

There's something about human life that is pressured, or experienced as pressured. Things come into our mind, and we wish we weren't thinking about them. It's too bad; it's on our mind anyway. Should I call this person, or shouldn't I? I should be thinking about something else, but I can't not think about it.

So what's with the pressure? What's with the experience of things being insisted upon, of being fated, of feeling somehow like I can't break my routine? I have to do it this way. I don't like it, but I have to do it anyway. Theories of the drives are trying to explain that.

FONG: How do you reconcile the conception of feeling pressured by the drives in a good sense, as in the case of love, with the more common conception, which is to feel like you want to be rid of them? People come to psychoanalysis saying that they have certain compulsions, certain constraints or things that they want to transcend. How do those two forms of pressure relate to one another?

LEAR: The problems will never go away, but the question is, can they be a source of creativity? Can they be a source of joy? Can they be a source of being with others in rich and intimate ways? Or do they always get in the way? Do they always imprison you? At their worst, they imprison us in these horrible repetitions that make us very unhappy and unable to live with others or ourselves well. But at the other end of the spectrum, they help us say, 'Well, this is my inheritance. I have freedom to deal with it in different ways, and I can't just ignore it.'

FONG: One of the ways in which that pressure manifests in analysis is transference – the unconscious mapping of earlier emotional structures onto the analyst by the patient – which some people have had a difficult time distinguishing from love. How do you think about transference?

LEAR: I think of transference as a ubiquitous human phenomenon going on all the time. What happens in the psychoanalytic situation is that there's a certain way that transference becomes useful. It's made conscious in a way that allows it to become much more directed and efficacious. Freud has this phrase that you can't burn somebody in effigy. Roughly the idea is that if you can get this in the room where it is focused on in the right sort of a way, it can have a direct effect on the mind via the mind's own understanding of its functioning.

This is why I think of psychoanalysis as a master craft. Great pianists can get better at playing a Bach concerto all their lives. The technique of making good use of transference, right in the here and now, when you might say the two of you are making music together, lies at the heart of the psychoanalytic practice.

FONG: So what begins as a pressure that's unwanted becomes something that is occasion for growth?

LEAR: Yes. This is one of the reasons why it's not just about having the right story. You have to deal with your defenses, even the defensive use of stories. What you want to develop is the capacity to understand the workings of your own mind, in the presence of another, in such a way that in the liveliness of your own understanding, you can change your mind in a direct, causal, efficacious way via the very understanding that's changing it. That's the deal. Psychoanalysis can do that when it's working well.

*

FONG: In your most recent book, *Imagining the End* (2022), you open with an anecdote from a lecture on climate change that you attended. A young academic gets up during the Q&A and proclaims, 'We will not be missed.' The audience laughed, but I took it that you didn't. Why not?

LEAR: From a psychoanalytic point of view, it's always interesting to find out why people laugh. Why do people find this funny? There's a weird relationship between the involuntary and the voluntary. Someone tells you a joke, you laugh at it, you find it funny – a lot of that is not up to you. It's not like you chose to find it funny. You laugh; it's a spontaneous and automatic reaction. And sometimes that can be embarrassing. When people respond to a comment by laughing, they're showing something about themselves that is not completely up to them.

So here's this person saying that human beings are going to vanish from the Earth, and we're not going to be missed. And everybody finds that funny. That's worthy of inquiry.

Part of the way the joke works is that the phrase 'we will not be missed' is ambiguous. It has layers to it. One is just the brute fact that there won't be any creatures around who will be capable of missing us in a way that we would find appropriate to be missed – if the humans get wiped out, but cockroaches survive. But it's also a way of saying 'Good riddance!' Nature is going to go on beautifully without us. And guess what? We don't deserve to be part of it. We will not be missed in the sense that we don't deserve to be missed. A little bit of a punishment gets sneaked in.

FONG: You take this joke to be a confrontation with death, but part of what seems to interest you about it is the way that it sidesteps mourning.

LEAR: I want to help people understand that mourning is not just an important thing that we do, but that it is a very important part of being human. We are creatures who mourn. We have the capacity to form attachments to other people, to ideas, to works of art, to all sorts of things. This makes us vulnerable: when these people or things go away or die, we mourn them. Our imaginations become active thinking about loss, thinking about what we've lost, thinking about what that means for us now and what that might mean for us into the future.

Freud wrote an essay at the beginning of the twentieth century called 'Mourning and Melancholia'. He takes himself to be giving a differential diagnosis between two very interesting psychological categories, mourning on the one hand and melancholia on the other. But the way I read him, speaking beyond himself, is that mourning is not just a psychological category of differential diagnosis. He's really laying down an existential category of the human, in response to our human vulnerability. Do we mourn, or are we melancholic? And melancholia here isn't just a depression that you could take a pill for. It's a refusal to mourn. So mourning is a crucial ethical category, in my opinion, not just one more psychological process among others. We are finite, dependent beings, who by our very nature and in our very living have to deal with loss.

FONG: You're now working on a book about gratitude. How does gratitude come into your thinking about mourning?

LEAR: At the end of her career, Melanie Klein wrote a classic article called 'Envy and Gratitude'. Klein placed envy and gratitude at two opposite poles of the axis of human suffering and flourishing. She didn't say a lot about why that is. That was just her intuition after a life of clinical work.

I wanted to think hard about what gratitude is and why one might think of it as fundamental to the human, not just one nice thing among others. The word gratitude has a family of meanings. Gratitude is not one single thing. But among the family of meanings, there is one that I think is very special. And it goes back to Aristotle. Aristotle defines gratitude as the appropriate response to a gift, favor, or benefaction that is given to you for your own sake, and not with any expectation of return. What is the role of *that* in human life?

It's very important in our contemporary culture because we live in a world of reciprocity and exchange, goods for services and commodities. Education is a commodity. We buy it, and we get an expert service back. We pay an analyst, and we get analysis back.

Even if you throw a surprise birthday party for me and it's for my sake, you sort of expect that I'll invite you to a picnic, or there'll be a museum opening someday, and I'll take you as my guest. There is an exchange going on. A lot of late nineteenth- and twentieth-century anthropology conveys this lesson: we think there are these great acts of generosity, but really they are social exchanges of very high complexity. It's all very fascinating work. But it's led to the cliché that the kind of social interaction that Aristotle defined as for the other's sake and with zero expectation of return, genuinely no strings attached, is not possible.

FONG: It seems as if you're linking Freud's 'Mourning and Melancholia' with Klein's 'Envy and Gratitude'. Is mourning necessary for gratitude, and is there some essential connection between melancholia and envy?

LEAR: Not all melancholia is envy, but I think you're absolutely on the right track. Gratitude in its essence has to be a form of remembering. That's what you're grateful for. Somebody in the past helped you. The gratitude lies in the memory of 'this person helped me' or 'this deed helped me'. And it's forward-looking. Past, present, and future are all there because I look backwards in gratitude, but I also take it up in the present, and I project myself into the future: How am I going to live now that I've been the beneficiary? It's not by paying this guy back; it's by something else. What is that other thing?

I don't want to equate envy with melancholia. Envy is a very special and unusual case. As with gratitude, there are a lot of different meanings of the word 'envy'. But there is a use of the word 'envy' that gets to a negativity in human life that is very hard to understand.

The family of mourning and melancholia, gratitude and envy, provides a very basic ontological choice. It's not just an emotional or psychological choice. It's about how to be as a human being. That's my next book. It's my last book too. I think I can take another step forward. ■

Robert Hass

To Adam Zagajewski

Poets gathered around heat lamps on the deck
of the old ski resort. I think you can imagine it.
Cold air breathing its way down from the snow fields
between peaks, a young moon stating its case
to the night sky, frogs singing in the pond. They –
the poets, not the frogs – are reciting poems
to each other for the pleasure of it. I don't
remember if we ever talked about Keats and,
if we had, I suppose we would have talked
about poetry and death, the way he saw it coming,
and, like you, believed fiercely in not wasting joy.
I thought of you because one of the young poets
stood up in the night air and recited Keats
to the accompaniment of the frogs, and another
recited that poem of Linda's that amused you
in which she is watching TV with the sound off
and reading Chinese poetry. The young man
reproduced her rhythms exactly, as if her breath
visited us, as the breath of John Keats whose breath
failed him, visited us, and I remembered you
told me of Linda's death as we were leaving
the reading in the market square in Kraków.

'What things,' I could quote her lines then,
'are steadfast? Not the birds. Not the bride and groom
who hurry in their brevity to reach one another.'
Your Maja was with us. You both seemed happy,
the summer crowds were drinking wine in the cafés
and the world seemed as full as your poems
wanted it to be. It's late, I'm a little groggy,
but I thought you might like this report. The mountain air,
the moon, Adam, and the faces of the poets.

Thinking of Adam

So, belatedly, after the great and monstrous war,
He put on a once elegant trenchcoat
He acquired in the Sunday flea market
In Kraków in the cathedral square
And hunched his shoulders, and walked
The streets of the twentieth and twenty-first centuries,
Brooding on what Kierkegaard said about Hegel
And why people, given the chance,
Had not chosen the great flood of beauty to live in
And who was the Elise Beethoven had in mind
When he heard and wrote down 'Für Elise'.
And if people couldn't hear it, why couldn't they
Be irradiated by the sunflowers like exploding stars
And stars like deep blue and bright yellow explosions
Of light in van Gogh's eyes, he lived long enough
To ask a clever machine to estimate for him
How many of the thirty to sixty million people
Who died in the great and monstrous war
Would have died anyway in those five or so years
His parents lived through, and his aunts and uncles,

When a thin music of keeping one's head down
And just scraping by was replaced by another decade
Of keeping one's head down and just scraping by,
So he could not, shoulders hunched, walking
The streets of many cities, understand why,
Given the chance to dive into a summer pond
Or sit in the back row of a converted synagogue
Listening in the dark to what Bruckner did with the shock
Of love and the timbre of a clarinet, chose instead
To enlist in the green and black armies
Facing one another across the gulf
With its swift current, into the indifferent waves
Of which they pitched large, murderous abstractions
And real lives. He suffered from headaches,
Which taught him to be still and patient.
He's gone from us now, but we have the poems
That praised softness in a hard time, and plurality
In a narrow time and the broken world
In a broken time, and recommended to us
The next transformation, and mint, and cellos.

Politics

In the bad lip-sync of the dubbed video of Costa-Gavras's *Z*
You stop being driven crazy only when Yves Montand is killed
And Irene Papas who plays his wife falls silent.

A man who lives in a country ruled by a military junta
Walks across a square to give a speech against them.
The generals can't kill him themselves; there is the question

Of NATO, of US foreign aid. (This was years before a Saudi prince
Sent a squad of murderers with a surgeon to torture and kill
A journalist he didn't like and dismember the body and pack it

In suitcases and bring them to him.) As I recall two thugs drive up
In a comically small blue car and turn into the square.
The blue Citroën, or whatever it is, is fate.

The two thugs surge from the car with bats and crush his skull
And, in the ensuing panic in the crowd, with police collusion,
Lean back into the car and drive off. As if they were never there.

Here we leave the politics behind. His wife,
With her strong, severe looks, receives the news
In her hotel room. She sits in the dark for a long time

With no expression on her face. Finally, she gets up,
Goes to the bathroom, turns on the faucet, splashes water
On her cheeks, her eyes, then still without expression,

Pauses, turns the water off and reaches for his aftershave –
She is looking at herself, at her eyes, in the mirror –
And twists the cap and smells it. The rest of the film

Is politics. An investigator is appointed who is expected
To protect the generals, but he doesn't. He finds the killers
– this is what makes the story an entertaining procedural –

Names their bosses, from a purely professional sense
Of justice he's been educated to. So the generals
bury the story, and the audience of middle class

Urban intellectuals who watch things like Costa-Gavras films
Is left with an aching hunger for justice and the memory
Of a woman before a mirror sniffing a bottle of aftershave.

CONTRIBUTORS

Jesse Barron is a journalist and a contributing writer at the *New York Times Magazine*. His article 'The Girl From Plainville' was adapted into the TV series of the same name.

Christopher Bollas's recent publications include *Essential Aloneness* and *Streams of Consciousness*. *Pitching to the Dream Team* and *Being in Analysis* are forthcoming in 2026.

Louise Bourgeois was a French-American artist. From drawings to large-scale installations, she expressed a range of psychological states through continuous formal experimentation. Her work has been exhibited internationally and features in a number of public collections.

Dushko Petrovich Córdova is a painter, writer and publisher. His observations about the visuals of the second Trump administration were recently published in *n+1*.

Benjamin Y. Fong writes about labour and logistics and is an editor at *Damage* magazine.

Olive Franklin's work has appeared in *Poetry* and the *Poetry Review*. Her debut pamphlet, *Dyke Juvenilia*, is forthcoming in 2026.

Justin Greene is a poet and translator. His poems have appeared in *Pleiades* and *Hayden's Ferry Review*.

Camilla Grudova is the author of *The Doll's Alphabet*, *Children of Paradise* and *The Coiled Serpent*.

Lidija Haas is a writer, editor and candidate at the Institute for Psychoanalytic Training and Research in New York City.

Rosalind Harvey is a translator of contemporary Spanish-language fiction, including Guadalupe Nettel's *The Accidentals* and Luis López Carrasco's *The White Desert*, forthcoming in 2026 with Granta Books.

Robert Hass's most recent book of poems is *Summer Snow*. *A Third Commonness: Essays in Poetry, Poetics and the Natural World* is forthcoming in 2026.

CONTRIBUTORS

Victor Heringer was the author of the poetry collection *Automatógrafo*, the two novels *Glória* and *The Love of Singular Men*, as well as a collection of non-fiction writing, *Vida desinteressante*.

Sheila Heti is the author of eleven books, including *Alphabetical Diaries*, *Pure Colour*, *Motherhood* and *How Should a Person Be?*

Gitta Honegger has translated work by Elfriede Jelinek, Elias Canetti, Thomas Bernhard and Peter Handke. Most recently, her translation of *The Children of the Dead* by Elfriede Jelinek, was published in 2024.

Mark Hutchinson's translations from French include René Char's *Hypnos: Notes from the French Resistance*, Emmanuel Hocquard's *The Garden of Sallust* and four books by Anne Serre.

Elfriede Jelinek has written novels, plays, poetry, essays translations, radio plays and opera librettos. In 2004, she received the Nobel Prize in Literature.

Rinko Kawauchi is a photographer whose books include *Utatane*, *Hanabi*, *Hanako* and *M/E*. In 2024, her solo exhibition *a faraway shining star, twinkling in hand* was held at Fotografiska Stockholm.

Paul Keegan has written the introduction to the Penguin edition of *The Psychopathology of Everyday Life*. He was formerly the poetry editor at Faber and Faber.

Benjamin Kunkel's short story 'Prairie Dogs' appeared in *Granta* 167. He is currently at work on a novel.

Jonathan Lear was the John U. Nef Distinguished Service Professor in the Committee on Social Thought and the Department of Philosophy at the University of Chicago. He was the author of *Love and Its Place in Nature*, *Open Minded*, and, most recently, *Imagining the End*.

Deborah Levy's novels include *Swimming Home*, *Hot Milk*, *The Man Who Saw Everything* and *August Blue*. Other books include *The Position of Spoons*, the story collection *Black Vodka* and her trilogy of 'living autobiographies'. Her new novel, *My Year in Paris with Gertrude Stein*, is forthcoming in 2026.

Juliet Mitchell FBA is an author, psychoanalyst, literary critic and emeritus professor at the Universities of Cambridge and London. Her books include *Psychoanalysis and Feminism*, *Woman's Estate*, *Women: the Longest Revolution*, *Mad Men and Medusas*, *Siblings: Sex and Violence* and *Fratriarchy*.

Guadalupe Nettel's work has been translated into more than twenty languages. Her most recent novel, *Still Born*, was translated into English in 2022; *The Accidentals*, her new collection of short stories, was published in 2025.

Musuk Nolte is a Peruvian photographer and editor whose work moves between documentary and artistic practices. He has published eight photography books and in 2013, founded KWY Ediciones.

Anne Serre is the author of nineteen works of fiction, including *The Governesses* and *A Leopard-Skin Hat*. Her latest book, *Vertu et Rosalinde*, will be published in English in 2026.

Nigel Shafran is a photographer whose work has been exhibited at Tate Britain, the V&A, Photographers' Gallery and Fig-1 London. His publications include *Ruthbook*, *Dad's Office*, *Teenage Precinct Shoppers*, *Dark Rooms*, *The Well* and *Workbooks*.

Natalie Shapero is the author of, most recently, the poetry collection *Stay Dead*. She teaches at the University of California, Irvine.

Missouri Williams is the author of the novel *The Doloriad*. Her latest book, *The Vivisectors*, is forthcoming in 2026.

James Young is a translator and writer. He has translated two books by Victor Heringer, *The Love of Singular Men* and – together with Sophie Lewis – *Glória*.

GRANTA TRUST

Granta would be unable to fulfil its mission without the generosity of its donors. We gratefully acknowledge the following individuals and foundations:

Ford Foundation
British Council
Jerwood Foundation
Pulitzer Center
Amazon Literary Partnership
Sigrid Rausing
The Hans and Marit Rausing Charitable Trust
Anonymous
Bloomsbury Publishing Plc
SALT
Open Society
The Common Humanity Arts Trust
Jonathan and Ronnie Newhouse Fund
Hawthornden Foundation

We also thank the following readers, including those who wish to remain anonymous, for their kind support:

Anonymous
Alex Fardon
Jared Hameloth
Michael Isard

GRANTA MAGAZINE EDITIONS
is a paperback original series of
exceptional literary voices, published
by *Granta* magazine.

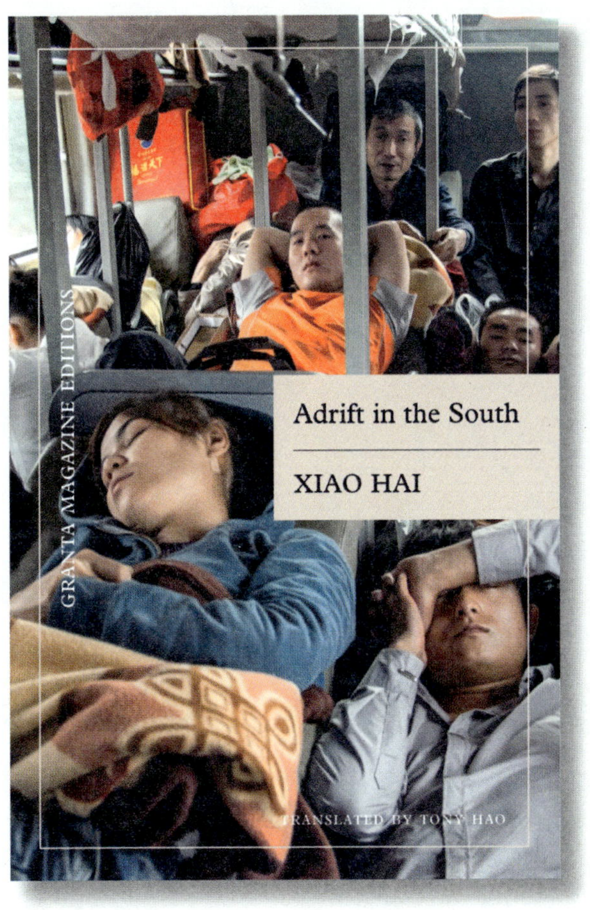

Adrift in the South by Xiao Hai
Out May 2026